Mineke Schipper studied French and Philosophy at Amsterdam Free University, and Literary Theory and Comparative Literature at the University of Utrecht. She started her teaching career at the Université Libre du Congo. In 1988, she became the first Professor of Intercultural Literary Studies in the Netherlands, first at the Free University of Amsterdam and from 1993-2008, at Leiden University. She is Emeritus Professor of Intercultural Literary Studies at the University of Leiden, with visiting professorships in Nigeria, Kenya, Zimbabwe, Burkina Faso and China. She has a Royal Order of Knighthood (Officier in de Orde van Oranje-Nassau) for 'building intercultural bridges nationally and internationally, inside and outside the academy.'

Schipper writes literary non-fiction and fiction and is the author of several books, essays, and novels, including *Never Marry a Woman with Big Feet* (2004), *Naked or Covered: A History of Dressing and Undressing Around the World* (2017) and *Imagining Insiders: Africa and the Question of Belonging* (1999). Her internationally acclaimed *Never Marry a Woman with Big Feet* won the Eureka Intermediair Prize 2005 (Best Non-fiction Book) and was also nominated for the Eureka Furore category: best female achievement.

Also by Mineke Schipper in Speaking Tiger

Naked or Covered: A History of Dressing and Undressing Around the World

Never Marry a Woman with Big Feet

HILLS OF PARADISE

Power, Powerlessness and the Female Body

Mineke Schipper

SPEAKING TIGER

SPEAKING TIGER BOOKS LLP
125A, Ground Floor, Shahpur Jat, near Asiad Village,
New Delhi 110049

First published in the Netherlands as *Heuvels van het paradijs: Een geschiedenis van macht en onmacht* by Prometheus 2018

Published in English in India as *Hills of Paradise: Power, Powerlessness and the Female Body* by Speaking Tiger 2023

ISBN: 978-93-5447-517-7
eISBN: 978-93-5447-508-5

10 9 8 7 6 5 4 3 2 1

For sale in South Asia only

Typeset in Athelas Regular by SÜRYA, New Delhi
Printed at Shree Maitrey Printech Pvt. Ltd., Noida

CONTENTS

PART II: DESIRABLE AND TERRIFYING

Pregnant Woman by Aat Veldhoen. Rotaprint, 1964.

PROLOGUE

A Precarious House of Stories

> The eye is not satisfied with seeing,
> nor the ear filled with hearing.
>
> Ecclesiastes I: 8

Despite major cultural differences, there are striking similarities between all people: we share the same bodies and bodily functions—except for the few parts that physically distinguish women and men. The power and powerlessness of both sexes run like a thread through human history, even though women have had little demonstrable influence on written tradition. Myths have played a major role in our history, in ways so prevalent that they were rarely questioned.

In the twentieth century, women started occupying positions that had previously been inaccessible to them. This relatively recent development has been accompanied everywhere by discomfort, awkwardness, inconvenience, frustration and worse. For all the gains and moves towards equality in the recent past, gender norms restrict women's access to education and employment, exclude them from decision-making, and expose them to violence and abuse. In conflict zones, women are the targets of systematic rape and sexual violence, which is used as a weapon to terrorise and destroy communities. One in three women around the world will experience sexual or physical violence in their lifetime.[1] Sharing privileges, it seems, does not come easily.

The Taliban's immediate rebranding of the Women's Affairs Ministry back to the Ministry for Propagation of Virtue and Prevention of Vice soon after regaining power in August 2021 is an eloquent example of the disappointing discord between promises and policy, and not only in Afghanistan. To make sense of the present structure, and how and why it is sustained by stubborn traditions, media outlets, advertisers and governments, we need to understand its foundations.

This book takes a wide-ranging look at a global house of stories and ideas about the body parts that only women are naturally endowed with. From time to time, some social and cultural bricks have been removed from the walls, and some spaces have been radically rebuilt over the years. But we are still enmeshed in traditions passed through the ages, which connect us more closely to our ancestors than we may realise.

A laden legacy

Since time immemorial, an order has been established on the basis of differences between the sexes that still strongly determines the wellbeing and woes of men and women. Power generates fear—the fear of losing one's acquired power. Both power and fear manifest themselves in an unstoppable torrent of male comments on wilful and uncontrollable female body parts, while female ideas about these body parts have been swept under the carpet. Information from women about their own sex is rare before the twentieth century. No doubt they had ideas about their own bodies (and

---

1. https://www.who.int/news-room/fact-sheets/detail/violence-against-women; see also https://womenforwomen.org.uk/work-we-do/why-women-conflict.

about those of men), but until recently their views have had little impact on social relationships. The knowledge they had was either silently taken over by the other sex or dismissed as unprofessional.

A European example is the exclusion of female doctors and midwives in the establishment of medicine as a scientific profession. Until the thirteenth and fourteenth centuries the term *medica* referred to a female doctor next to *medicus* for a male. Female doctors did not confine themselves to gynaecology or female patients. Some women, like the twelfth-century abbess Hildegard von Bingen, wrote authoritative medical texts in Latin. Nonetheless, women were excluded from secondary education and the study of medicine, and therefore, from access to more respected forms of medical practice. As a result, women's medical knowledge has rarely been preserved in books. An exception is Jane Sharp's *The Midwives Book, or The Whole Art of Midwifry Discovered* (1671), a medical handbook based on rich experience with the female body. Hardly any knowledge is available about her, barring the detail on the book's title page that she practised as a midwife for over thirty years. There were no guilds for female doctors or midwives. In their medical handbooks, male doctors were inclined to describe female colleagues as incompetent. By the end of the sixteenth century most medical acts were exclusively reserved for members of medical guilds, to which women had no access.[2] Evidently, 'scientific men [...] do not live in a vacuum; on the contrary, the directions of their interests are ever conditioned by the structure of the world they live in.'[3]

Most of what has been said and written about the female body originates from male sources or have been coloured by

---

2. Margaret R. Miles, *A Complex Delight*, 2008, Chapter 4.

3. Needham, *A History of Embryology*, 1934: xvi.

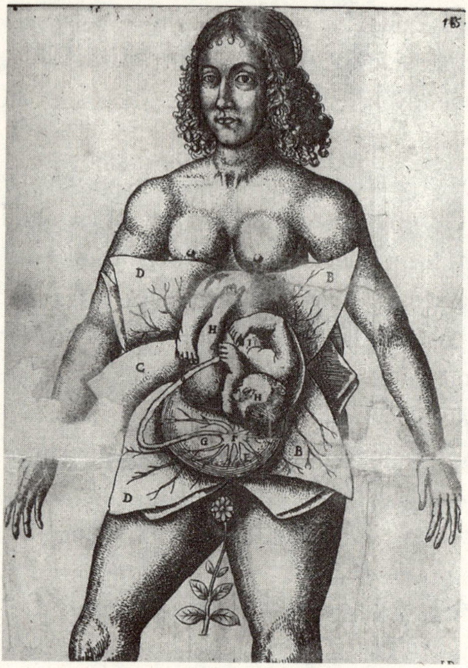

Woman with Unborn Child. Jane Sharp,
The Midwives Book, 1671.

male perspectives. Over the centuries, research on human society has been led by men. Research from the female perspective at local, national and global levels is relatively recent: we do not know what women were saying or thinking among themselves, they wrote relatively little, and their own oral traditions have only attracted interest since the 1970s. Before that time there was usually less attention for female than for male contributions to society, the more so because most anthropologists were men who had concluded from personal experience that women's business was of little interest. Moreover, they often had less access to women in the cultures where they did their fieldwork research. Thus, women were reduced to 'muted groups'. The term is Edwin

Ardener's, who concluded that in the social sciences there is an enormous discrepancy in knowledge about men and women: 'There is a real imbalance. We are, for practical purposes, in a male world. The study of women is on a level little higher than the study of the ducks and fowls they commonly own—a mere bird-watching indeed.'[4]

Of course, this does not mean that women always agreed with their submission to inherited views. Without female resistance, male fear of and need to control the female anatomy would have been unnecessary. That fear resulted everywhere in two mechanisms that are still alive and kicking: to belittle women as much as possible, and to warn men against destructive female power. Even though the two messages contradict each other—why should you be afraid of someone who is completely insignificant?—they reflect two sides of an ancient coin forged from an emotional mixture of power, fear and insecurity.

Holders of power, great and small, have managed and controlled female sexuality, as if women were their property. The need to nullify bodies with breasts, a vulva and a womb, the need to negate the female contribution as much as possible and to act as if everything and anything sexual was your domain is remarkably widespread. It can be found in countless handed-down images, stories, symbols, rituals and commentaries that concentrate on the body parts that distinguish women from men.

Ideas about men's and women's rights and duties run parallel with political and economic developments. Male poets, storytellers, artists, clergy, scholars and spouses began determining the differences between the sexes based on their desired answers to fundamental questions such as who is active and who is passive; who looks and who is looked at; who speaks and who should listen?

---

4. Edwin Ardener in: *Perceiving Women*, (Shirley Ardener ed.), 1977:1-2.

This book's title comes from a medieval student song in Latin, which explores an undulating feminine landscape:

> Softly shines her virgin bosom,
> And the breasts that gently rise
> Like the hills of Paradise.
> Oh, the joys of this possessing! [...]
>
> From her tender breasts decline,
> In a gradual curving line,
> Flanks like swansdown white and fine. [...]
> 'Neath the waist her belly turneth
> Unto fulness, where below
> In Love's garden lilies blow.
> Oh, the joys of this possessing![5]

The song eulogises the girl's beauty, but in passing also declares her naked body the property of the man looking at it, touching it, describing it, praising it.

In the twenty-first century, male students and rappers still sing about girls as property, but in Western culture some songs have changed considerably and some are strikingly violent. In the Middle Ages girls didn't yet study and now they do—would that explain the difference in tone? Bragging about one's potency conceals the fear of one's personal performances in 'Te lam Om te Zingen' ('Too Blotto to Sing'), a recent song popular in Utrecht University's Earth Sciences student union: 'My sledgehammer is my third leg / It rams rocks to pieces / but I'd rather shove it in your cave.' The girl submitted to this ramming finds it 'a bit strange', because she is only fourteen. The greater the male insecurity, the younger and less experienced the girls that are targeted. The Groningen student association Vindicat published

5. 'Flora' in *Wine, Women, and Song: Medieval Latin Students' Songs*. 1840:112-113.

an almanac that listed and commented upon the hottest girls of that year's intake, while expressing the heartfelt wish 'to pull the cunts of the dirty ones over the pistol.'[6]

Oddly enough, female students hardly ever protest publicly against this kind of humiliating language. A recent public protest came from indignant parents. They objected to a song entitled 'Viva Vagina': 'The sexism, hatred of women and rape fantasies are abhorrent and unacceptable,' they wrote to the board of the student association, but they did not want their names to be made public, probably to prevent problems for their daughters.[7]

Perhaps female students let such verbal violence pass because it belongs to a widely shared way of thinking in terms of weak-willed flesh about humans with female body parts. In 2017, columnist and microbiologist Rosanne Hertzberger drew attention to this legacy, reporting on a behind-the-scenes documentary showing ingrained sexism in the Fox News studios, and in a Dumpert web broadcast from the Telegraaf Media Groep, in which male commentators would routinely remark on whether a parade of female bodies merit having a dick in them. The format was a tremendous success, with about eight million viewers per month.

> Humiliating women is big business. Fortunately, capitalism offers a beautiful solution to these kinds of situations. The fact is that women are not only breasts, bellies and buttocks, they are also America's most important consumers. They are the ones who decide which kind of car to buy, where to go on holiday and they do the shopping. So, when all those Fox women began to collectively express complaints

---

6. https://www.erasmusmagazine.nl/en/2016/09/23/groningse-vindicat-meisjes-op-banga-lijst/.

7. https://www.nrc.nl/nieuws/2018/01/09/seksistisch-zo-had-de-studieclub-het-niet-bekeken-a1587722.

> against their bosses, fewer and fewer advertisers wanted to be associated with the show.[8]

The awareness that not only you, but also others are entitled to respect can bring people together. Asking advertisers to think about the contents of the programmes they sponsor is an excellent idea, now that the urge to belittle is expressed so openly and on such a large scale. The sad need to humiliate women offers no solution to make the present bearable. It will only end when we dare to look our mutual history of fear and uncertainty in the eyes.

At the cradle of an established order

Even though both sexes are needed for procreation, from ancient times one sex was selected for preferential treatment in most societies. In the case of newlyweds, only one of the families decided where the couple would live: with the family of the groom (patrilocal) or with the family of the bride (matrilocal). In cultures where hunting and gathering were replaced by large-scale agriculture, when men got more of a grip on planting thanks to the invention of the plough, family relations began to move from matrilocal to patrilocal residence, and more and more often young women had to put up with the man's family instead of the other way round.[9] The young women ended up in unfamiliar surroundings, under supervision of and submitting to the rules of the 'others', whereas the husband had the comfort of staying with his kinfolk on the family compound.

---

8. https://www.nrc.nl/nieuws/2017/04/21/vrouwen-vernederen-big-business-voor-geenstijl-wiebetaaltdumpertreeten-8355536-a1555513.

9. Ruth H. Munroe, Robert L. Carol R. Ember and Melvin Ember, 'The Conditions Favoring Matrilocal Versus Patrilocal Residence'. *American Anthropologist* 73 (1971): 571-594.

In-laws are not direct relatives, and mothers-in-law and daughters-in-law are commonly presented as being suspicious of or even hostile to each other. In Congo, where I lived, mothers warn their sons who want to marry: 'To eat with a woman is to eat with a witch.' A daughter-in-law comes from outside and brings 'foreign blood' into the family. For the family of the girl, this means her destiny is to leave for a foreign family, and her children will also belong to others.

In many cultures girls are considered to be 'in transit' in their own homes. Indeed daughters, destined to depart, are considered 'spilt water' (Chinese) or 'cigarette ashes' (Arabic). Children come to belong to the clan of the husband, whereas their mothers never entirely belong anywhere. Or in the words of a Luba proverb: 'A daughter is like a raindrop, she will fertilise the fields of others.' Evolutionary psychologists show that in patrilocal societies wives risk more violence in the form of harassment, abuse, rape and exploitation than in matrilocal family contexts.[10]

Women have often been considered male possessions. Therefore, rape was not so much seen as a violation of a woman's honour, but as a defilement of her owner's property. In the case of an unmarried girl, her rapist would pay compensation to the original 'owner', her father, and the victim was passed into the hands of the rapist, her new 'owner'. This arrangement is outlined in the Book of Deuteronomy (22:28-29) in the Hebrew Bible, and in many societies, it is still a common course of events—although nowadays there are more protests against it. The reasoning is that the owner has authority over his property: he can exchange it or give it away as he likes. Damage or injury gives him the right to a reasonable compensation.

---

10. Vandermassen, *Darwin voor Dames*, 2005:189. More about violence in Chapter 10.

In all cultures, the exchange of gifts is one of the most important ways to sway the delicate balance between love and hatred in human relationships. Giving and receiving create ties that prevent the group from falling apart. When a man wanted a wife, she had to be ceded by another man, usually her father or a brother—as Claude Lévi-Strauss observed.[11] This almost universal principle is based on the much wider concept of reciprocity: humans as social beings must exchange property with others.

The exchange of this most precious property—women—created that much-needed reciprocity of give-and-take between groups. This form of barter-trade made men see themselves as the managers of society, and 'their' women as commercial family property. The exchange of those living goods increased the autonomous status of men and turned women more or less into 'moveable assets'. The exchanged were no longer seen as humans on an equal footing with the exchangers.

Patriarchal societies were organised in the same way as the family model in which fathers exercise authority. The term patriarchy consists of the Greek words *pater* ('father') and *archè* ('beginning' or 'reigning principle'). The establishment of patriarchal relations was a long process that took place at different moments in different parts of the world. In the Middle East this development took place over 2,500 years (about 3100-600 BC). The oldest known laws are engraved in clay tablets dug up in Mesopotamia (now Iraq). Inscriptions in cuneiform characters make clear that sexuality and female birth-giving capacity were controlled by men very early, as Gerda Lerner convincingly demonstrates in *The Creation of Patriarchy*, a fascinating book.[12]

---

11. Claude Lévi-Strass, *The Elementary Structures of Kinship* (1955). Boston: Beacon Press, 1969:481.

12. Here I gratefully refer to her Chapter 1: 'Origins'. (OUP, 1986).

The existence of matriarchies, societies in which women had a dominant position, has been certain feminists' wishful thinking. Convincing proof has never been found—though there are many (mostly negative) stories about societies that in the past consisted of women only, or in which women reigned.[13]

A few communities have been described in which women and men shared their power in several respects, for example, in Çatalhöyük in Anatolia, a matrilocal urban settlement from the late Stone Age (six or seven millennia old), where about 6,000 to 8,000 people lived.[14]

In times of crisis, when group survival was in danger due to ecological or demographic circumstances, there was a great need for more birth-giving capacity—so more women. Agriculture was keeping ever-greater numbers of people alive, and wherever the population increased and the space was limited, farming had to be intensified or territories extended. This resulted in tensions and conflicts between neighbouring clans. When expansion resulted in war, the infrastructure of the defeated clan was destroyed: the menfolk were eliminated or dispersed, and women and children were regarded as spoils of war for the victors. Hierarchies were reinforced, with only slaves a lower category than women, and as populations grew male-dominated family and kinship structures were reflected in broader class-based societies.

Agricultural communities developed into urban centres, and around 4000 BC the first cities were built in Mesopotamia and Egypt. Early states came into being, first in Asia and Mesoamerica; later also in Africa, Northern Europe and other parts of the world. In places where security increased, people's confidence grew, and

---

13. As explained in my earlier book *In het Begin was er Niemand*, (*In the Beginning There Was No One*) 2010:171-175.

14. Lerner, ibid. 30-32.

gradually godly and secular power became embodied in a single male ruler.

Thanks to the inscriptions on clay tablets from the earliest known period (*c.* 3000 BC) we know that women actively participated in economic, religious and political life, but even then, women depended on a man for their position in society. Wherever male dominance was established, an iron rule was that women who no longer pleased their menfolk lost their power. Thanks to their family line, men had their own home, whereas women belonged to men who had acquired rights over them, according to local tradition. Women's place in the hierarchy was determined by the status of the men on whom they depended: their fathers, brothers and husbands.

> All women had to accept as given the control of their sexuality and their reproductive processes by men or male-dominated institutions.[15]

This held even more for women who had been looted or bought: for them economic exploitation included sexual exploitation. Women mostly went along with the dominant ideas, as they hardly had any choice—and most likely these ideas were internalised at an early age to become the accepted norm and ever more self-evident.

In early societies, physical violence existed in almost every community, and that was one of the reasons women were forced into 'breeding arrangements'.[16] The life for children of a mother without a male protector was so risky that the mother simply couldn't go against the norm. Such a protector wanted to be sure about his own offspring. Battles with rivals resulted in male property of and control over women's bodies for personal use.

---

15. Ibid. 100.

16. The term is Sarah Blaffer Hrdy's in *Mother Nature*, 1999:258.

Men have mapped out the history of society from their own perspective and experience, and so far, in most societies, masculinity has been more appreciated than femininity. Men have more political power, and 'men's work' is valued more highly than 'women's work'.

The power of myths

In his bestseller *Sapiens*, Yuval Noah Harari concludes that biology makes lots of things possible which culture then restricts or forbids. That male dominance has developed almost universally cannot be a coincidence, he says, but he is unable to explain why this hierarchy still remains so widely in force:

> Maybe males of the species *Homo sapiens* are characterised not by physical strength, aggressiveness and competitiveness, but rather by superior social skills and a greater tendency to cooperate. We just don't know.[17]

Disappointing, really. In spite of the claim in the subtitle of his book—*A Brief History of Humankind*, the author has a blind spot for the revealing light that myths and popular culture throw on the origins of sexual inequality. Two of the key issues in origin and creation myths are the changing roles of goddesses and gods, and the superiority of the first man over the first woman, leading to a history that gradually justified inequality on the basis of sexual differences. Thanks to the success of shared myths, ever larger groups of people began working together, first in clans and urban communities, later as nations or in international communities and world-spanning religions. The author of *Sapiens* rightly insists on the importance of such stories as the cement for the functioning of societies[18], but like Lévi-Strauss, he has a blind spot for the

17. Yuval Noah Harari, *Sapiens*, 2011:178.

18. Harari: 30, 36.

revealing light that myths and popular culture throw on the development of sexual inequality.

Myths deal with crucial issues that affect all of society. They lay the foundations for human existence and are passed down from generation to generation. As long as people believe in their own stories, the established order depicted in those stories persists. If a society changes fundamentally or heads in a new direction, the house of stories is reconstructed.

Gods inevitably acquire human traits, and over time, the basic creative and life-giving functions of mythical goddesses are remarkably often taken over by male gods. Many stories are recast so that one sex is elevated over the other, appropriating most power and delegating most opportunities to itself. In some stories the new divine leader radically eliminates his primeval mother in a dramatic battle.

Myths justify this turn of events by explaining that female power had to be curbed because women were capricious, unjust and demanding. A Gikuyu story I was told in Kenya describes how women were once in charge. They were cruel and ruthless, and ruled like tyrants. The men did everything for them—they hunted, worked the land, cooked, cared for the children (in some versions they even breastfed the babies) and protected their families against enemies. The women just handed out orders and did nothing. However zealously men did their best to meet the women's demands, they were exploited as slaves. The female rulers were never satisfied. No wonder the men resorted to a ruse: they agreed amongst themselves to impregnate all the women at the same time. And while the women were giving birth, their unjust regime was overthrown. 'The men created a new order and strengthened their grip on society. Since then justice and peace have reigned in Gikuyu society.'

This story gives the impression that matriarchal power was

superseded by patriarchy but, as indicated earlier, matriarchy never actually existed as a societal order. Men's theft of female power, also called the theft of 'women's secret', is a striking theme in several parts of the world (Chapter 10 deals with this in more detail).

Myths devote a great deal of attention to the body, and link messages about sexual hierarchy in a community to stories about the first people. Proverbs prescribing 'how things should be' in sexual relations can be found just about everywhere, for example, in the popular metaphor of the horse and its rider: 'The one who mounts is in charge.'

The inescapable fact that men were dependent on women for their ardently desired sons must have upset the balance between the sexes from the very start, creating a strong male desire for compensation, the need for power and control over women's fertility, and the tendency to declare important areas out of bounds to women.

Contact between the sexes has also been complicated by male fear of the vulva—in which, in cautionary tales in many cultures, the desire to devour is said to lurk. This fear is also reflected in strange prohibitions. The power of this primal gateway spurned the delusion that a man who looks at female genitals will be punished with children born blind.[19]

The female capacity to produce life became associated with an uncontrollable nature that had to be tamed. Many myths tried to muzzle this frightening life force by introducing a reassuring male supreme god or ancestor as the creator of all life. In an Egyptian story, the primordial ocean god Nun bears the sun god Atum, and this second male creator subsequently copulates with his own hand. He masturbates and puts his semen in his mouth,

19. Satlow, *Jewish Constructions of Nakedness*, pp.441-442.

and by spitting it out, he creates his children Shu and Tefnut. In an ancient Egyptian tomb text, he manifests himself as an autonomous procreator:

> Before heaven came into being,
> Before earth came into being,
> Before the ground and the reptiles had been created here.
> I was the great one who came into being out of myself,
> All alone I fulfilled all my desires,
> I considered in my heart and planned in my head
> How I would shape and create myriad forms.
> So it was I who spat forth Shu and vomited up Tefnut.
> This happened when I was still alone...
> I masturbated with my fist, I copulated with my hand,
> I spat from my mouth, out of myself.[20]

In many traditions, a male god creates life by uttering a powerful word, or with his own hands from mud, dust or other materials, including from his innermost body. An innate lack of male birth-giving power is transformed into success stories about a divine masculine order that overcomes and regulates female chaos.

Female chastity prior to and in marriage became a self-evident requirement to control this feared and presumed chaos, because women's virtue determined the family's and its offspring's status. In a world without DNA testing, motherhood was indisputable, while the father's name was the mother's secret.

Myths and other handed-down texts are permeated with suppressed male fear and doubt. That the step from uncertainty to aggression is small is shown by countless exhortations to violence

20. Free translation from Papyrus Bremner-Rind 26, 21-27, 1 Bibliotheca Aegyptica 3, Brussels 1933:59-61 and other magic tomb texts referring to myths. With thanks to Egyptologist Jacco Dieleman for personal information.

against women: 'the more you hit them, the more they love you' is a widely heard exhortation (more on this in Chapter 9).

As a result of the many disparaging messages about their nature and outward appearance, women have been and are no less tormented by fear and uncertainty than men. Compulsive preoccupation with appearance led to a vicious circle: women competing with their bodies to attract attention from men for self-preservation. Women reduced themselves to objects, there being hardly any options to improve their lot other than looking sexy and finding a husband. Once this had been achieved, there was little else left in life to attain than giving birth to (preferably male) offspring.

Centuries-long overdoses of belittling commentary have provoked in many women a hypersensitivity to negative criticism. No wonder today's advertising is keen to tap into the age-old female need for approving glances, a need that insecure mothers are still tacitly passing on to their daughters.

Myths present a desired social order and hold people in the binding grip of their stories. They forge a tight singularity that persists as long as there is no viable alternative. Most myths confirm an order in which men are in charge, even though they remain dependent on women for offspring. This dependence has not only led to control over female sexuality, but also to an ostentatious male need for compensation in political, cultural and religious terms, and to a striking propensity to territoriality—excluding women from positions in which gender differences are totally irrelevant. On top of mythology and popular culture, philosophers and theologians have frequently warned that the female body can disrupt the prescribed order and cause disaster.

The bias of a male perspective was additionally safeguarded in societies where women were not allowed to recite or comment in public on holy texts, myths, epics, sometimes even proverbs, further reducing the female contribution to the shaping of traditions. In many cultures and religions women are still not permitted to engage with sacred texts or lead religious services.

Over the course of the twentieth century, women acquired freedoms that their mothers could only dream of, and female experiences of their own bodies and those of the other sex are no longer a closed book. The good news is that the once strictly delineated boundaries between men and women are starting to blur. Relations between the sexes are changing, and the transition areas between them are becoming more crowded.

In many places, sexual differences are now less socially charged. Wherever this happens, people no longer have to pretend to be dogged winners or angry losers. Relationships take on new forms, and the need to meet on an equal footing generates mutually liberating openness.

In the twentieth century, artists began to respond ironically to the old value-laden legacy. Niki de Saint Phalle's giant sculpture *Hon—en katedral* (*She—A Cathedral*, 1966; see Plate 1) of a reclining woman with her legs spread wide invited visitors to come and look at her body from within. A gigantic vagina was the entrance to an interior full of cheerful attractions, including a twelve-seat cinema, a planetarium, an aquarium, a milk bar in the breast cavity, and even a library. No wonder men, women and children queued eagerly to enter.

Relatively new collective changes were preceded by millennia in which one half of humanity was continually restricted on the basis of 'deviant' body parts, and often designated as the 'source of all evil'. Gender differences have given rise to distorted attitudes that many still regard as normal.

Body parts unique to women have played a decisive role in this legacy. Male fascination with the parts that physically separate women from men has always been great, and there is no lack of male commentary on them. Male appraisal of women overflows with mixed sentiments ranging from absolute power to absolute powerlessness, from delight to insecurity, distrust and fear. This book is about those ambiguous feelings towards indispensable, coveted, reviled and envied female body parts.

PART I

FROM FEMALE TO MALE CREATORS

Cycladic marble female figures, Syros, 2800-2300 BC; the one at the centre is pregnant. Archaeological Museum, Athens.

1. MOTHERS OF ALL LIFE

To the Mother of the Gods

Divine are your honours, O mother of the gods and nurturer of all,
Yoke your swift chariot drawn by bull-slaying lions
And, O mighty goddess who brings things to pass, join our prayers.
Many named and revered, you are queen of the sky,
For in the cosmos yours is the throne in the middle, because
The earth is yours and you give gentle nourishment to mortals
Gods and men were born of you.[21]

Before the oldest prayers were written down, there were already figures of women, images in stone, bone or ivory, with prominent breasts, bellies and vulvas. Usually aged between 10,000 to 20,000 years old, they have been found in many places—from Europe to East Asia. In 2008 a small ivory figure was unearthed in six fragments in a hollow rock in southwest Germany, a statuette with strikingly big breasts and a marked vulva, carved from a mammoth tusk. This so-called Venus of Hohle Fels—almost 6 cm high and between 35,000 and 40,000 years old—is so far the most ancient in a series of mother images that archaeologists

21. 'To the Mother of the Gods,' in: *Orphic Hymns: Text and Translation* by Apostolos N. Athanassakis: https://allaboutheaven.org/observations/orphic-hymn-to-the-mother-of-the-gods-007316/221.

called Venuses. The next oldest is the Venus of Willendorf, at around 30,000 years old.

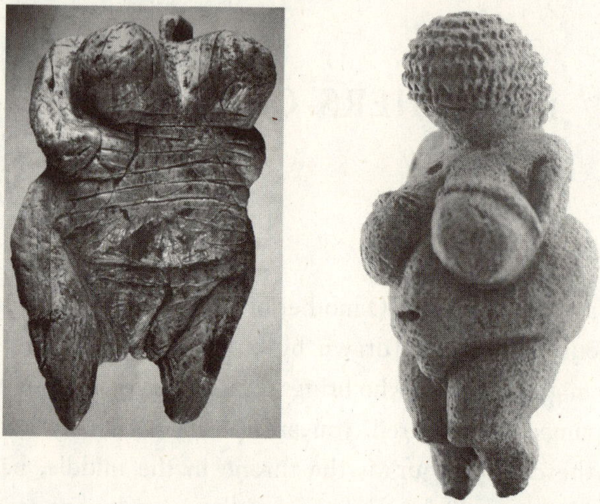

Left: Venus of Hohle Fels. Blaubeuren Museum of Prehistory, Germany.
Right: Venus of Willendorf. Museum of Natural History, Vienna.

The label 'Venus' is a problematic anachronism, because Venus, the goddess of love, arrived considerably later—just one of the many Roman goddesses, ranked below a supreme reigning Father God. So the term 'protecting mother figure' or 'fertility symbol' seems more appropriate here:

> Looking back so many thousands of years later at these earliest figures, it seems as if humanity's first image of life was the Mother. [...]. Images of giving birth, offering nourishment from the breast and receiving the dead back into the womb for rebirth occur in the Palaeolithic as they do 10,000 years later in the Neolithic and 5,000 years after that in the Bronze and Iron Ages—and, indeed, are present to this day in Western culture in the rituals surrounding

the Virgin Mary. It is not surprising that these images of the goddess appear throughout human history, for they all express a similar vision of life on Earth, one where the creative source of life is conceived in the image of a Mother and where humanity feels itself and the rest of creation to be the Mother's children.[22]

The breast that never dries up

Everywhere on earth mothers have been placed on a pedestal. In the words of an English proverb: 'God could not be everywhere, that's why He created mothers.' Praise for the mother is sung all over and sometimes it looks as if she was and is the divine presence herself. The human longing for godly mothers has always been huge, and divine breasts are perhaps even more worshipped by those who are unendowed. The earthly breast is no less cherished than the heavenly. A Spanish proverb knows it for sure: 'My home is my mother's breast', and a contemporary Chinese poem sighs yearningly:

Mother, my mother
Hold me tight in your warm embrace
Because the dark night is imminent.[23]

The pronouncement in the ancient Greek Orphic hymn that opens this chapter is confirmed in prayers to Mother Earth worldwide. 'The earth, our mother, feeds us, waters us and clothes us' is a Russian saying. The human need for cherishing mothers has sometimes considerably enlarged the breasts of mighty goddesses in stories and images. In the same way that some origin stories

22. Anne Baring and Jules Cashford. *The Myth of the Goddess*, 1993:9-10.

23. Quoted by poet and minister Jidi Majia, at a conference I attended in Xining, Western China.

tend to lengthen the first penis to such extreme dimensions that the owner has to wrap it around his middle to be able to walk unhindered, the breasts of goddesses grow to unlikely dimensions as well as gaining special powers.

The powerful breasts of the Greek goddess Hera even left their mark on our galaxy. This is how it happened: Hera's husband, supreme god Zeus, was so fond of Hercules, his mortal son by a terrestrial lover, that he wanted to immortalise the newborn. He placed the baby at the breasts of his sleeping spouse, but the baby sucked so hard at Hera's nipples that she woke up. As soon as she realised this was not her own child, she angrily pushed him off, causing her her divine milk to squirt high into the air. Its remains continue to brighten the Milky Way, and the incident inspired fine artists such as Rubens, many centuries later (see Plate 2).

Some stories about the pre-Islamic Arab goddess al-Uzza say that her breasts were so huge that she would throw them over her shoulders to let them hang on her back.[24] A dry human breast was seen as a curse, but mother goddesses blessed the devout human community with their abundantly nourishing breasts:

> The mother as breast is the Alma Mater, the Mother of Corn in ancient Greece and Asia and the Americas and, where agriculture was unknown, the Old Woman of the Seals of the Eskimo, the mother of Walruses of the Chukchi.[25]

On Babylonian clay tablets of millennia ago her name is 'The Mother with the faithful breast' or 'She whose breasts never failed' or went dry. This much-cherished body part was sometimes

24. Aicha Rahmouni, *Storytelling in Chefchaouen Northern Morocco*, 2015:60.

25. Wolfgang Lederer, *Fear of Women*, 1968:122.

depicted in stylised spirals or circles, sometimes impressively emphasised, or multiplied as in the case of Artemis, also referred to as Diana of Ephesus. Stories tell how milk or honey, blood or wine—or in an Inuit story, fish—flowed from her nipples.[26]

Creation goddesses

The shamanistic goddess Xiwangmu ('Queen Mother of the West') is one of the oldest Chinese deities. The first inscription referring to her is found on an oracle bone from around 1600 BC. The Chinese side of the Himalayas known as the Kunlun Mountains was considered a paradise where immortals live. This is the abode of Mother Xiwangmu; nobody knows her beginning and nobody knows her end, according to the well-known Taoist writer Zhuangzi in the fourth century BC. Her dazzling beauty was glorified by poets, and according to local tradition she is the one the Bible refers to as the Queen of Sheba—who went to visit King Solomon and gave birth to his son Menelik, to whom she would hand over the throne of her earthly realm. In the Kunlun Mountains, Xiwangmu attained a high state of spiritual enlightenment, and there she still reigns over the cosmic powers thanks to her peach tree, which stands as the axis between Heaven and Earth, and bears the fruits of immortality (see Plate 3). The gods are fond of these peaches that ripen only once every thousand years, and at these rare moments they join Xiwangmu in a heavenly banquet.

If a human succeeds in eating one of those peaches, he/she will be blessed with miraculous longevity. According to the stories, this mother goddess always wears a rainbow-coloured dress with winged sleeves; she helps, protects, gives excellent advice and takes care of humanity's elixir of life, nurturing her favourites.[27]

26. Ibid. 14ff.

27. https://www.suppressedhistories.net/goddess/xiwangmu.html.

She continues to be ceremonially worshipped, as I found out some years ago when attending a Mother's Day festival in the countryside near the city of Xining where many people gathered in her honour (see Plate 4).

With no contact between them, disparate cultures thought up stories in which a powerful goddess manifested herself in all the living earth, water and air (see Plate 5). The earth was her body, stretching out to the horizon, and all that existed belonged to her. She gave birth to and nourished all life without any intervention or contribution from a male god. Not only plants, trees and animals came up from her birth canals, but also tiny human beings: 'The little people crawled out in the dark like grasshoppers, their bodies naked and soft. Their eyes were closed; they hadn't opened them yet.' (Acoma Pueblo, New Mexico)[28]

The oldest stories confirm that everything came forth from the generous body of this (grand)mother:

> The mother of our songs, the mother of our seed, bore us in the beginning of things and she is the mother of all types of men, the mother of all nations. She is the mother of the thunder, the mother of the streams, the mother of the trees and of all things. She is the mother of the world and of the older brothers, the stone-people. She is the mother of the fruits of the earth and of all things. She is the mother of our youngest brothers, the French and the strangers. She is the only mother we possess. (Kagaba, Colombia)[29]

At the end of life this mighty mother figure took all and everything back into her hospitable womb. But gradually she underwent

28. Weigle, *Creation and Procreation*, 1982:46.

29. Konrad Preuss in Weigle, *Spiders & Spinsters: Women and Mythology*, 1982:45-46.

metamorphoses. She petrified, she no longer fulfilled her creative tasks, her sex changed, or someone snatched her creative powers.

> We can no longer see her in the way we can see a person, even though she has legs and arms, a head, a heart, flesh, bones, and blood. Her flesh is the soil now; her hair has become trees and vegetation; her bones are the rocks, and her breath is the wind. As she lies there, spread out, we live on her. When she moves, there is an earthquake.[30]

The story of Mother Earth bringing forth everything takes an abrupt turn when a new character is introduced with the name Old Man. In some variants he sits down upon the Mother's body and, without further comment, begins to transform her—he pulls bits from her flesh and rolls them into tiny balls. The last balls look 'different from any of the preceding ones. He called them men and they looked like Indians, and when he blew on them, they became alive.'[31]

In transitional stages of origin stories it is sometimes unclear whether the creator is male or female, but ultimately the creation of life has almost everywhere been disconnected from the earlier independent, birth-giving and nourishing Mother Goddess.[32] In Chinese stories, originally the goddess Nüwa created the first people with her own hands, without male intervention:

> This is what people tell: when heaven and earth had been created, there were no human beings yet. Nüwa, the primeval goddess, wandered through the quiet world and

---

30. Boas, Franz, James Alexander Teit, Livingston Farrand, Marian K. Gould, Herbert Joseph Spinden. *Folk-tales of Salishan and Sahaptin Tribes*, 1969:80.

31. Ibid.

32. e.g. Baring and Cashford, 1991; Lerner, 1986; Graves and Patai, *Hebrew Myths, 1964:26; David Leeming, Myth. A Biography of Belief*, 2002:41, 79.

> the silence filled her body with loneliness. Near a spring she found yellow soil, picked some up and began to mould a creature like herself. When she put it down beside the spring the creature began to laugh. Nüwa enjoyed the sound of laughing so much that she made another one, and still another one, and many more, shaping each of them carefully and beautifully with her hands. [...] She placed them on the earth. They all laughed and danced and enjoyed themselves, and Nüwa called them her sons and daughters. (Han, China)[33]

In later versions Nüwa lost her creative independence to become the sister and/or wife of Fuxi—and they were represented together with a human upper body and an underbody in the form of two intertwined snakes.

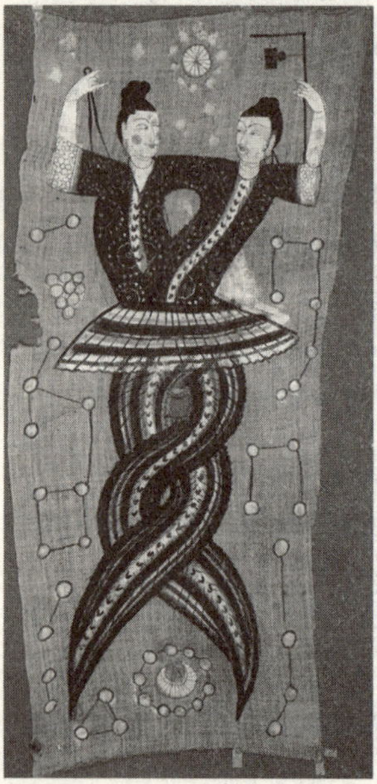

Nüwa and Fuxi. Silk painting, mid-eighth century. Xinjiang Uighur Museum.

33. Lihui Yang and Deming An 2005:170-172; Yuan Ke 1993:4; Mathieu 1989:63.

In Chinese, the key concept 'god' originally meant 'the ability to bear children'. In the course of history, the idea of 'bringing forth' completely disappeared from the ancient meaning, and in Chinese myths—no less than in other parts of the world—the mother goddess ended up in a submissive role as the partner of a male god, or she herself changed into a male character. Nonetheless, traces of her earlier independence are still detectable in ancient versions.[34]

The glass ceiling of sacred marriage

In many stories, procreation—creating life by giving birth—has been transformed into fabrication: creation from nothing by word or gesture, or from materials by means of creative handwork. In a Hrusso myth, the Sky God took the initiative from the earlier Earth Goddess who had previously proceeded all by herself. Her power crumbled away and she was ordered to literally shrink:

> The Earth was too big for the Sky to hold in his arms. 'Though you are my wife,' he said, 'you are greater than I. How can I take you? Make yourself smaller.' The Earth complied, and thanks to her adaptability the mountains and valleys came into being. The Earth became small and the Sky was able to go to her in love. From their lovemaking every kind of tree and grass and all living creatures came into being. (Hrusso, India)[35]

Mother Earth had to make way for an almighty Father God; an idea that became widespread. In the human world the small look up to the bigger, the younger have to respect the elder,

34. cf. Ye Shuxian, 2011; Bret Hinsch, 2004:77. Robert H. Lowie, *Primitive Religion*, 1925:275.

35. Elwin, 1958:15-16.

the weaker have to bow down to the mightier. In our day most men stick to this very reasoning when it comes to finding a wife, consciously or subconsciously obeying traditional proverbs warning those who are courting to look for a woman who is 'inferior' in stature, age, education, in brief, less bright than him. 'A woman without talents is already doing very well' is a well-worn saying in China.

This message is echoed from Africa to Asia and the Americas in the warning, 'Never marry a woman with bigger feet than your own', which I adapted for the title of my collection of proverbs about women from around the world, *Never Marry a Woman with Big Feet* (2004). Apparently, this message is universally recognisable. The book has been translated all over the world, with ever more translations forthcoming.[36]

Researchers generally agree that early agriculture was invented by women, whose task was to collect seeds, fruits and eggs while the men were hunting. They noticed that seeds or parts of tubers spilled on the compound germinated and matured on their own, so they began to plant seeds and root vegetables around the cave or hut where they lived. Aside from the sowing and harvesting of crops, the baking of bread, the creation of clay pots for ritual and household use, the weaving and dyeing of clothes and the use of healing herbs have all been attributed to women transmitting their knowledge and abilities to each other.[37]

Thanks to agriculture, people attained new insight into their own situation. As much as hunting had been a sacred activity, farming was surrounded by rituals and ceremony. People looked with religious awe upon the hidden forces of the earth containing

36. http://www.womeninproverbsworldwide.com/the-book/editions/. The complete data of more than 15,000 proverbs can be consulted at http://www.womeninproverbsworldwide.com/.

37. Sierksma, 1962, Chapter 9.

and bringing forth all creatures, plants, animals and humans as from a living womb. Most agricultural activities were projected onto the particular powers of a goddess, encouraging belief in the necessity of sacrifices. The earth as the nourishing mother of life was considered full of magic power, bridging the visible and the invisible order.

Gods, humans, animals and plants were part of the same nature and constituted an organic whole. In order to guarantee a successful harvest, sacrifices were made. Usually, the first corn was left standing in the field and the first fruits were left on the trees—as a gesture of restitution. There were sacrifices of animals or humans, as a means to recycle holy energy.

Human sexuality became more and more connected to the divine power that fertilised the earth. In Neolithic mythology, the harvest came to be seen as the fruit of a sacred marriage. The rain united Heaven and Earth. The earth was female, the seed from Heaven, male. In some cultures, people had ritual sex when planting their crops. The belief that dying and coming back to life were inextricably linked, developed into a reasoning with dramatic consequences—in the eternal cycle irreparable disasters will take place if no sacrificial blood has been shed. The mother goddess, though still considered loving and generous, began to change into a rather capricious or even cruel being, because of all the offerings she was believed to demand from her children.

Cybele, a widely worshipped fertility goddess, is a prime example. Most likely her foremother was a local Anatolian mother goddess, a precursor found in the earliest settlements of Çatalhöyük, where various images of plump women have been dug up. Physical birth-giving was a weighty topic in the Çatalhöyuk sanctuaries of Anatolia (around 7500-5700 BC). Archaeologists found giant stone reliefs of impressive female figures with huge breasts, bellies and thighs; left and right of the throne, their arms rest on a leopard or lioness. They are flanked by the horns of a bull or skulls of wild pigs—remains of successful hunting. These Stone Age images may well have been appropriated in later manifestations of Cybele and the Greek goddesses Artemis and Demeter.

Hunting was a male activity, but the god of hunting was often a female character and the gods of agriculture were originally female too. Artemis was mistress of the animals as well as the source of life. The hunters who risked their lives in order to keep their wives and children alive, understood that women were the source of new life. They were the ones who guaranteed continuity of the group, while men were replaceable.[38] Depictions of Cybele, the Great Goddess of Anatolia with a lion in her lap or on a chariot pulled by lions and leopards, are certainly reminiscent of the much older Neolithic stone reliefs found in Çatalhöyük.

Anatolian goddess with a newborn baby, flanked by lionesses, Çatalhöyü, *c.* 6000-5500 BC. Museum of Anatolian Civilizations, Ankara.

38. Karen Armstrong, *A Short History of Myth*. Edinburgh/New York/Melbourne: Canongate 2005, Chapter 2.

For centuries, several stories insisted that Cybele's lover Attis was also her son. According to others, Cybele drove him insane with jealousy, while some variants insist he killed himself because she no longer reciprocated his love. Whatever the cause, whether seen as a simple shepherd or a god of fertility, Attis castrated himself and bled to death, and from his blood sprang the first violets. After his death, a ritual was performed in his honour during which Cybele brought him back to life. The Cybele cult spread from Anatolia to Greece, Rome and many other places.

Inspired by Attis' example, all those who served Cybele as her priests were eunuchs. In Rome, where they were called Galli, they dressed in women's clothes, 'mostly yellow in colour, and a sort of turban, together with pendants and ear-rings, they also wore their hair long and bleached, and wore heavy make-up.'[39] After an ecstatic spring celebration on the 'Day of Blood', during which they mourned Attis, the priests castrated themselves. Running around, messy and disordered, they threw their testicles haphazardly into the houses they passed, a gesture the inhabitants appreciated as a special benediction.

This cult of the mother goddess with a son/lover was popular among many believers in the region, from the sixth century BC till the end of the fifth century AD—the end of the Roman Empire. Like other great goddesses, Cybele protected fertility and the dead, as much as untamed nature and the animals. For Lucretius (99-55 BC), Cybele as Magna Mater symbolises 'the world order'. Her image signifies the Earth, she is the mother of all, and the yoked lions that draw her chariot show the offspring's duty of obedience to the parent. She herself is uncreated, and thus essentially separate from and independent of her creations.[40]

39. https://en.wikipedia.org/wiki/Galli.

40. Ibid. and https://en,wikipedia.org/wiki/Cybele#Roman_Cybele. The Greek historian Strabo (c. 64 BC-23 AD) wrote about the sexual implications of Cybele's veneration.

Gradually myths were permeated with violence—believers thought the goddess provided them with food, but they felt that the harvest would come to nothing if no male had been sacrificed to the mother goddess. Those consorts were, in the words of Karen Armstrong, 'torn apart, dismembered, brutally mutilated, and killed before they can rise again, with the crops, to new life.'[41]

Surreptitiously the powerful, loving goddess turned into a demanding one who needed, all for herself, endless bloodshed and immolation of men and animals. That image matched the idea that women were the source of new life and men just disposable objects. From the anxious belief that the goddess would take it out on followers who did not comply with the required sacrifices, terms such as demanding, irreconcilable and vengeful became more applicable to this goddess than cherishing motherly love. No doubt such beliefs inspired stories about men 'stealing women's secret'.

After the invention of agriculture, women began to grow food near their homes. Thanks to their more and more substantial provision to the common daily food stores, female prestige increased, especially when the hunting men came home empty-handed—a situation that no doubt led to tensions. In places where the social status of women began to dominate social life, men developed secret societies in order to improve their position in relation to women. On three continents in areas around the equator, these tensions caused such disharmony that they inspired mythical stories about men grabbing power (more on this in Chapter 10).

The supreme power of the goddess is to be found in early images and myths revering female fertility in various forms, from snake goddess to sea goddess or moon goddess or virgin goddess or a goddess fabricating human beings from clay. The original key to the mystery of life was femininity. Originally Mother Earth

41. Armstrong 2005:49-50.

had all the potential for stepping up to the echelon of Supreme Goddess, but her career was blocked by the glass ceiling of her sacred marriage with Heaven.

The male invention of the plough and the taming of oxen and other animals to draw it through the soil, brought a new balance between male and female contributions—economically speaking, male plough agriculture was superior to the older corn and tuber cultures invented by women, producing a much more considerable harvest. More people stayed alive longer, more children were born, and small villages grew into bigger ones.[42]

From around 4000 BC people began to build cities with fortified walls to feel safer. Increasing male self-confidence inspired myths in which the creative role of goddesses was transferred to male gods and first male ancestors, and those new stories served as the cement to bind society together. The creation of life continued to be a crucial theme in every society, but the tenor of the stories changed—with striking consequences for the ways in which the creation of life was represented.

In many myths about the creation of humans, a male god creates the first man before the first woman. Often, she is created from lower-quality material. Three examples:

> Hinegba took some earth and made man out of it. He then took some more earth and made woman out of it. Man is physically stronger than woman because he was created first, that is before the strength of the earth had been sapped by the creation of an earlier human being out of it. (Kwotto, Nigeria)[43]

---

42. Sierksma 1962:152.

43. Kwotto: J.R. Wilson. 'Ethnological Notes on the Kwottos of Toto (Panda) District, Keffi Division, Benue Province, Northern Nigeria.' *Journal of the African Society* XXXVII (1927-1928), p.145.

> The Lord of Heaven decided to fashion first ten men and then ten women out of the flesh and bones of fowls. As soon as he began working on the women he ran out of material, and had to take clay instead. As a result, the women created had no strength and were too weak to labour. The Lord of Heaven then infused strength into their bodies. However, the women now became so powerful that the men were no match for them. Considering this to be unsuitable, the Lord took back half of their strength. (Oroqen, China)[44]
>
> Aware of Adam's loneliness God created the first woman out of dust. Her name was Lilith. However, he had not used pure dust but filth and sediment instead. (Jewish Apocrypha)[45]

In a lot of cases a male Supreme Being first creates a complete man, then a female human being out of an insignificant body part of this first man, for example, a toe, a rib or a thumb. Or he urges the first man to make himself a wife from his own urine, sperm or foreskin, or from a piece of flesh from his thigh. So many small details include such blatant messages of sexual hierarchy, it becomes difficult to consider them all accidental.[46]

One could of course argue that being created later does not necessarily mean being inferior—on the contrary, a second creative effort might well turn out more perfect than the first thanks to errors encountered and overcome in the earlier effort. However,

---

44. With thanks to Ye Shuxian who generously shared with me his unpublished collection of myths, p.6: Narrator: Meng Xingquan; recorded by Meng Shuzhen.

45. Louis Ginzburg, *The Legends of the Jews*. Trans. Henrietta Szold. Seven vols. Philadelphia: 1967-1969. Vol. I:65.

46. More details in *In het Begin was er Niemand, (In the Beginning There Was No One*), Chapter 6.

appearing second came to be equated with 'less valuable'. This and many other elements in creation and origin stories reflect male responses to female birth-giving—apparently experienced as an imbalance between the sexes.

How Eve lost her life-creating status

The story of the first ancestral couple in Judaism, Christianity and Islam is one of the best-known origin myths. Verbal and visual variants of the Adam and Eve story have spread globally—from Scandinavia to South Africa, from Mexico to Southeast Asia. In the first book of the Bible, the first human being is created in God's image and likeness, male and female. Originally it is just a 'mud creature', shaped from *ha-adamah*, the earth, as a piece of pottery. Only their separation turns the two parts into gendered humans. Some scholars have argued that the name of Eve (in Hebrew, *Havah*) is close to *Yahweh*, the name of God: 'The potential of procreation justifies that closeness. [...] Eve was not born from the first man, but split off from the first creature, bi-sexual, as the first part of the story says: he created the human in his image and likeness—man and woman he created them (plural).'[47] Moreover, she is described as 'the mother of all the living', an impressive name.

In the most popular translation and interpretation of the next part of the story (Genesis 2), God's creation of Eve out of a rib from Adam's body, Eve ends up as 'a help fit for' Adam, immediately establishing Eve's inferiority, which would descend automatically on all women after her, and serve as a justification of sexual hierarchy practices in Judaism, Christianity and Islam.

What is more, some researchers have stated that the translation 'rib' is not correct in this context. The bone that Eve had been

47. Personal comment: Mieke Bal.

made of was no rib, but a *baculum* or 'penis bone', a part some animals (such as lions, chimpanzees and gorillas) still possess. After Adam had to sacrifice it for Eve's 'creation', men have ever since had to do without this helpful little pillar.[48]

That God created the human male and female is explained by some rabbis as the creation of two separate beings. Others suggest that originally Adam consisted of a male and a female body in one. That first back-to-back creation was not very practical for moving, or having a conversation. Which is why God sawed them apart and gave both a back of their own, and placed them in the Garden of Eden.[49]

An androgynous Adam and Eve, sharing two legs
and having one arm each, eleventh century.
Capital in the church of Anzy-le-Duc, Burgundy.

48. Ziony Zevit, http://www.biblicalarchaeology.org/daily/biblical-topics/bible-interpretation/the-adam-and-eve-story-eve-came-from-where/.

49. Ginzberg: *Genesis Rabba in Graves and Patai*: 66; Kvam, Schearing and Ziegler 77-78; Elaine Pagels 1976:298.

The number of artistic creations of Eve grew considerably in ninth-century Europe. In some, the first humans are created separately 'in God's own image', in others, they are imagined as a combined hermaphrodite creature, or God takes a rib from Adam's body and goes on to build Eve from that rib (see Plate 6).[50]

Halfway through the eleventh century, the successive scenes culminate in a crucial reversal—Eve's creation was presented as an act of Adam's giving birth. She lithely pops out of the sleeping Adam's right side, her two hands raised in devotion. As an accomplished midwife, God—represented as a man with a beard—pulls Eve from Adam's body with his left hand, while his right hand makes a blessing gesture (see Plate 7).

In Christian Europe the image of a birth-giving Adam was a popular visual theme between the twelfth and the sixteenth century, as can still be seen in churches, cathedrals and museums. Representations of Eve born from Adam's body turned the natural roles of men and women upside down, thereby downgrading Eve's status. If, in human terms, the one who gives birth is superior to the one who does not, and should rule over the one given birth to, the church had a problem. By underlining that Adam had been Eve's birth-giver, the matter was immediately resolved. Images of Eve appearing from Adam's side or groin as a euphemism for his genitals made clear to the illiterate masses of believers that the man has to dominate the wife—he was created first and she came from him and therefore had to be subservient. This reasoning resulted in the hierarchical message that it is 'in the natural order of things' that women serve their husbands, children their parents, and servants their lords and masters. That logic justified the position of the man as the head of the family, and his lasting power over his wife and children—a logic still cherished in many contexts.

---

50. Englard: 24.

The reversal of roles was confirmed in pedagogic texts, for example, in the words of the Italian merchant and writer Paolo da Certaldo (1320-1370): 'A good son loves his father, has respect for him and obeys him, because he has given birth to him, even though his mother provided practical aid.'[51] The idea that man and woman had been created as equal partners in God's image receded further and further into the background.

The 'crooked rib' in Islamic tradition

The Christian representation of Eve born from Adam was based on wishful thinking about hierarchical marriage relations, a representation that went against the biblical creation story and also against its rendition provided in the Quran (Sura 4:1), where no rib is mentioned. Nonetheless, Islamic versions of the rib story spread in Islamic traditions just as freely as in Christian ones.

The character of women was associated with the rib from which their foremother Eve was created, according to an Islamic belief that is still quite popular, and therefore a man must learn to live with female 'crookedness'—women's crooked arguments and unreasonable behaviour are due to the crooked rib she originates from. In short, a woman cannot help it and men must try to make the best of it, according to the respected Islamic scholar Bukhari (810-70) in a frequently quoted commentary:

> A woman is like a rib; [...]. If you want to straighten her, she will break: if you want to benefit by her you can do so despite her crookedness.[52]

This text comes from the Islamic Hadith, the most respected commentaries on the Quran. In matters of creation, intelligence

---

51. Paolo da Certaldo, *Livre des Bons Usages*, quoted in Zapperi: 31.

52. Sahih Bukhari, Arabic-English translation, Vol. VII, Hadith:113: http://www.shariahprogram.ca/status-rights-women/woman-crooked-rib.shtml.

and religion, these scriptures present man as superior to woman; therefore, he is more suited to the role of judge and to lead religious services. His testimony is twice as valuable as a woman's. That is why greater responsibilities have been granted him, with accordingly greater privileges. Moreover, a woman's intelligence is deficient, her lust too vast, and if she has too much money, she will end up corrupt.

Various old Islamic texts insist that a man's status is so much higher than a woman's that the two can never be on an equal footing. In 1985, Muslim writer Ahmad Zaky Tuffaha, seriously and reverently, quoted the following text:

> If a woman offered one of her breasts to be cooked and the other to be roasted, she still will fall short of fulfilling her obligations to her husband. And besides that, if she disobeys her husband even for a twinkling of an eye, she would be thrown in the lowest part of Hell, except if she repents and turns back.[53]

Hadith scriptures about the relations between men and women visibly reflect the desperate need for emphasis on the superiority of men. The *Book of One Thousand Questions*, a sort of Islamic catechism in Q&A form, confirms this logic of male superiority on the basis of creation story elements:

Q. Was Adam taken from Lady Eve or was Lady Eve taken from Adam?

A. Lady Eve was taken from Adam. If Adam had been taken from Lady Eve, all men certainly would be obedient to women. So, it is clear that Lady Eve was taken from Adam.

---

53. 'Men's Superiority and Women's Deficiency' in: http://www.answering-islam.org/authors/newton.html.

Q. Was Lady Eve generated from the body of Adam or from something outside Adam's body?

A. Lady Eve was generated from the body of Adam. If Lady Eve had been generated from something outside Adam's body, all women in this world certainly would go around naked and not feel ashamed in front of men.

Q. Was Lady Eve generated from the left or right side of Adam?

A. Lady Eve was generated from the left side of Adam. If she had been generated from his right side, all women would inherit two parts. Lady Eve was generated from the left side of Adam and therefore all women only receive one [third] part of the inheritance, according to the word of God the most high in the Quran.[54]

'The mother of all the living' receives harsh judgement in a number of commentaries, as the one who disrupted the harmony of paradise and saddled humanity with the finiteness of life. Stories and images of Adam and Eve have left deep scars in the thinking of believers and non-believers alike, and do so even today. In the three monotheistic religions many theologians were keen on deploying Eve's sin as an easy means to project negative qualities on the female sex.

In older myths from Mesopotamia, Egypt and Greece, life and death were still taken care of by the Great Mother. In the biblical story, life-confirming images—the garden, the four rivers, the Tree of Life, the Serpent and the world parents—make way for fear and guilt.[55] In a number of interpretations, death is mainly blamed on Eve because it did not exist before her disobedience. Augustine (fourth century), one of the most influential Christian church fathers, alleged that 'even before her sin woman had been

54. Quoted in Steenbrink, *Adam revivus*, 1998:55. Quran Sura 4:1.

55. More details about interpretations of Eve's story in Baring and Cashford, Chapter 13.

made to be ruled by her husband and to be submissive and subject to him.'[56]

In the Genesis story the life-creating role is attributed to God the Father, but gradually the most widespread visual image made clear that Eve, the first female creature, came forth from the first man's body and was held responsible for the mortality of all humans.[57]

Slowly but surely, the room of Mother Earth in the house of origin stories was remodelled as a space where male gods gradually took over her life-giving activities. The urge to embezzle the female share in the production of offspring must have been pressing. Or in Erich Fromm's words, halfway through the twentieth century, in *The Forgotten Language*:

> There are good reasons for assuming that even before male supremacy was established there was a 'pregnancy envy' in the male, which even today can be found in numerous cases. In order to defeat the mother, the male must prove that he is not inferior, that he has a gift to produce. Since he cannot produce with a womb, he must produce in another fashion; he produces with his mouth, his word, his thought.[58]

In origin stories this 'other fashion' doesn't seem to fully make up for the lack.

Mysteries surround us, and our human limitations try to reduce incomprehensible godliness to human proportions. In images and stories of gods, human desires filter through, providing the gods with strangely human features—divinities are believed to want to own and to achieve everything.

---

56. Augustine, *The Literal Meaning of Genesis*, Book XI:37.

57. Baring and Cashford: 494.

58. Fromm, 1956:233. More examples of 'pregnancy envy' stories in Chapter II.

Bumba, creator god of the Kuba-speaking people in southeastern Congo, throwing up people from his inner body. Woodcut by South African artist Motshile wa Nthodi, 1979.

2. MALE CREATORS

> In the beginning there was only darkness and nothing existed on earth except water. Bumba the Chembe (creator god) ruled alone over this chaos. Bumba had the shape of a man, but was of enormous size [...]. One day he felt a terrible pain in his belly, and soon he began to throw up.[59]

Stories about Mother Earth never refer to her longing for her own penis, although she might readily have made that demand. Later goddesses of agriculture were presented with frequent sacrifices of young men, and phalluses were placed on their shrines ready for use.[60]

Creating life with and without a womb

Except in some matrilocal myths, the high-profile creator of life is usually represented as a male divine being. Male gods are not just presented as creators of all life, but are often given anatomical extras in the form of a womb or breasts. When they create from 'nothing', a word, a dream, a breath, a shadow or a gesture suffice. When they create from matter, they achieve no less spectacular results than the mother goddess.

---

59. Torday and Joyce, *Notes ethnographiques*, 1910:20-21. My translation.

60. Lederer:216.

The aforementioned Bumba vomits all of creation from his own insides:

> He first vomited the sun, then the moon and lastly the stars, and that is how there came to be light. [...] And Bumba started to vomit again and this time he choked up in sequence the leopard, the crested eagle, the crocodile, a small fish, the tortoise, thunder and lightning, the white heron, the beetle and the goat. He then vomited out a great many people.[61]

Producing the world and humanity, Bumba did as easily without a wife as some birth-giving female creators managed without a husband in earlier traditions. With the exception of thunder and lightning, which soon began to wreak havoc, the Kuba god's life-giving work was flawless.

Similar examples can be found in Hindu mythology, where androgynous gods are a regular occurrence. Shiva and his partner Parvati (see Plates 8 and 9) are often represented in one person: one half is male and the other half is female—with the male Shiva usually being the right half.

Prajapati (Lord of Creatures), the creator god of the Vedic period of ancient India, later became associated with the Hindu god Brahma. He brings biological creation into existence, and is sometimes seen as the 'motherly male' or referred to as the mythical divinity of birth: 'His structure, his actions, his feelings are all analogous to the human reproductive process; even his lassitude after creation, and his need for refertilisation pertain to this model.' In order to create the world from his insides, he starts with the procreative ritual wish, 'May I propagate myself.' Then, as the creator, he provides himself with a womb-like

61. Torday and Joyce, ibid.

Androgynous Shiva: right half male,
left half female, tenth century.
Khajuraho temple complex, Madhya Pradesh, India.

organ (*prajanana*), from which he begins to emit 'progeny and animals'.[62]

Male gods lacking a womb sought different solutions to the problem of procreation, often in stories about one and the same god. Sometimes Prajapati is represented as a bisexual divine being in the shape of a man and a woman in an intimate embrace, able to divide itself into two halves in order to copulate:

> Prajapati became pregnant and created posterity from his right thumb, nipple, and other organs, without the benefit

62. Doris Meth Srinivasan. *Many Heads, Arms and Eyes*, 1997:60-61.

> of mothers. But he became dissatisfied with this creation, and so he divided his body in half and made one half a woman. He tried to make love to her, and although she and her brother were shocked at this incestuous act, he eventually married her and created progeny with her.[63]

This raises the tricky question of whether a person originating from your body is your child. If the answer is yes, then having sex with that person is a matter of incest—a universal taboo. From a mythical perspective this problem is done away with as an unavoidable case of *force majeure*: in the beginning, there was simply no one else available with whom to multiply and provide an empty world with the first progeny.

What about Adam and Eve? In Christianity the miraculous creation of Eve was sometimes presented as a riddle:

> I died and was not born,
> I married my father
> When I was one day old,
> And a mother I have none.[64]

The problem of incestuous relations between Adam and Eve was resolved by the influential medieval priest, professor and philosopher Thomas Aquinas—only in the case of a 'natural' birth one could raise the matter of incest, but Eve's was an absolutely exceptional birth. Therefore, Eve was not Adam's daughter.[65]

---

63. Wendy Doniger O'Flaherty, *Women, Androgynes and Other Mythical Beasts*. Chicago: Chicago University Press, 1980:312.

64. German riddle.

65. Zapperi, *L'homme enceint*, 1983:25ff.

Does God have breasts?

The images we came across earlier of goddesses with striking breasts and swollen bellies, found in Europe and up to 40,000 years old, resemble later images from Mesopotamia and Syria's Halaf culture.

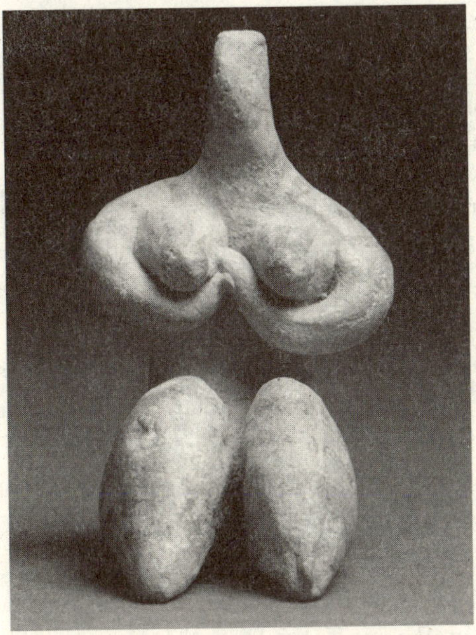

Ceramic fertility figurine, Mesopotamia/
North Syria, c. 6000-5100 BC.
Musée du Louvre, Paris.

Here too believers begged the divine mother to share with them the powers of her mysterious fertility. And here too, since time immemorial, stories were told in which all life sprang from her fertile motherly body.

Most myths surviving in the Middle East originate from a time in which the exclusive rights of the mother goddess had already been transferred to a male partner or a pugnacious rival.

That transfer was sometimes far from peaceful. Sometimes the primal foremother was literally butchered by vindictive posterity, as in the famous Babylonian *Enuma Elish* (probably composed in the late second millennium BC). In this story, the matriarch Tiamat succumbs in a decisive battle with her ambitious offspring Marduk who then claims power for himself:

> [Marduk] placed his feet on the lower parts of Tiamat
> And with his merciless club smashed her skull.
> He severed her arteries
> And let the north wind bear up her blood...

Showing no mercy, he splits her colossal body in two 'like a dried fish', and stands triumphant over her dead remains, which he uses to create the clouds, winds, earth and mountains.[66] His violent settling of accounts renders her powerless.

This cosmic conflict from the Babylonian tradition has been usurped by the biblical myth of one creating God, but in poetic biblical texts the actors from previous stories return in references to sea monsters, dragons and storm gods that were fought against by the Hebrew God. The primal deep, controlled by God's wind sweeping over the 'face of the waters' in the Hebrew Bible is referred to as *tehom*, a term related to Tiamat.[67] The dramatic defeat of the mother goddess in Babylonian myth and in the Hebrew Bible is far from unique. Comparable stories emerged in many societies where changing social relations gave rise to new stories in which the starring role is assumed by a supreme deity or God of Heaven.[68]

---

66. W.G. Lambert in *Imagining Creation*, (Geller and Schipper, eds.), 2008:20.

67. E.g., in Genesis 1:2; 7:11; 8:2; http://www.oxfordbiblicalstudies.com/article/opr/t94/e1913.

68. Anne Baring and Jules Cashford. *The Myth of the Goddess. Evolution of an Image*, 1993:420ff.

Differing views exist on the development of the Hebrew religion—depending on the starting point. In contrast to Marduk, the Father God has no ancestors. He was there right from the beginning, what he said was true, and all he created was good. In the Jewish tradition God had no proper noun, His name was too holy to be uttered aloud, but reverently referred to as Elohim or El ('God') or as Jahweh (usually translated as 'the Lord'), and in expressions such as 'He is One and Only' or as eternal, omnipotent, omnipresent, omniscient, aphysical (and therefore invisible), inscrutable and incomprehensible. Being pure spirit, from the strictly monotheistic perspective of traditional Judaism, He has no body and possesses no sexual traits. Nonetheless, since in the Hebrew language every noun is either masculine or feminine, 'every verbal statement about God conveyed the idea that He was masculine', as Raphael Patai observes in his fascinating book *The Hebrew Goddess*.[69] In spite of the strict message in the Bible and the Talmud, daily life offered a different view, in which an intense veneration of Ashera, Astarte, Anath and other goddesses continued. Polytheism was current among Israelites until the second century BC, as the author demonstrates on the basis of old Jewish traditions in the context of other cultures in the region. He finds this unsurprising 'in view of the general human, psychologically determined predisposition to believe in and worship goddesses.'[70]

Like earlier representations of mother goddesses, Ashera figures from the eighth and seventh century BC support or offer up their divine breasts with both hands. Referred to in the Canaanite pantheon as 'mother of the gods' and 'wet-nurse of the gods',

---

69. Raphael Patai, *The Hebrew Goddess*, 1968:18ff.

70. Ibid.; https://thequeenofheaven.wordpress.com/2011/08/17/does-god-have-breasts/.

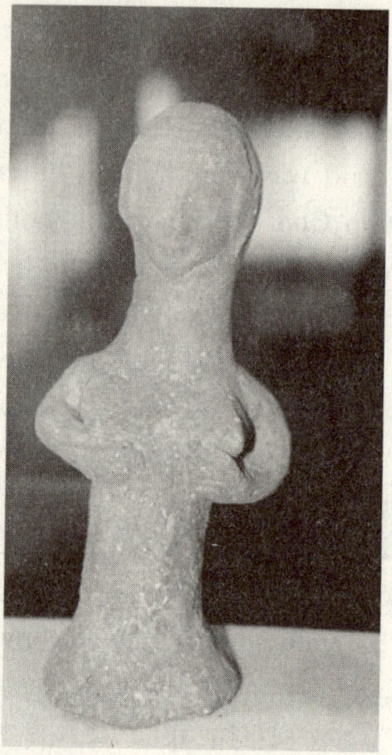

Goddess Ashera. Earthenware, eighth to sixth century BC. Eretz Israel Museum, Tel Aviv.

she was also depicted suckling certain humans of high birth.[71] According to archaeologists, Ashera—whose name appears more than forty times in the Bible in a negative context—was the wife of the God of ancient Israel, and was worshipped alongside him. Unearthed inscriptions from the eighth century BC invoke blessings 'by Yahweh and his Asherah'. On an old shard of pottery excavated near Kuntillet Ajrud in the Northern Sinaï, the Egyptian god Bes is the central figure (he looks after sexuality and birth giving), and beside him is another god (perhaps the militant god Aha). On the same shard, a nameless Jewish merchant has carved: '[...] May

71. Patai: 330.

you be blessed by the Lord who protects us and his Ashera'.[72]

The monotheistic editors who put the Bible into writing twisted the existing stories in a new direction and gave them new meaning. So the Hebrew Bible was bold enough to do what earlier patriarchies hadn't yet dared—to radically obliterate each and every trace of female veneration. The Bible is the first holy book without any female godly presence, divine spouse or lover. In contrast with ancient Middle Eastern deities, Yahweh is the first God unhindered by female competition.[73]

He is usually characterised by labels such as 'Man of War', 'Hero', 'King', 'Lord of Hosts', 'Master of the Universe', 'Our Father in Heaven', and yet theologians maintain that God is absolutely not to be seen in terms of sex or gender. Obviously, this was not self-evident to all believers.[74]

The Hebrew Bible emphatically warns against idolatry and the worship of images, which was firmly adopted in Islamic tradition. Christians, on the other hand, frequently represented God visually, mostly in the form of an impressive man with a beard. All three religions refer to God as an anthropomorphic male character, in Judaism and Christianity also called Father—a Father who can get mad at his children:

> The Biblical God-concept [...] reflects the strictly patriarchal order of the society which produced it; this patriarchal

---

72. Ze'ev Meshel. Kuntillet 'Ajrud. An Israelite Religious Center in Northern Sinai' in *Expedition* 20 (summer 1978): 50-55.

73. Robert Graves and Raphael Patai. *Hebrew Myths: The Book of Genesis*. New York: Anchor Books/Doubleday, 1964: 26-28; https://www.encyclopedia.com/environment/encyclopedias-almanacs-transcripts-and-maps/israelite-religion; http://www.bbc.co.uk/programmes/b00zw3fl: Bible's Buried Secrets, 2: Did God Have a Wife?; https://matricien.org/matriarcat-religion/judaisme/asherah/.

74. Elaine Pagels, 'What Became of God the Mother? Conflicting Images of God in Early Christianity' in *Signs* (2) 1976:293-303.

> society gave rise to a religion centred around a single, universal deity whose will was embodied in the Law, but who was abstract, devoid of all physical attributes and yet pronouncedly male, a true projection of the patriarchal family-head.[75]

As the Jewish tradition developed into a religion with one spiritual and incorporeal supreme God, believers struggled with this inexorable requirement. Many still longed for a female element, and found what they needed in local goddesses—which can be inferred from the many biblical texts in which Hebrew prophets demonise the worship of goddesses, and demand that believers only worship Him. There are obvious similarities between the blessings of the breasts and the womb found in Genesis and the fertility cults of Israelites' Canaanite neighbours, who cherished goddesses such as Ashera and Anat represented with prominent breasts.[76]

In the biblical story in which God makes a covenant with Abraham, He is referred to as El Shaddai, translated as 'God the Almighty', but the Hebrew word *shad* means 'breast':

> The sacred breast found in early Judaism is directly connected to God Himself. El Shaddai, the name of God that is always associated with the fertility blessings, meant something like the 'God (El) with breasts' or the 'God who suckles'. Even if this language was to be understood only metaphorically, it is obviously a masculine appropriation of a fundamentally female attribute. God could be seen as both male and female, transcending the narrow confines of human gender.[77]

---

75. Patai: 23-24.

76. Marilyn Yalom. *A History of the Breast*, 1998:25.

77. Yalom, ibid. 27.

By assimilating Ashera's nurturing breasts, the monotheistic God could not only be a Father for his people, but also a comforting Mother, and a source of life. The Hebrew Bible refers to God speaking of Himself as a mother 'bearing the Israelites in His bosom'.[78] No less than in the surrounding religions, Judaism celebrated fertility, and considered a woman 'complete' once she had given birth to male offspring.[79]

The end of Arab goddesses

As in the Hebrew tradition, the heaven of the pre-monotheistic Arab world was inhabited by male and female gods. Al-Uzza, Al-Lat and Al-Manat were cherished goddesses in the Arab pantheon of the seventh century. Al-Uzza, the mother of the earth and the equivalent of Demeter, controlled fertility and everything related to the origin of life. Her cult was respected among all the Arabs, 'extended throughout Arabia as far as Mesopotamia [and] enjoyed a privileged importance,' according to Ibn al-Qalbi (737-819) whose *Book of Idols* is one of the most important scriptures about pre-Islamic religions. Evidently, the Prophet Muhammad had to radically shed the surrounding world of Al-Uzza and other Arabian goddesses:

> The cult of the goddesses presented a thorny problem for the messenger of Allah. He would not be able to monopolise power and establish the basis of the monotheistic religion unless these three goddesses were not only discredited but destroyed. Goddesses of fecundity, of generation, of sexual reproduction, they had to be liquidated if Allah and Islam were to triumph. This liquidation was carried out in

78. e.g. Isa. 49:1; 49:15; 66:11-13, as mentioned in Walker Bynum, 1982:125.
79. Yalom, ibid.; Patai 162.

> two ways: ideologically, through discourse; and concretely, through the physical destruction of the sanctuaries of these goddesses.[80]

As in the history of the Hebrews, confusion now spread among the Arabs, who thought the three goddesses were the daughters of Allah (*Banat Allah*). No less than Jewish monotheism many centuries earlier, Islam was confronted with the question of how to get rid of popular goddesses, as Fatima Mernissi explained in her daring book (for safety's sake written under a pseudonym) *Woman in the Muslim Unconscious*:

> By robbing woman of the giving of life and reducing her to a mere passive envelope in the creation process, God is confronted with the problem of sexual duality: how to retrieve the couple and how to recreate it. It will be reconstituted, but after having undergone a metamorphosis that negates the attribute of femaleness, the capacity to give birth. [...] In sacred reality, it is man who gives birth to woman. [...] For the sacred order to exist, the female element (along with the child as a manifestation of it) has to be liquidated, because it is the incarnation of the finite, the mortal. The pre-Islamic Arab goddesses had to be destroyed to make possible the assertion in heaven and on earth of the domination of the male element—that is, monotheism.'[81]

Al-Uzza's temple in the region east of Mecca was destroyed in 630, and sooner or later other sanctuaries suffered a similar fate. Muhammad had to cut the umbilical cord that allied believers

---

80. Fatna A. Sabbah (Fatima Mernissi), *Woman in the Muslim Unconscious*, 1984:104.

81. Ibid. 99, 103.

with these goddesses. They appear in the Quran, but in several passages are deemed a disgrace. According to Ibn al-Qalbi the Quran did succeed in solving the problem.[82] Negative stories about Al-Uzza were brought into circulation. An old Berber story contains a warning along those lines of thought:

> Walking through a cemetery at night, you will hear beautiful singing. Whether you want to or not, you will go after it until you find a small, black, but very beautiful girl. She flees from you, first slowly, then more and more rapidly. You are forced to keep up with her and follow her [...]. Her breasts grow longer and she ends up by throwing them backwards over her shoulders. Then suddenly she jumps into a grave and the follower, jumping after her, is doomed to jump to his death.[83]

In other words: never go where Al-Uzza and other goddesses are found, because they will mercilessly drag you to your death.

As we have seen, in Judaism, Christianity and Islam, the One, the Eternal, the Almighty, the Supreme God, has mostly been presented as a male character. But in each of the three monotheistic religions, female elements kept sneaking in through unexpected back doors.[84] In Christianity, the Virgin Mary was called upon to fulfil the missing female role, in particular in its maternal function (more about that in Chapter 4).

---

82. Ibid. 103ff.

83. Ploss and Bartels, *De Vrouw in Natuur—en Volkenkunde Anthropologische Studiën*:128-129. My translation.

84. As Raphael Patai convincingly demonstrates in *The Hebrew Goddess*. For Jewish gnosticism including female elements, cf. Elaine Pagels, *The Gnostic Gospels*, 1989.

Jesus as a woman and a mother

Jesus as a mother is referred to in texts of the earliest Christian church fathers.[85] Around the twelfth century, the image of Jesus with nourishing breasts became very popular in religious scriptures, and various sermons refer to Christ nursing his children.

> The Bridegroom [Christ] has breasts, lest he should be lacking any one of all duties and titles of loving kindness. He is the father in virtue of natural creation...And also in virtue of the authority with which he instructs. He is a mother, too, in the mildness of his affection and a nurse.[86]

'Natural creation' suggests here that it is the man who is responsible for procreation (an idea that stubbornly stayed alive for centuries, also outside Christianity), but the metaphor of the nurturing mother perfected that 'natural' image. Of course, the celibate clergy who popularised these motherly depictions had renounced their own families and were obliged to refrain from all contact with women. Their poetic language served as a spiritual substitute for the world they had relinquished, often at an early age.

The union with God has sometimes been represented as a physical attachment at the nursing breast or within the protective womb. Some monks describe themselves or their souls as brides of Christ. 'One should not exclude that in such texts men could

---

85. Teresa Shaw, The Burden of the Flesh, 1998:16-17; Rolf Quaghebeur, *Eigenzinnige Christusvoorstellingen, over het moederschapsthema in de mystieke beeldtaal van de Middeleeuwen*. With thanks to Elise Bocquet who drew my attention to this unpublished thesis.

86. Caroline Walker Bynum. *Jesus as Mother: Studies in the Spirituality of the High Middle Ages*, 1984:119, 122. In the Christian Middle Ages there was limited knowledge about the origin of the foetus. Following Aristotle, people believed that the woman contributes the matter for the child and the man provides the superior parts: life and soul.

deal with their sexual longing: playing at the breast or penetrating the female body in references (perhaps with womb overtones) to the soul entering the side of Christ.'[87]

A sixteenth-century painting in clear light colours depicts a dead Christ dressed in a loincloth lying on a shroud, surrounded by mourners. His eyes are closed and his knees slightly bent. This Christ has breasts, which is emphasised by the way his arms are folded and he holds his right index and middle finger close to the nipple of the left breast, like a woman about to suckle her baby. This gesture has a metaphorical meaning—Jesus' tragic death bestows life on believers and nurtures them, just as a woman gives birth to and nurses her child. Around the body stand angels, praying women and the onlooking disciple John, while Mary Magdalene kneels devoutly at Jesus' feet next to her ointment pot (see Plates 10a & 10b). This anonymous painting, entitled *The Lamentation of Christ*, is part of a tradition of representing Christ with breasts.[88] By the end of the fourteenth century, this tradition made way for more emphasis on the suffering of Christ and the sinfulness of man.

In the human need for a nursing bosom, androgynous solutions also crop up in other parts of the world. Returning to the birth-giving Indian god Prajapati:

> Prajapati gave himself breasts, so that the creatures he created could suckle and live. Prior, his creatures had famished for want of mother's milk [...]. He then made

87. Idem, *Holy Feast and Holy Fast*, 1982:162-163.

88. The painting is part of the collection of the Musée Hôpital Notre-Dame à la Rose in Lessines, Belgium (with thanks to curator Elise Bocquet who provided the photograph. See also Elaine Pagels, 'What Became of God the Mother? Conflicting Images of God in Early Christianity' in *Signs* (2) 1976:293-303, and https://thequeenofheaven.wordpress.com/2011/08/17/does-god-have-breasts/.

> two breasts teeming with milk in the front of his own body. He (again) emitted offspring. These offspring, having been emitted and rushing to the breasts, thus came into existence; they are those that have not succumbed.[89]

The Egyptian god Hapi, who lived in a cave next to the first cataract of the Nile at Elephantine, is another such divine androgynous apparition. His sagging breasts and big belly represented his responsibility for the annual flooding of the Nile and the fertility of its valley.

The androgynous Nile god Hapi, with papyrus and lotus flowers. *Encyclopaedia Biblica*, 1903.

89. Doris Meth Srinivasan, *Many Heads, Arms, and Eyes*: 62-63.

In many cultures male gods adopt characteristics of the other sex,[90] and since time immemorial people have converted their faith in the divine into images that reflect human needs and desires. After mother goddesses were removed or displaced from the religious sphere, crucial female body parts and functions were apparently dearly missed in representations of male gods, so patriarchal cultures adroitly projected female features onto them.

In the twenty-first century, Ariana Grande reversed the roles once again in her affirmative song, 'God is a Woman.'[91] But the question remains, why should the divine be equated with either sex?

---

90. About Androgyny Worldwide: Hermann Baumann, *Das doppelte Geschlecht*, 1955.

91. https://genius.com/Ariana-grande-god-is-a-woman-lyrics.

Mary shares her breast milk with the (later canonised) Bernard of Clairvaux. Flemish School, *c.* 1480. Grand Curtius Museum, Luik.

3. GOD THE MOTHER BECOMES THE MOTHER OF GOD

> Men and women share equally imperfection, and are to receive the same instruction and the same discipline. For the name 'humanity' is common to both men and women; and for us 'in Christ there is neither male nor female'.[92]

> It is not permitted for a woman to speak in the church, nor is it permitted for her to teach, nor to baptise, nor to offer [the eucharist], nor to claim for herself a share in any masculine function—not to mention any priestly office.[93]

In the first two centuries of Christianity, male and female believers sat together during the service of worship, but it didn't take long before orthodox communities adopted the traditional Jewish habit of separating men from women. The above quotations represent diametrically opposed views of women by church fathers Clemens of Alexandria and Tertullian from around 180 AD. By the end of the second century, women were forbidden to take charge of any activities in the church, and groups ignoring this prohibition were branded heretics.

---

92. Clemens of Alexandria, quoted in Elaine Pagels, *The Gnostic Gospels*, 1979:87.

93. Tertullian, ibid. 81.

Immaculate conception

Both Christians and Muslims consider Mary as holy and elevated above all women. Under her Arabic name Maryam, she is mentioned more often in the Quran than in the Bible. Medieval Islamic scholars saw Maryam as the willing vessel for God's spirit and the Prophet Jesus, chosen for her privileged genealogy, carefully preserved chastity and unconditional submission to God.

While the Virgin Mary provided believers with the nourishing and cherishing maternal breast, time and again the church had to suppress a natural inclination to deify the mother of Jesus: no one was allowed to call her the Mother Goddess.

After some centuries of Christianity, Mary was granted special status—during the ecclesiastical Council of Ephesus in 431 she was officially declared to be the 'Mother of God'. It was certainly not by chance that this decision was taken in Ephesus, where the temple of the many-breasted goddess Artemis stood (see p.122). Early Christianity had been in conflict with this ancient fertility goddess, who had been revered for centuries by Greeks and Asians. In Europe, the Mother of God took the place of the Mother Goddess. The Virgin Mary occupied a special position as a virgin who gave birth to and suckled a divine son. Yet in the Bible only the evangelists Matthew and Luke remark on the virgin birth, and even in the book of Luke, Mary calls Joseph the father. Critical Bible specialists consider stories about Jesus's virgin birth more as legends.

Over the centuries, Christian theologians and high clerics elaborated on the metaphor of Mary's virginity. Popes continued to insist that Mary's body was 'intact'. According to Pope Siricius (fourth century AD), Jesus would certainly have rejected Mary as a mother, had she ever been besmirched by male seed. Some clerical scholars asserted that Jesus' delivery had been painless and without afterbirth, and that her hymen remained undamaged.

Even though some theologians, especially Protestant ones, disputed such matters, Roman Catholic and Eastern Orthodox doctrines held on to the virginity of the mother of Jesus.[94]

The oldest images of the Virgin Mary with her child Jesus at the breast originate from the Coptic tradition in Egypt. They were clearly inspired by the example of the goddess Isis affectionately breastfeeding her son Horus.

Isis with her son Horus. Bronze, c. 600 BC.
Wellcome Collection, London.

94. Uta Ranke-Heinemann, *Eunuchs for the Kingdom of God: Women, Sexuality, and the Catholic Church*, 1990:32 and 340ff.

Egyptian kings were frequently represented at the breast or in the lap of Isis or another goddess, symbolising that they had absorbed the divine powers and status of their powerful nurse.[95] People all over the Mediterranean knew the story of Isis, and images of her as a divine nurse have been found throughout Europe. Only after Christianity had become the most powerful religion in Rome, were the temples of Isis forbidden in the city. The Madonna with child invoked the same feelings of compassion as the Egyptian mother goddess. Mary as a human mother with her divine child Jesus appealed to everyone—learned or illiterate, rich or poor.

Maria lactans

The nursing Mother of God (referred to in Latin as *Maria lactans* or *Madonna lactans*) inspired many stories and became an important theme in European art. Several famous images depict the miracle of Mary sharing her breast milk with the abbot Bernard of Clairvaux (see p.49). In paintings and drawings, he kneels down in a white religious habit and the Virgin appears to him while nursing her baby. According to the story, as she takes little Jesus off her breast, a jet of her breast milk curves down to the lips of the clergyman to ease his thirst. In some images the jet of milk lands on his forehead in order to express that this is all about spiritual nourishment.

Some statues of Mary in places of pilgrimage send holy water out through her saintly breasts, so as to generously share the healing forces of the Mother of God with the pilgrims. From a double-sided Maria Fountain in Austria, the curing water wells from four breasts at the same time.

Mary's popularity is affirmed in the many stories of sightings

95. More in Baring and Cashford 250; Yalom: 11-12.

of the Holy Virgin over many centuries across the globe. They have all been mapped by *National Geographic*, both those approved and not approved by the Vatican.[96]

In Europe, Mary's multiple apparitions of 1858 at Lourdes are well-known, but more than three centuries earlier, in 1531, she appeared in Mexico City on four occasions to Juan Diego, a poor Indian who was belatedly canonised in 2002. A basilica dedicated to the Virgin of Guadalupe (as the Mother of God is called there), near the site of the apparitions, is visited every year by twenty million pilgrims.

Religious becomes secular

Symbols can make an invisible reality accessible but, like human beings, they hit their peak and gradually lose their power—and ultimately their meaning. This is what happened, slowly but surely, to the symbol of Mary's bared breast. Although representations of the maternal breast had been consistently portrayed, unnoticed changes tainted its symbolic structure, as Margaret Miles explains in her book *A Complex Delight* (2008). Studying hundreds of images of Mary suckling her child, she noticed a shifting meaning and function of women's breasts in early modern Western Europe—a meaning visibly evolving from the religious to the secular:

> In early modern Western societies in which Christianity was the dominant religion, her bared breast, appearing in paintings and sculptures, signified nourishment and loving care—God's provision for the Christian, ever in need of God's grace. Moreover, referencing every human being's earliest pleasure, the breast pointed to and 'opened up'

96. https://www.nationalgeographic.com/science/article/151113-virgin-mary-sightings-map

the greater reality of the universe's provision of life and the sustenance of life. The believer's acceptance, pleasure and gratitude expressed by the appropriate responses, reminding viewers of the foundational moment of their existence.[97]

Two statues of the Virgin breastfeeding Jesus.
Left: Lorraine, France, early fifteenth century, Musée des Arts Décoratifs, Paris.
Right: Lower Austria, c. 1380, German National Museum, Nuremberg.

From the fourteenth to the eighteenth century, Mary was frequently depicted with one bared breast suckling Christ as an infant. The image aligned with the natural act of mothers everywhere, whether at home or in the public sphere, exposing a breast to feed their baby without embarrassment. Thanks to Mary's indispensable nursing breast, Jesus could later give his life to save the world. Thus, in a certain sense, the Virgin Mary's

97. Miles, 2008: ix.

milk was equated with the blood of Jesus.[98] The Mother of God was often seen as a mediator: she pleaded with her divine son for the sake of mortals who were terrified of the Last Judgement. In some stories her breasts even alleviated the concerns of those who had already died. In an Italian painting by Nicola Filotesio dell'Amatrice (1506), Mary with Jesus on her right arm stands high above Purgatory, where she lets the milk from her breasts rain down upon the thirsty souls.

In early images, a tiny breast about the size of a billiard ball pops up from a small aperture in Mary's royal raiment, often placed awkwardly high on her shoulder (see Plate II). And until well into the fifteenth century believers associated Mary's one bared breast with her virginal motherhood:

> No more bare flesh than was absolutely necessary surrounded this single nourishing breast—it was solemn and not sensuous, and the clothing worn by the Virgin in all early-fifteenth-century art was equally solemn. These gowns were similar to a type of dress actually in use, but they were much enriched and manipulated for hieratic purposes in art.[99]

By 1750 the symbolical meaning of the nursing mother's breast was no longer understood, thanks to increasing eroticisation and medicalisation of this body part.

From as early as the fourteenth century, people had started to adapt their bodies by all manner of artificial means: both men and women embellishing their contours with shape-improving ribs and paddings, according to the reigning aesthetic rules. Corsets

98. Saxon, Elizabeth, *The Eucharist in Romanesque France: Iconography and Theology*, 2006:205-207.

99. Anne Hollander, *Seeing Through Clothes*, 1978:187.

became fashionable and breasts were constricted or pushed up.[100] Female commentary from that time has not been preserved, and changing views of the female breast in word and image are only presented from a male perspective, just like the majority of myths about the beginnings of humanity.

Buttoned up

Little by little, three changes took place in paintings of breasts, as Margaret Miles discusses in great detail in *A Complex Delight*. First, the breast was depicted more and more realistically, and the increased emotional and erotic implications provoked clerical fear of arousal. Male priests in Catholic regions became aware that the increasingly lifelike images no longer produced the same unequivocal meaning. No wonder then that in December 1563 the Council of Trento rejected realistic images of the nursing Holy Virgin as unseemly.

From the end of the fifteenth century, biblical maternal breasts were not the only breasts to be painted or sculpted. Aside from the Virgin Mary, breasts played a role in other biblical topics—such as representations of the story of the elders peeping upon the bathing Susanna—and in tragic classical themes such as Lucretia committing suicide after being a victim of rape. A seventeenth-century example is *The Prodigal Son* by Johannes Baeck, a painting expressing the moral degradation of a young man whose hand is carelessly groping the naked breast of a woman.

Other paintings on a biblical theme depict the wife of Potiphar trying to seduce the innocent slave Joseph with her breasts. The moral lesson of chastity was given less and less emphasis:

---

100. As shown in the exhibition La Mécanique des Dessous in the Musée des Arts Décoratifs, Paris, 2013.

The Prodigal Son by Johannes Baeck, 1637.
Kunsthistorisches Museum, Vienna.

> By the seventeenth century, naked breasts presented frankly erotic images, though often still with scriptural warrant [...]. In thc cighteenth century, unapologetically secular breasts, larger and rounder than a century before, were frequently painted.[101]

A third change to be seen in early modern art was that not only one but two breasts were depicted, whether or not framed in a décolleté. A transitory figure in this development was Mary Magdalene. As a former prostitute, good and evil come together in her sexualised body, 'migrating between the repentant sinner and the erotic sex worker'. A Donatello statue hides her breasts chastely behind her long hair, but in Titian's painting the nipples are clearly visible through her long hair.[102]

101. Miles: 8-9.

102. Miles: 11-13.

In the second half of the fifteenth century décolletage became fashionable in Europe thanks to Agnès Sorel, a renowned beauty of her time who became famous as the mistress of Charles VII of France. In the mid-fifteenth century this celebrity courtesan modelled for Jean Fouquet's *La Vierge de Melun.* He painted her with her eyes piously lowered, crowned and surrounded by angels, with a naked baby Jesus sitting upright beside her and one uncovered breast directly in view. In an anonymous later painting she is wearing a long black dress and a gauze veil, repeating the same pious downward glance. From her loosely-laced bustier, one naked breast emerges, even though there is no child on her lap. Instead, she holds a book in her hand with a finger halfway between the pages, suggesting that she was reading while waiting for the painter.

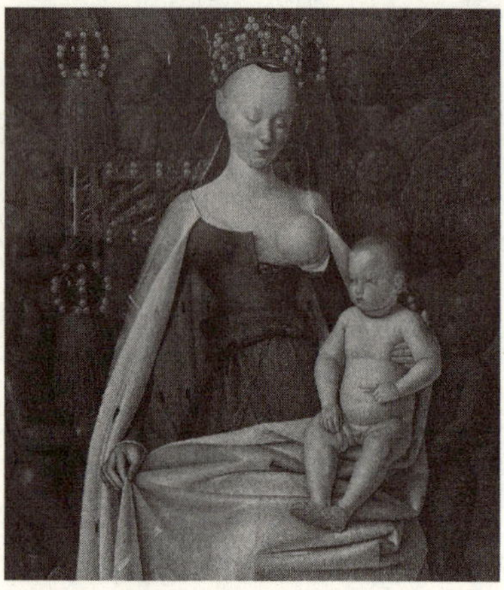

Left: *La Vierge de Melun* by Jean Fouquet, *c.* 1450.
Royal Museum of Fine Arts, Antwerp.
Right: Sixteenth-century portrait of Agnès Sorel. Anonymous, after Fouquet.
Château de Loches, Indre-et-Loire.

No doubt this painting shocked spectators at the time, as it went against the unwritten rule that the artist must convey religious meaning to believers:

> [...] contrary to pictorial custom, [Agnès Sorel] wears a very low décolletage and fashionable tight bodice, ostentatiously unlaced to liberate a most attractive large white breast. This breast bursts out of its confinement while the other one, for once equally visible under the dress, submits to its pressure with equally sexy effect.[103]

Such paintings reflected the transition from religious images with no implicit aesthetic purpose to 'art for art's sake'.

Sorel introduced her daring fashion of keeping her bodice unlaced to expose her naked breasts at the French court shortly before her untimely death at twenty-eight in 1450. Many women followed her habit, as can be seen in other European paintings. Piero di Cosimo's portrait of Simonetta Vespucci as Cleopatra is a famous example (see Plate 13).

The familiar natural image began to show cracks, and the long-cherished symbolism of Mary's bare maternal breast gave rise to opposing views: either degraded as an object of lust, or rejected on the grounds of chastity. From now on, the owners of flesh-and-blood breasts could be dismissed as wicked seducers or eulogised as pious, chaste madonnas. Breasts became a social standard by which to judge women's chastity, or lack of it.

Within a century of the invention of printing in around 1440, Europe was inundated with illustrated pornographic literature.[104]

---

103. Anne Hollander, 1978:187-188.

104. cf. Miles 132: 'A search of *Art Resource* in New York, the largest image collection in North America, produced not a single image of the virgin with one bare breast after 1750.'

By the seventeenth century, images of the female body were circulating in numerous medical textbooks, such as Vesalius' famous book on human anatomy, with its title page showing a female body being dissected before a mass of male spectators. So through the twin rise of pornography and medical research, those body parts that only ornament the female body became special objects of attention.

Title page of Andreas Vesalius' *De humani corporis fabrica*, Basel, 1543. Leiden University Libraries.

On the run-up to the French Revolution in the late eighteenth century, the rising middle class was increasingly prudish and critical of the earlier aristocratic display of luxurious dress and plunging necklines.

But what of Mary? As the Mother of God she had been the indispensable link between God the Father and ordinary men and women since time immemorial. Local colour was projected onto her everywhere. In Europe artists gave her white, Western features: blue eyes, rosy cheeks and even fair hair. On other continents her skin colour, eye shape, facial features and dress matched those of local believers, so that people could more easily identify with her. In Africa and Latin America, she became darker skinned (see Plate 12). In China she resembled Guanyin, the kind and compassionate goddess of mercy, while in Vietnam she became popular as 'Our Lady of La Vang', wearing the *ao dai* national dress. It was in La Vang in 1798 that Mary appeared in that outfit to believers who had fled to the jungle, at a time when the Vietnamese emperor was persecuting and killing Christian believers.

Over time, European Catholic missionaries distributed millions of devotional pictures of Mary all over the world. They all have one striking feature in common: the Mother of God no longer suckles the baby Jesus, but wears buttoned-up dresses in accordance with the decree of the Council of Trento, thereby effectively obliterating the previously familiar and well-understood image of the Blessed Virgin as a nursing mother.

PART II

DESIRABLE AND TERRIFYING

Above: Fertility ornaments, vulva with womb. Flores, Indonesia.
Below left: Necklace pendant, silver with cedar wood, Tuareg, Sahara;
right: Necklace pendant, leather triangle with fertility cowrie shell, Dogon,
Mali, twentieth century. Author's collection.

4. THE GATEWAY OF LIFE

The nameless is the beginning of Heaven and Eearth.
The named is the mother of ten thousand things.
Ever desireless, one can see the mystery.
Ever desiring, one can see the manifestations.
[...] Darkness within darkness.
The gate to all mystery.[105]

Mother of the feast, little stone in your vulva.
Oo! Oo! The vertical column of the clitoris, vulva. Oo-ee-ee!
Penis. O! Penis. O! Vagina is calling you.[106]

Dutch columnist Frits Abrahams rightly marvelled at the negative language referring to the female sex apparatus in his part of the world. The male member having already been verbally reduced to a powerless appendix, now the female genitalia had begun their negative slide. In Dutch, an off-day is called a 'cunt day': 'Cunt is nothing, cunt is feckless, cunt is something extremely bad.' He noticed that women use the word for their own body part as derogatively and as indifferently as men. Moreover, in his recollection, the absolute lowest term 'supercunt' was used

105. *Tao Te Ching*, translated by Gia-fu Feng and Jane English (1972), Chapter 1.

106. E.E. Evans-Pritchard, *Some Collective Expressions of Obscenity in Africa*, 1929:323.

by women only.[107]

The time has come to speak up for this unjustly reviled body part, the pathway to life for all humanity. This chapter sets out to explore the vulva by removing some of the veils that usually obscure it from view.

Mystery

In contrast to today's often crude candour about sex, my grandmother never ever spoke about the subject—words were simply lacking for this heavily laden phenomenon. Only once in her life and with great hesitation she referred to the vagina as 'The Mystery'. In her reticence, she aligned herself, without being aware of it, with a long tradition of cultures worldwide expressing the belief that this gateway of life possesses unknown powers.

In different parts of the world women were believed to be able to protect their family or the whole community against impending disaster thanks to this hidden mystery. The idea that even just an amulet with this image would scare away the enemy and protect against evil, comes from a much older belief that animals would flee, natural disasters be calmed, people's fertility and a good harvest be secured if only one or several women dare to expose their awesome genitals to a rainless sky, infertile fields, turbulent seas and dangerous enemies.

This custom may appear vulgar to contemporary onlookers, but the word 'obscene' includes the meaning 'inauspicious', and in times of danger during the historical transition from hunting to agriculture a large part of humanity used to practise this rite. Anthropology provides many examples. Deliberately and solemnly exposing one's usually covered genitals was considered an act of exceptional courage, and only applied in extreme situations:

107. 'Van kut naar superkut', *NRC Handelsblad*, 27 February 2017.

'In normal times the abnormal is taboo, but in abnormal times abnormal things are done to restore the normal condition of affairs.'[108]

In ancient China, in times of serious drought female priests were ritually undressed and exhibited to the heat of the sun in order to call down rain. Indeed, magic power was attributed to the naked female body:

> As the ultimate embodying of yin, people attributed to the publicly shown female genitals the power to eliminate all yang. In emergency cases Chinese generals sometimes resorted to naked prostitutes to silence the cannons of their adversaries.[109]

Deterrence of the enemy by the display of genitals was also practised in other parts of the world. By revealing their vulva in public in dramatic circumstances, women could guarantee the wellbeing of their own clan. In times of war, the effect was twofold: the soldiers on one's own side were encouraged, and opponents were paralysed by this deadly threat.

Such exposure, as documented by Edward Schafer in his long paper, 'Ritual Exposure in Ancient China', was a rare event, filled with magical power. The shaman's exposed yin counteracts the yang of the burning sun or, in another explanation, the nudity shames the rain-dragons into action.

In the Niger Delta in July 2002, a group of 600 unarmed mothers and grandmothers drew on this ancient curse during

---

108. E.E. Evans-Pritchard, 'Some Collective Expressions of Obscenity in Africa', in *The Journal of the Royal Anthropological Institute of Great Britain and Ireland*, 1929:323.

109. Wilt Idema, 'Bespied in bad', p.31 in *De Boekenwereld* 2017; Edward H. Schafer, 'Ritual Exposure in Ancient China', in *Harvard Journal of Asiatic Studies* Vol. 14, No. 1/2 (1951):130-184.

an oil protest by threatening to remove all their clothes—and it worked.[110] In the context of the ancestral tradition that 'we all come into the world through the vagina', the wordless gesture of exposing the vulva includes a powerful message: 'Herewith we take back the life we have given you.' The curse publicly punishes men with social execution and considers them to be dead: as from now all women would refuse to cook for them, marry them or do business with them. Here, as in earlier days, the 'Curse of Nakedness' proved to be a most effective female weapon to ward off misery and disaster.[111]

Sheela-na-gig at the church of Kilpeck, Herefordshire, twelfth century.

110. https://www.theguardian.com/world/2002/jul/22/gender.uk1.

111. More information in *Naked or Covered*, pp.28-29.

In northern Europe there are many examples of old stone carvings of female figures with a gaping vulva. In Great Britain and Ireland they are called *sheela-na-gig*. These images were believed to serve similar purposes, to avert death or evil spirits. In the Pacific island country of Palau, carved wooden female figures were fixed over the doorway of a chief's house: their hands rested on the thighs, and the splayed legs revealed a striking vulva and clitoris marked by a dark triangle. As elsewhere, such images, called *dilukái*, were meant to protect health and fertility, guarantee a good harvest and fend off evil spirits. Each of these iterations represent the vulva as 'the primordial gate, the mysterious divide between non-life and life.'[112]

Dilukái, Palau, *c.* 1900. The Michael Rockefeller Memorial Collection.

112. Juliette Dor, 'The Sheela-na-Gig: An Incongruous Sign of Sexual Purity' in Bernau, Evans and Salih, 2003:33–55; Bertling 96ff; Mircea Eliade in the *Encyclopedia of Religion*: http://en.wikipedia.org/wiki/Sheela_na_gig#cite_we-14.

Dark threat

Mythological stories present scenes in which a 'goddess of obscenity' unveils her intimate body parts in a ritual dance at times of crisis, evoking the sacred cycle of fertility, life and death. In ancient Japanese myth, Susanoo, brother of the Sun Goddess Amaterasu, is a disruptive element in the realm of the gods. His rage makes the lush green landscape wither, threatening human life. His parents, the creator gods Izanagi and Izanami, decide to ban this uncouth son to the underworld of Yomi. Before his departure Susanoo is granted one last visit with Amaterasu in the Plain of High Heaven. As soon as he ascends, he causes violent commotion in the sea and deafening groans in the hills and mountains. He then desecrates the sacred Weaving Hall where the garments of the gods are woven, and the consequences are disastrous. The raging Sun Goddess gathers her radiant robes about her, enters a cave, obstructs the entrance with a rock, and hides in seclusion. Suffocating darkness swallows every trace of daylight: a fatal catastrophe threatening all life.

As the gods ponder how to persuade Amaterasu to show herself again in all her lustrous glory, the heavenly maze goddess steps forward. Dancing in a trance, she first takes out her breasts and then lowers her robe below the vulva. The gathered gods roar with liberating laughter, awakening Amaterasu's curiosity. As she eases the cave door ajar and her divine light comes forth again, the god of force Tajikarao takes her hand and pulls her out into the open. All the gods align behind her so she can't go back inside. As the Sun's light shines again in Heaven as on Earth, Susanoo is punished and the end of humanity has been averted.[113]

---

113. F. Hadland Davis. *Myths and Legends of Japan*, 1912. This story originates from the *Kojiki, or Records of Ancient Matters* (translated from the Japanese by

In Greek mythology the goddess of agriculture Demeter curses the fertile earth after her beloved daughter Persephone had been kidnapped by the god of the underworld. Because of that curse no more children are born, corn refuses to grow, flowers stop blooming, and people lose their faith in the gods. After gloomy wanderings over the earth, Demeter sinks down near a well, where Baubo crosses her path. This mysterious figure succeeds in making the goddess smile again. Was she another deity, an old midwife, or perhaps Demeter's former

Demeter on her throne, with ears of corn, poppies and a torch. Corinthian earthenware, late fifth century BC. National Archaeological Museum, Athens.

Basil Hall Chamberlain in 1882). At the order of Empress Gemmyo, this old and very long oral story was performed in 712 by an old woman narrator who knew it by heart. It was then transcribed for the first time—cf. Nobuhiro Matsumoto. *Essai sur la Mythologie Japonaise*, 1928 and Pierre Lévêque, *Colère, Sexe, Rire: Le Japon des Mythes Anciens*, 1988.

nurse? There are different opinions. Her name 'Baubo' means 'lap' or 'belly', and she personifies sexuality—images show her with a vulva on her chin or conspicuously visible between her spread legs. She gestures to her naked genitals, and puts her hand there. To please Demeter, Baubo has shaved her pubic area and begins to dance with swinging breasts and wriggling hips suggesting the act of sex. As the goddess of agriculture, Demeter's anger is a threat to humanity's future. In the Greek as well as in the Japanese story, unveiling the vulva is the only way to undo the spell.[114]

During festivities in honour of Demeter, the central secret ceremony was accessible to women only. The cakes eaten there were in the shape of genitals, and women amused each other by telling obscene jokes during a meal accompanied with abundant wine. The Baubo ceremony of Anasyrma—the exposing of the genitals—concluded the fertility rites.[115]

In agrarian contexts, obscenity served to 'reanimate' fertility. In both Japanese and Greek mythology obscene gestures were part of ancient belief in the magic of this vital body part. The gesture of exposure was unprecedentedly powerful and interpreted as a favourable portent. Thanks to their birth-giving gateway, women had the power to dispel imminent catastrophe, to melt away anger in contagious laughter, and to create space for new vigour and a future full of new life.

---

114. Images of Baubo have been found in many places, mainly in Greek settings. With thanks to Leiden University colleagues Ineke Sluiter and John Miguel Versluys for personal information about Baubo.

115. P-L. Couchoud, 'Le mythe de la danseuse obscène' in *Mercure de France*, July-August 1929. Paris.

Mounds of terracotta, gold or lapis lazuli

As long as the Great Goddess was in high esteem, holy rivers welled up from the vagina of the earth, and all life crept out of her birth canals on to the earth. Nature and culture have always been deployed to represent sexuality and fertility with symbols referring to the origin of life. The best-known symbol for the vulva is the inverted triangle. The Greek letter Δ (delta) refers

Ishtar among water animals, representing fertility.
Larsa, Mesopotamia, second millennium BC. Musée du Louvre, Paris.

to both a river mouth and the vulva. In ancient Greece, Delta was the name of a place of sanctuary for Demeter, originally worshipped as mother goddess and later held responsible for agriculture.

The inverted triangle indicates ancient foremother or goddess images in many cultures. Corresponding to the *Dilukái* figure from Palau we saw earlier, an image of the Sumerian goddess Ishtar on a water pot uses the triangle to symbolise the vulva and the womb. Ishtar was the Sumerian goddess of love and war. In ancient Mesopotamia her vulva was admired and praised as 'sweet as beer' and 'sweet as the mouth'.[116]

Aside from the triangle, the vulva is represented as a lozenge or diamond in many cultures. A gold pendant from the third millennium BC unearthed in Syria shaped as a triangle includes an inserted lozenge of twisted gold wire representing the vulva. Before the civil war in Syria this fertility ornament was on show in the Museum of Aleppo.[117] An easily recognised contemporary stylised diamond is the Renault logo (below)—though it is doubtful that many car drivers are aware of the profound meaning of the gateway of life as a protective object of power.

Renault logo (Wikimedia Commons)

116. With thanks to Assyriologist Theo Krispijn, Leiden University, for information and references to the *Reallexicon der Assyriologie*.

117. Cf. Rients de Boer, *De kleding van Ištar van Lagaba*, 2013:30ff.

In moments of existential crisis, threat or illness, a votive or oblation would often be left on a shrine to appease a god or goddess, confirm an entreaty or express thanks for a wish fulfilled. Such ornaments in the form of female genitals exist in many cultures. On the opening page of this chapter are two examples from the island of Flores in Indonesia, which were worn as power objects generating new life. In ancient times warriors wore them as a means of protection when they went to war. Two more originate from Africa—one logenze-shaped and one incorporating the natural contours of a cowrie shell. Vulva-shaped objects dedicated to the goddess were sometimes made of expensive materials. On a detailed lists of votives, one vulva in gold and eight in silver, all dedicated to Ishtar, are mentioned on millennia-old clay tablets. Ishtar received those, and many other kinds of objects from worshippers, especially from women. One of the associated prayers runs as follows:

> Merciful Ishtar, who reigns over the universe,
> Heroic Ishtar, who creates humanity,
> You who walk on ahead of the flock, you who love the
> shepherd [...]
> Without you the river will not open,
> The life-giving river will not be blocked up,
> Without you the channel will not open,
> The channel from which people drink far and wide
> Will not be closed [...]
> Ishtar, charitable lady,
> Hear me and bestow your grace upon me.

At the end of this prayer Ishtar is discreetly reminded of all the sacrifices the humble servant has brought her, a comprehensive inventory ending with the most expensive gifts: 'a vulva of lapis lazuli and a [missing word] of gold.'[118] Vulva- or womb-shaped votives made of stone, terracotta and other materials exist in many traditions. For an ancient Roman votive example, see the opening page of this chapter.

As well as being an ancient fertility symbol, the vulva has always been a thoroughly discussed object of attention in manuals devoted to eroticism and sex. The Indian *Kama Sutra* dates back to the second century and served as a walk-through for men and women in whose arranged marriages love did not usually spontaneously bloom. Sex manuals also circulated early in China, and Robert van Gulik's *Sexual Life in Ancient China* (1961) is an erudite and detailed book on this topic. In Arabic there is *The Perfumed Garden of Sensual Delight*, the long treatise written by Sheikh al-Nefzawi, each edition of which looked different. Such books give an idea of the kind of women the various authors consider 'worthy of praise' or 'deserving nothing but contempt', as al-Nefzawi put it.[119] This is how he saw the ideal woman:

> In order that a woman may be relished by men, she must have a perfect waist, and must be plump and lusty. [...] her breath will be of pleasant odour, her throat long, her neck strong, her bust and her belly large; her breasts must be full and firm; her belly in good proportion, and

118. Erich Ebeling, *Quellen zur Kenntnis der Babylonischen Religion*, Leipzig, 1918, II:12. My translation.

119. *The Perfumed Garden of Sensual Delight* (رطاخلا ةهزن يف رطاعلا ضورلا) رطاعلا ضورلا) is an Islamic sex manual, similar to the Hindu *Kama Sutra*. It is believed to have been written between 1410 and 1434. Published in Paris in a first full French edition in 1886 as *Le Jardin Parfumée du Cheikh Nefzaoui: Manuel d'Erotologie Arabe: xvi Siècle*, Sir Richard Burton took care of an English translation from the French in the same year. Also see: https://en.wikisource.org/wiki/The_Perfumed_Garden and https://burtoniana.org/books/1886-Perfumed Garden/index.htm.

> her navel well-developed and marked; the lower part of the belly is to be large, the vulva projecting and fleshy from the point where the hairs grow to the buttocks; the conduit must be narrow and not moist, soft to the touch, and emitting a strong heat [...]. If one looks at a woman with those qualities in front, one is fascinated; if from behind, one dies with pleasure.[120]

And so forth. Such handbooks deserve separate comparative research with careful attention to the commentator's perspective on the experiences described. Finally, a brief quotation from a Chinese manual (Ming Dynasty, 1368-1644) in which the author discerns different kinds of vulvas—apt for all those who carefully follow the instructions for use:

> All vulvas, whether in the high, middle, or low positions, possess desirable qualities, provided that someone knows how to use them well. A woman whose vulva is in the middle [...] is suitable for copulation in all four seasons of the year and for induction into all sexual positions. [...] A woman whose vulva is high is suitable for cold winter nights. A man can have intercourse with her by lying on her under the coloured quilts of a square bed. A woman whose vulva is low and placed further towards the back is suitable especially for hot summers. A man can have intercourse with her by sitting on a stone bench under the shade of bamboo. [...] This is what is called utilising the particular advantages of the shape of the woman one copulates with.[121]

---

120. Sheikh Nefzawi, *The Perfumed Garden*, 1886:96.

121. Quoted in R.H. van Gulik, *Sexual Life in Ancient China: A Preliminary Survey of Chinese Sex and Society from ca. 1500 BC till 1644 AD*, 1974:272-273.

Gnashing teeth and other obstacles

Literary genres from origin myths to fairy tales to proverbs refer to something beyond desire: 'Before the time, great courage; when at the point, great fear,' runs the English and Spanish proverb. Almost without exception, the outlined scenarios reflect a male perspective, even in the advice mothers and grandmothers provide to girls before their wedding night, as in the Bulgarian exhortation

The Ill-Matched Couple, copper engraving by Hans Baldung Grien, 1507. State Art Collections of Dresden.

to submissiveness, 'Endure, young bride, it's a man.' Or in an Ethiopian Oromo instruction, 'Be quiet and lie down at his side!'

Men have their own anxieties. In contexts where an exposed vulva is believed to eliminate negative forces or drive away hostile armies, it is understandable that individual fears give rise to fantasies about fearsome vaginas and insatiable female lust. A man needs boldness and self-confidence, and uncertainty about one's potency and achievement, especially for older men, is obviously a delicate point: 'Old man, cold bedfellow' is just one revealing statement.

In the old man's nightmare his young wife runs off with a younger, more adequate sex partner. As far as ageing is concerned, Bette Midler's wisdom in her twentieth-century TV show applies to all times and places: 'It is easier for a man of twenty with a woman of eighty than the other way round.' But insecurity is not always a matter of age—far from it.

Anthropologists working in different parts of the world have described quite a number of incidents involving men who believed that women's special powers deliberately caused male impotence. Among the Australian Aranda, for example, it was feared that a woman might have scattered a handful of bewitched dust on the place where the man usually went to pee, which would give him a burning feeling in his urethra and unbearable pain. Or, another trick, she sings a magic song over her own forefinger and then inserts it in her vulva, and the man who has sex with her will 'become diseased and may lose his organ altogether'.[122] No doubt, the very thought had a paralysing effect.

Male fear changes women into inhuman creatures, as in this Khond story from India: 'In the old days, woman had four breasts and two vaginas, one in front and one behind. But she had only

122. Ernest Crawley, *The Mystic Rose: A Study of Primitive Marriage*, 1902:182ff.

one face, looking forwards. Most *people* were so frightened of *women* that they never got married'[123] (italics mine). In stories from Asia and America, the first created women used to consume their food with vaginal teeth—no wonder men were scared to approach them. *Vagina dentata* stories in which women eat or rob men's most vulnerable body part reflect male nightmares. A Jicarilla Apache demon daughter with teeth in her vagina changes herself into a beautiful girl as soon as she sees a man, seduces him, bites off his penis and eats it. Increasing the drama, the vulnerable penis is confronted by all sorts of extreme threats: elephant tusks, poisonous snake teeth, a saw at the entrance of the vagina, or hungry piranhas waiting within. The horror, the horror![124]

In some stories the woman herself doesn't seem to realise how dangerous she is, even though the man hears the gnashing teeth under her skirt from afar. Of course, a real hero does not give up, but employs smart tactics. Before knocking at her dangerous gate, he may lovingly rock the woman to sleep, courageously remove those horrifying teeth by pulling them with a cord or destroying them with an iron rod and, to his great relief, discover a 'normal' vagina beneath. As soon as the woman (read: vagina) has been tamed, the threat disappears once and for all.[125]

Sometimes the woman is completely innocent: in a Gond story from Central India, a small snake slips inside the vagina of someone squatting down to relieve herself. There the intruder

---

123. Elwin 1954:452.

124. Yukaghir story from Siberia, other examples and details: *In the Beginning There Was No One*, Chapter 8.

125. Bogoras, Waldemar. *Chukchee Mythology*, 1913: 667; Ho Ting-jui, *A Comparative Study of Myths and Legends from Formosan Aborigines*. Unpublished thesis, Indiana University, 1967:388.

grows so rapidly that her husband thinks she's pregnant, but one day, in full public view at a bazaar, the head of the snake pops out from under her sari. A passer-by who sees it immediately realises how much danger her husband is in (in the story, no one seems to care much that the woman too might be in peril). The snake is killed and from then on, the couple live happily ever after.[126]

Origin stories about sex reveal fear of 'the first time'. From his creation the first man has to manage without any wise advice from experienced fellow sufferers. What awaits the inexperienced man, when his newly created sexual organ has to enter that dark passage? He knows he must take the initiative, because female sexual initiatives are suspect or taboo. Stories in which the first, still untamed woman dares to take the initiative or wants to lie on top, concern themselves with the need to radically eliminate that threatening female power.

How does one stay lord and master over one's own member once in contact with the opposite sex? 'The penis comes erect as if it intends to kill, but the vagina swallows and tames it,' is a concise Nigerian Igbo observation. And a Chilean Mapuche proverb classifies women as sexually violent: 'They overthrow even a man's penis.' From that fearful perspective the vagina is blamed for bad intentions. In New Zealand the Maori tradition warns against it as 'the house of death'. There are also cultures that go for facts without fear, like the down-to-earth Palau islanders who soberly observe that 'everyone on earth comes out of the crack.' The widespread idea that female powers must be 'tamed' by men fits with earlier lines of thought about the need for the power of the Great Goddess to be usurped by an almighty male

---

126. Elwin, 'The Vagina Dentata Legend' in *British Journal of Medical Psychology* 19:443.

creator god. The creation of hierarchy functions as reassurance against fear of the gateway of life.

The Jewish Talmud tells the story of Lilith, Adam's first wife, who demanded the impossible:

> Adam said, 'I will not lie beneath you, but only on top. For you are fit only to be in the bottom position, while I am to be in the superior one.'
> Lilith responded, 'We are equal to each other inasmuch as we were both created from earth.'[127]

Following that line of argument, Lilith insisted on lying next to him, or on top. When Adam tried to force her into his preferred position, she refused to give in, sneered at him and flew away, out of paradise. Lilith went to the shores of the Red Sea where she cohabited with lascivious demons, and her favourite pastime was having sex with them. Angels wanted to bring her back to Adam, but she refused and became a demon herself, giving birth to a hundred evil demons daily. To this day Lilith and her daughters, the *lilim*, kill babies, preferably uncircumcised little boys. Taking inspiration from their mother, the *lilim* hang around in men's dreams, sit on their victims' bodies, and gulp down the poor men's semen as they ejaculate. With the stolen semen, they continue to produce yet more new demon children. Though there are many different versions of this story, there is one thing all the storytellers agree upon. This assertive wife wanted complete equality—even in matters of sex. God took pity on Adam, let him fall into a deep sleep and created Eve, 'flesh of his flesh' (Genesis 2:23).

---

127. The *Alphabet of Ben Sira* 5:23a and b. This is the oldest source of the Lilith story (eighth to tenth century). For more references see Kvam, Schearing aand Ziegler 1999: 204. An earlier reference to Lilith as Lilake has been found on a Sumerian clay tablet of 2000 bc, cf. Graves and Patai: 68. The only reference to Lilith in the Bible is in the book of Isaiah (34:14).

By describing or reversing the mythical roles and functions of the first humans, origin stories enable those in power to shape and adapt daily life according to their own interests. In the words of the thirteenth-century Islamic scholar al-Qurtubi:

> The female sexual organ was created for men. [...] Allah made it known that that place of the woman was created from man for man's sake. So the woman must yield it whenever the husband calls her. If she refuses then she is an oppressor and in a grave position. Sufficient proof of this was reported from Sahih Muslim in the Hadith that says, 'When a man calls his wife to his bed, and she refuses, the One Who is in the heaven will be angry with her until he [her husband] is pleased with her. All the woman's piety is considered useless if she disobeys her husband. Her disobedience to her husband represents an unlawful and irrational act. But obedience to her husband is the key to Paradise.'[128]

Mythology and anthropology are full of threatening examples of frighteningly dominant women. In contemporary reality patients tell psychiatrists stories about earthly mothers whose powerful arbitrariness plays no less threatening havoc on vulnerable children's souls than powerful mythical mothers did in the Stone Age and the Bronze Age. Obsessive images about fear of castration in erotic dreams, sometimes in combination with penis envy projected onto the mother, are now submitted to therapists:

> Castration anxiety will mean man's fear about the possibility of losing his penis; penis envy will mean woman's resentment at man's possession of the penis,

128. Tafsir al-Qurtubi commenting on Ahadith 42-44: https://answering-islam.org/Authors/Newton/women.html#woman#woman.

> and her wish to have one herself. This sort of envy could, of course, result in the destructive attack on the penis, thus giving rise to legitimate castration anxiety. And penis envy and castration anxiety could be considered as the two sides—male and female respectively—of the same problem: 'I have it, she wants it; he has it, I want it.'[129]

Although there is no indication in myth or anthropology that a woman would actually want to have a penis on her own body, she is just interested in *using* it, many examples in therapeutic literature suggest ego-damaging mothers are the cause of castration fears. I mention a few from a rich supply: selfish or loveless, rigidly controlling or tyrannical mothers, suffocating mothers unable to let their children escape a symbiotic relationship, mothers who exploit their children or turn them into scapegoats or chase them into criminality. According to psychiatrists, they all represent, metaphorically speaking, the castrating mother. Girlfriends, brides and wives may have a similar effect on adult men. One sneering remark can do the job:

> Whatever he does, and whichever way he does it, he risks the possibility that his penis may be just a little smaller, and just a little less adept, than someone else's. And yet, so often it is only this cold-nosed, derogatory bitch he is after, because his real interest is not in her, but in beating the competition; he risks the snipping away at his phallus because he not only wants her to love him, but to love him for being bigger and better than the others.[130]

---

129. Lederer: 214.

130. Ibid. 219.

The legacy of his own fears is a tragic fate with 'a frightened bride and a frigid wife'. And Wolfgang Lederer refers to a story about a neurotic girl—an American example from the 1960s—who prepares a first-aid box at her bedside, with iodine tincture and gauze bandages, and a small basin with hot water. A paralysing nightmare suggesting mutilation rather than the promise of mutual pleasure.

A little stone in the vulva

Does a man enjoy sex more than a woman, or the other way around? Even the gods once wondered. Jupiter believed that women enjoyed it more than men, but his wife Juno disagreed. They submitted their question to Tiresias, a wise soothsayer and prophet in Thebes who had lived in a female body for seven years. Tiresias became a woman after he struck two copulating snakes with a stick. Seven years later he saw the same snakes copulating again. A second blow with his stick changed him back into a man. Having experienced sex as both man and woman, Tiresias sided with Jupiter, observing that women enjoy sex nine times more than men! Juno was so disgruntled with the answer that she struck him with blindness.[131] This punishment was too much for Jupiter. He couldn't undo Juno's divine punishment, but alleviated it by providing Tiresias with the ability to predict the future. But was Tiresias wrong? Proverbs worldwide allude to fearsome female insatiability:

> The rat will die, and the hole will not be satisfied. (Arabic, Tunisia)
> Water, fire and women will never say 'enough'. (Polish)
> Women and fire: if you have to, take just a little. (Fulfulde, West Africa)

131. Ovid, *Metamorphoses*, Book III:82-83.

> The man as long as he can, the woman as long as she wants to. (Spanish, Bolivia)

Did the fear of female voraciousness result in clitoridectomy? The Dogon of Mali justify excision in their origin story. The small 'potent' termite mound of the Earth is not allowed to 'stand up' against the supreme male creator and sky god:

> After Amma had created the Earth, he wanted to copulate with his partner. But the Earth had not yet been purified by excision, and the termite mound stood up against Amma. He cut it away and had sex with the Earth, while she was still bleeding from the wound.[132]

The mound literally rises up against male sexuality at the moment of penetration and is considered a threat to the existing order. In this story excision is presented as a necessary measure—the clitoris of the Earth must not become equal to the penis of Amma, the male god who created her.[133] Do the many variants of female genital cutting originate in fear and envy, and is that the very reason why power has to be exerted over the vagina, menstrual blood and the hymen? Does the presumed proof that men have the power to make women bleed from the vagina function as a means to appease their own fears?[134]

In myths that explain that women were once in charge, the clitoris is sometimes referred to as a 'small penis'. It is quite likely

---

132. Marcel Griaule, *Dieu d'Eau*. Paris: Fayard, 1966:16.

133. Elisabeth Bekers, *Dissecting Anthills of W/Human Insurrection: A Comparattive Study of African Creative Writing on Female Genital Excision*, 2002: 34. In the case of infibulation the complete clitoris is cut off, along with all of the inner and much of the outer labia, followed by stitching up to close most of the vagina. Only a small opening is left for urine and menstruation blood. The friction caused by the artificially narrowed vagina increases male sexual pleasure.

134. Bruno Bettelheim, *Symbolic Wounds* 1954:120-121.

that jealousy or fear of this little source of pleasure inspired the practice of female circimcision. Cutting parts of male and female genitals have been presented as taking away the 'remainders' of the other sex—for men, the foreskin and for women, the clitoris—often including parts of the labia as well.

A reassuring order is established via surgical intervention intended to make girls 'completely feminine', in order to prevent them seeming like men. In rural areas in Egypt rumours still prevail that the clitoris of an uncut girl will grow into a long penis. Removal of the androgynous part will 'purify' female genitals—just as the male foreskin is considered 'female' and must be circumcised.

Puberty rituals serve to symbolically separate boys from their mother's body, as initiation and circumcision inaugurate them into the secrets of the adult men's world. As their 'last bit of femininity' is cut away, the surrounding ceremony is meant to mark their 'second' or 'real' birth—the moment they become men, independent from their mothers.

The consequences of circumcision and excision, however, are completely different, physically as well as socially. Male circumcision 'unveils' the glans. The removal of the foreskin and the phallic exposure represent male licence to venture into the outside, non-domestic domain, whereas excision and infibulation of women's genitals lead to confinement and restriction.[135]

This difference in outcome is confirmed in proverbs worldwide, even in cultures without circumcision rituals. Expansive male spaces contrast with restricted female spaces. 'The home is the wife's world, the world is the man's home' is an Estonian saying. As for travelling, men should and women shouldn't. 'A son who never leaves home always thinks that his mother's is the loudest fart,'

---

135. Eric K. Silverman, *Anthropology and Circumcision*, 2004:429.

as a Kenyan Gikuyu proverb has it. Or, in a piece of Malaysian wisdom, 'A travelled woman is like a garden trespassed by cattle.'

The male need for hierarchy and control over women is confirmed in metaphors contrasting male expansion with female immobility. Open, outward male dynamic activities are set against closed, inward female realms. 'Woman' is equated with 'womb', 'house', and all that is 'inside' and needs to stay there, with the kitchen as dominion, and infibulation an extra lock on the womb to allow women to keep their good name. Neatly-circumcised men go into the world without endangering their status.

The Quran condemns mutilation of the body, and female genital cutting is not referred to anywhere. The Prophet Muhammad even emphasised women's right to be sexually satisfied. A few Ahadith traditions claim that female genital cutting existed in the early Islamic world, but Islamic scholars have dismissed such statements as 'weak' and historically unsubstantiated: genital cutting existed long before Islam and was sometimes absorbed from local pre-Islamic traditions.

The Byzantine Greek physician and medical writer Aetius of Amida (sixth century AD) confirmed that the clitoris (*nymphê* in Greek) was removed when it became 'too large' or triggered arousal when rubbing against clothing. According to him, the Egyptians were inclined to remove a clitoris before it might grow too large, 'especially at that time when the girls were about to be married.' Aetius added accurate details on the procedure:

> Have the girl sit on a chair while a muscled young man standing behind her places his arms below the girl's thighs. Have him separate and steady her legs and whole body. Standing in front and taking hold of the clitoris with a broad-mouthed forceps in his left hand, the surgeon stretches it outward, while with the right hand, he cuts

> it off at the point next to the pincers of the forceps. It is proper to let a length remain from that cut off, about the size of the membrane that's between the nostrils, so as to take away the excess material only; as I have said, the part to be removed is at that point just above the pincers of the forceps. Because the clitoris is a skinlike structure and stretches out excessively, do not cut off too much, as a urinary fistula may result from cutting such large growths too deeply.[136]

The practice of infibulation also became linked to slavery. In 1609 the Portuguese missionary João dos Santos referred to a group near Mogadishu who had a 'custome to sew up their Females, especially their slaves being young to make them unable for conception, which makes these slaves sell dearer, both for their chastitie, and for better confidence which their Masters put in them.' Thus male control of the female body became 'associated with shameful female slavery [and] came to stand for honour.'[137]

In nineteenth-century Europe and in the United States, gynaecologists sometimes removed the clitoris of women in order to prevent masturbation and perceived insanity. The first Western clitoridectomy was carried out in 1822 in Berlin on a fifteen-year-old girl who masturbated excessively. The operation was described in *The Lancet* in 1825, but there are also nineteenth-century examples from England. In the United States this surgical intervention was

---

136. Aetius quoted in https://en.wikipedia.org/wiki/Female_genital_mutilation; see also Mary Knight, Curing Cut or Ritual Mutilation? Some remarks on the practice of female and male circumcision in Graeco-Roman Egypt. *Isis*, 2001, 92 (2): 317-338.

137. Mackie, Gerry. 'Ending Footbinding and Infibulation: A Convention Account' in *American Sociological Review*. 61 (December 1996) (6): 999-1017 (refs pp.1003 and 1009).

applied until the 1960s as a treatment of hysteria, erotomania, and lesbianism.[138]

More than 200 million women alive today have had to undergo this operation, mostly in Africa but also in some cultures in India and Islamic countries like Yemen, Malaysia, and more and more often also in Indonesia (see Plate 23).[139] Worries about virginity and nubility are put forward to justify female genital mutilation. A frequently used argument is that after the surgery a girl will be less likely to discredit family honour.

Usually it is the mothers, grandmothers and other female relatives who control the genital cutting of girls, and the procedure creates a strong group identity. Social pressure makes it difficult for many women to leave their daughters uncut. Research indicates that a large majority of mothers are determined to continue this tradition and apply it to their own daughters. The tradition is closely associated with ideas about purity, embedding in the community, sexuality and fertility.[140]

Since the second half of the twentieth century many people in the Western world have developed a strong awareness that the vagina and foreskin are a person's inalienable personal property. But this remains in conflict with traditional ideas in cultures

---

138. Sarah W. Rodriguez, 'Rethinking the History of Female Circumcision and Clitoridectomy: American Medicine and Female Sexuality in the Late Nineteenth Century' in *Journal of the History of Medicine and Allied Sciences.* 63 (3), July 2008:323-347.

139. http://www.womanstats.org/substatics/femalegenitalcutting_2015_2correctstatic.png; Kamran Paha in the *Huffington Post*: http://www.huffingtonpost.com/entry/why-female-circumcision-violates-islam_us_58fa2f46e4b0f02c3870e94a.

140. For some informative details, I made use of the nuanced article of Sandra D. Lane and Robert A. Rubinstein, 'Judging the Other: Responding to Traditional Female Genital Surgeries', 1996:31-40.

and religions arguing that the importance of genitals, foreskin, glans, clitoris and vulva reaches much further than their owner's individual body. In parts of Africa, the Middle East and Asia, Western views are often dismissed as another form of cultural imperialism in a long colonial history. Numbers in favour of abolishment are growing because this ancient tradition often results in the death of the victims, but many older women in rural areas still argue that women and society at large face more serious problems than a once-in-a-lifetime genital cutting.

In most cultures the first aim of sex is procreation, and stories rarely refer to masturbation. In the Bible the fact that Onan spilled his sperm on the earth 'was wicked in the sight of the Lord, and he put him to death' (Genesis 38: 10). Masturbating girls or women are almost entirely absent in oral traditions. In myths I have found just one example: an African Adam and Eve story told in the Congolese province of Katanga. It comes from the *Jamaa* movement, an African sect rooted in Catholicism, and refers to 'playing with one's own body' with obvious disapproval. This oral Swahili story blames the original responsibility for all that has gone wrong between men and women on a conversation between Satan (called Lucifer here) and Eve. In summary, Eve goes for a walk in paradise and hears the voice of Lucifer calling her from a tree. Feigning innocence, he asks her who she is and to whom her body belongs. Eve explains that her sex makes her female and her body belongs to her husband, as God told her right after he had created her: 'You are not a complete person; you will be a complete person when you give your body to your husband so that he may feel the beauty of your body. But if you play with it, this will be your death.' Lucifer, however, convinces her that this is a lie, and that by touching herself she can create new life:

> When Eve heard this she began to play with her body, all by herself. Her fecundity fell down on the ground.

> She saw it with her eyes. Now she began to feel shame and suffering and loneliness. She said to Lucifer: 'See what you did to me?' Lucifer laughed and went away quickly. Eve went back to her husband, silently, without saying anything and without asking for the body of Adam. And when Adam called her she wouldn't listen anymore. Adam thought, this woman has sinned, as God told us.[141]

Playing with one's own body may contribute to personal pleasure, but not to the production of offspring—an unacceptable outcome in a context where procreation is the main purpose of life. God descends to the earth and punishes Adam and Eve by depriving them of His love. From now on Adam and Eve will need to buy each other's love by the sweat of their labour.[142]

Most origin stories in which female genitals play a role reflect male awe and fear. The message is that sex is a dangerous enterprise, but a man must produce offspring—and this holds particularly true for the first man living in an otherwise empty world. Heroic male courage is needed to overcome sexual threats.

As for the answer to the question raised by Jupiter and Juno, disagreement continues to reign, and the 'little stone in the vulva' keeps its own secret.

---

141. Fabian 1997:1971:124ff; also in Karin Barber: 27-28.

142. Ibid. 125.

Pre-Columbian earthenware pot.
Museo Larco, Lima, Peru.

5. POWERFUL BLOOD

That is the time when we are powerful and the men are afraid [...] woman, at her periods, is the vessel of a supernatural power, the power that allows her to give birth.[143]

(Tohono O'odham people, Arizona and Mexico)

They both got very angry. There was a big palaver. Finally, the man in his anger plucked a poisonous fruit which God had forbidden them to eat. He nearly swallowed it, but remembered in the last moment that the fruit was forbidden. So the fruit got stuck in his throat and can still be seen there. But the woman also plucked the fruit and she swallowed it. The fruit burst open her womb, and she began to bleed.[144]

(Igala, Nigeria)

---

143. Statement of a woman belonging to the Indian Tohono O'odham people in the Sonoran desert, Arizona and Mexico, in Marta Weigle (1982): 173. Here, women were not considered unclean (as were menstruating women in a number of other cultures, e.g. in the Book of Leviticus in the Bible), but loaded with sacred power to take care of the growth of the clan.

144. In *Black Orpheus. A Journal of African and Afro-American Literature*, Vol. II, January 1958:6.

Bridal texts in cuneiform script from more than 4,000 years ago address Inanna, Queen of Heaven, as female friends sing in honour of a young girl who is preparing for marriage:

> Now our breasts stand up!
> Now our parts have grown hair!
> Going to the bridegroom's loins [...]
> Dance! Dance!
> Baba, let us be happy for our parts![145]

Baba was the pet name of Inanna, the Mesopotamian goddess of sex, love, war, justice, and political power, and wedding songs were performed to bolster the confidence of an inexperienced young bride. Child brides were the norm in those early days, but in our own times many girls with guaranteed virginity and small, budding breasts are still married off at a very young age, frequently to much older men.

Hymen, the god of marriage

Hymen is the Greek word for skin or membrane and also the name of the Greek god of marriage, most commonly held to be the son of Apollo and one of the Muses, or in some accounts the result of a coupling between Dionysus and Aphrodite. The anatomical usage originates from the idea of the vagina as a locked sanctuary of Aphrodite, the goddess of love, beauty, sexuality and fragility, who was also in charge of deflowering.

The hymen has traditionally been associated with virginity, as if it obstructed access to the vagina. That is not correct, because without an opening menstruation blood could not get out, and a

145. Thorkild Jacobsen, *The Harps That Once...Sumerian Poetry in Translation*, 1987:18; cf. Zainab Bahrani, *Women of Babylon: Gender and Representation in Mesopotamia*, 2001.

completely closed hymen would be an abnormality only to be fixed by surgical intervention. During childhood this thin membrane begins to wear away due to sporting activities or masturbation, but often small remnants survive. The idea that the breaking of the hymen must be a painful experience for girls and an impossible task for boys has caused a lot of needless stress.

In communities where family honour is a crucial issue—and an intact hymen a must for brides—girls panic about not being able to convincingly prove their virginity. Traces of blood due to a presumed 'piercing' of the membrane during the wedding night, must demonstrate that she had never 'done it' before. That is the reason why in some traditions both families still want to see bloodstained sheets as proof that the marriage has been consummated and the bride was indeed a virgin. A lack of bloodstains is interpreted as unchastity, which in some cultures may lead to repudiation or honour killing. A tragic and unnecessary drama, because the hymen of about half of all girls does not bleed during the first sexual experience. That is why medical doctors are unable to conclude from the state of the hymen whether a girl is a virgin or not.

In societies or groups with a virginity obsession, the demand for surgical reconstruction is huge—not just from brides, but also from prostitutes who can earn extra money as fake virgins. Considerably less complicated ways to suggest virginal loss of blood are the 'carmine pill' (a pill containing fake blood) that a woman can insert beforehand; a small finger cut; or the careful planning of menstruation with the help of the birth control pill.

Usually very little information is available about wedding-night performances. Bridegrooms are warned that a girl may dread penetration; older men are aware that a young girl may feel reluctant or even abhorrent towards a man with whom she is going to share a life that others have decided for her. In proverbs, the husband is advised not to appear too delighted on the wedding night or in subsequent days, because it will make the young wife unbearably presumptuous:

> Neither praise the bride after the first night nor the shepherd after his first year. (Hebrew)
>
> A praised bride turns out to be a slob. (Farsi, Iran)
>
> If you love your wife, do not praise her before she is dead. (Bengal, Burmese, Czech, Russian)

A groom's fear can be no less overwhelming than the bride's: it is his duty, he has been taught, to deflower the bride on the wedding night. He must pierce the hymen, in spite of inexperience or advanced age. Do terrifying *vagina dentata* stories reflect male anguish of defloration? Imagine if he fails...Sympathising with only his perspective, a Berber proverb laments: 'May God have mercy on the husband; as for the wife she knows what awaits her.'

Virginal bleeding

'The wind that opens the bedewed peach' is a poetic Chinese defloration image. 'Wind' refers to flirting here, but in combination with words invoking moisture or rain it carries more direct sexual connotations.[146] In some cultures the hymen is deliberately ruptured in the first days of a baby's life, by the mother herself, for reasons of exaggerated cleanliness or because the girl is being prepared for premature intercourse with adult men. Among the Sakalava in Madagascar, girls would break their own hymen before marriage, if their parents hadn't already seen to it. No reason at all for the groom to worry.[147]

---

146. Barnard Wolfe, *The Daily Life of a Chinese Courtesan Climbing up a Tricky Ladder: with A Chinese Courtesan's Dictionary*, 1980:18.

147. Ploss and Bartels, 1912:209-210.

There are also traditions in which the hymen was considered so dangerous that it drastically impeded enjoyment. In Vedic texts the blood of the wedding night was presented as poisonous and the virginal vagina as a seat of danger.[148] Although male fear of deflowering a girl does not exist everywhere, some inexperienced grooms still prefer to leave that acid test to someone else:

> [...] someone immune to its dangers—a woman perhaps, using an instrument; or, paradoxically, a person ordinarily taboo, such as a close relative, a brother or father; or, sometimes, a priest, may rupture the hymen.[149]

Ancient texts point out that, among the Phoenicians, a special slave was commissioned for the task of deflowering. Jehan de Mandeville (a.k.a. Sir John Mandeville), the fourteenth-century writer of a widely-read fictional travel journal suggests that on a particular oriental island a small group of men committed themselves to the precarious business of deflowering girls:

> Then you come to an island where is the custom, if one takes a wife, he does not sleep with her as the first man, but there are poor servants who do this and take the girl's virginity, and for doing so the servants are paid... The vagina of the daughters is sorcered and poisoned, that it is dangerous to sleep with a daughter for the first time, but later on it is not dangerous at all.[150]

---

148. Verrier, *Myths of Middle India*, 1949:365.

149. More examples in Lederer:44; Freud, 'Das Tabu der Virginität' in *Gesammelte Werke* XII:161.

150. *Les Voyages de Jehan de Mandeville* was probably written in 1356. Quoted in Jörg Wettlaufer, who provides more examples in his article, 'The *jus primae noctis* as a Male Power Display' in *Evolution and Human Behaviour*, Vol. 1, 2 (March, 2000): 116.

Perhaps the greatest surprise is that this task was performed by 'poor servants'. In most examples from India and South America, it is chiefs or priests who service the new brides.

Even in places where little attention is paid to the hymen of girls, such as New Caledonia, some men would refuse to deflower their own wives, preferring to rent for that task a *perceur attitré* (an official penetrator) as the French observer Léon Moncelon noted in the nineteenth century.

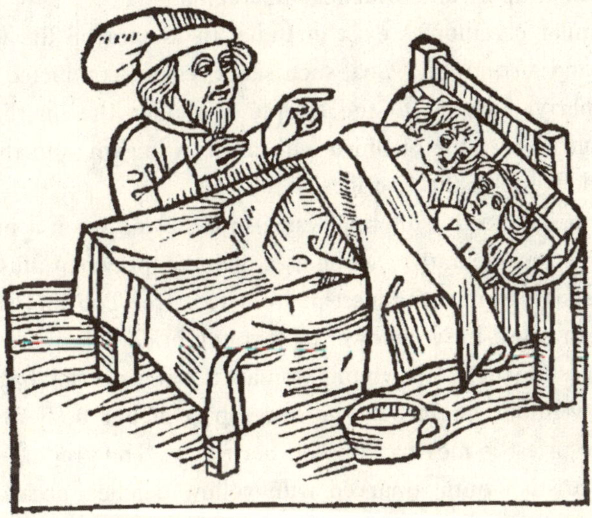

Ritual defloration woodcut in *Les Voyages de Jehan de Mandeville.* Strasbourg, 1484 edition.

According to the ancient Greek historian Herodotus (484-424 BC), the North African Nasamones, living in the area that is now southeast Libya, had a particular custom of their own. In their tradition, during the course of the wedding night, the bride was obliged to have intercourse with every male guest, who had to give her a present each in return. This male solidarity was indispensable not only to undo the power of a single hymen and to satisfy the violated bride, but also to placate the spirits whose task was to defend the young woman against intruders. Such a ritual serial rape served to dilute the dangerous supernatural power released during the tearing of the hymen, by spreading the risk among all the men.[151]

Other traditions, on the contrary, presented the defloration of a young girl as a particular honour or special gift offered to a god. In ancient Rome, 'The Roman bride sat down on the lap of the god Mutunus, so that his phallus entered her vagina, tore the hymen apart and widened the vagina.'[152]

Similar ceremonies exist in India. In Kanara on the western coast, and also around Goa, such sacrifices are conducted Before they marry, girls go to the temple and offer the 'firstlings' of marriage to a statue of Shiva with an iron lingam, and this God takes delivery of the 'sacrifice'.[153]

The right to this offering was also bestowed upon a priest as the god's representative, acting as a divine deputy. An illustration in a Persian Islamic manuscript from 1602 (see Plate 16) shows a Christian priest busy deflowering a young bride before the groom has access to her. The young woman is lying on her back with a pillow under her head. The lower part of her body is naked and the priest is moving between her thighs. The groom, dressed in a Christian outfit (marked with yellow patches, according to Islamic prescriptions) is patiently waiting outside until the priestly treatment is finished. According to the author of the manuscript, Muhammad Al-Qazwini, this was a typical Christian custom.[154]

151. Herodotus, *Histories*, Book 4:172-173.

152. Ploss and Bartels: 211.

153. Ibid.

154. This Persian manuscript of 1602 is a translation of an Arabic work by Zakariya al-Qazwini (1203-83) in the collection of Leiden University Libraries, with thanks to Dr Karin Scheper.

These stories about outsiders served to emphasise the gap between 'them' and 'us', the real believers.

Such examples of practical or ritual defloration—by the mother, a divine statue, a priest, a family member, a slave, a servant or a foreigner—were often inspired by paranoid fear of the magic powers or poisonous effects of hymenal blood. They had nothing to do with the so-called *jus primae noctis* ('right to the first night'), a medieval privilege often postulated as a *droit du seigneur* or the lord of the manor's right to have sexual intercourse with a vassal's bride on her wedding night. This right was also referred to as *droit de cuissage* (literally, 'a right to the thighs'); or in a free translation can be interpreted as the right of powerful men to have sex at will.

The first literary example of this presumed right dates back to around 1900 BC in the *Epic of Gilgamesh* from Mesopotamia. In that text, it is evident that Gilgamesh, as king of Uruk, is entitled to have sex with every betrothed woman or bride before any other man has access to her. In his *Histories*, Herodotus goes on to describe the Adyrmachidae, another tribe in Libya, where custom demanded that all girls who wanted to marry had to first visit the king, who had the right to deflower them all. The medieval Vikings also assumed this right in Irish monasteries where they overpowered Christian brides-to-be.[155] To this day, contemporary rulers and other powerful men continue to claim this right, with differing degrees of approbation and censure.

On the question of whether medieval landlords literally shared the bed with the virgin brides of their workers, scholars seem to disagree. The ancient rituals inspired by male anguish about deflowering a girl are largely replaced here by the hierarchical reasoning: owing to my status, I have a right to your body. Perhaps their powerful position gave them the reckless feeling that they

155. Cf. Wettlaufer.

were personally immune to the hymen danger, which would no doubt exacerbate the feeling of having a right to everything. In his book *Chimpanzee Politics*, Frans de Waal compares such modern-day characters to 'alpha males' among primates. A male of high status, in competition with his peers, will clock up more copulations and produce more offspring. In industrialised societies, life turns less on reproduction than on sexual prestige within one's group. Across cultural traditions, men have thought up rules by which their privileges regarding their sexual 'rights to women' are assured.

From my Congo years, I remember that wherever President Mobutu Sese Seko deigned to visit, young girls had to dance for him. *Nomen est omen* in this case: the name he chose for himself by decree, *Mobutu Sese Seko Nkuku Ngbendu Wa Za Banga* means 'The all-powerful warrior who, because of his endurance and inflexible will to win, goes from conquest to conquest, leaving fire in his wake.' The president was accustomed to selecting one or more of those gracious girls to have sex with. However, I am not sure that the family concerned considered it a great honour to have their young daughter deflowered by the nation's highest chief, as David Van Reybrouck suggests in his book *Congo*. I remember a friend's consternation after Mobutu sent her a preciously-ornamented belt, signifying that the president had a more than ordinary interest in her. For her own security she had to leave the country in haste, because the chief knows his rights: no one dares refuse him anything.

Sigmund Freud had his own ideas about outsourcing the breaking of hymens to someone other than the husband. He suggested that a woman always harbours revulsion and resentment towards the first man who penetrates her, often to the point of wrecking a marriage right from the start.[156]

---

156. Sigmund Freud, *Das Tabu der Virginität. Gesammelte Werke XII*, 1952:161; Lederer, Chapter 6.

Other dangers beyond a sorcerous, poisonous or mortal hymen loom on a wedding night. Some communities warn against the risk of conceiving a child on the night of defloration. If the very first coitus results in a pregnancy, the mighty hymenal blood will result in the birth of a sick or handicapped child. Unfortunately, the fear of female blood is not restricted to the once-only hymenal bleeding. In many cultures, blood originating from a female body has been associated directly with danger for the community in general and for men in particular. This holds especially true for menstrual blood.

Myths about menstruation

Every culture refers to the first menstruation in its own way. In Japan it is depicted as 'the year of the splitting melon'; among the Xhosa, the 'unbudding of the flower'; in Germany, as the beginning of the 'monthly flower' and in India as 'the five arrows of the god of love'.[157] Origin myths explain the beginning of this mysterious bleeding and its consequences, connecting it to monthly rules and prohibitions with both positive and negative connotations. In an Egyptian funerary text (eighteenth to sixteenth century BC), the colour red is associated with hostile forces and cosmic battles in the process of creation—although it is not quite clear whether it is the woman herself or her menstrual bleeding that was disapproved of.[158]

In stories that do not present menstruation as a punishment, the explanation postulated for this natural phenomenon is completely different. In a Saramo story from Tanzania, for example, the bleeding is due to an accidental disfigurement:

---

157. Ploss and Bartels: 169.

158. O'Rourke: 'The Wt-Woman' in *Zeitschrift für Ägyptische Sprache und Altertumskunde*, Vol. 134, 2 (2007), pp.170-171.

> Long, long ago, there were only two men, who lived on honey. One of the men climbed a tree. The bees had built a nest up there and he wanted to get the honey from inside the tree with his axe. Suddenly the sharp blade of the axe fell down and hit the other man, who was lying on his back asleep right there under that tree. The falling axe hit his penis and cut it off. What was left was a bleeding wound like women have.
>
> His companion climbed down and asked, 'What is that?'
>
> 'The axe cut it off,' he replied.
>
> Then they slept together and a girl was born. They slept together again and a boy was born. A world of people descended from those two men. Ever since then, women lose blood down there, just like that first woman. (Saramo, Tanzania)[159]

In a dramatic turn of events, a mutilated man becomes the first woman, who spontaneously starts bleeding from her fresh wound and is soon able to give birth to the very first children. No question of punishment here.

In a Koya story from Andhra Pradesh, India, there were women from the beginning, but they never bled. But as a consequence, babies were born without eyes or mouths and quickly died. The population did not grow, a worrisome situation. So one of the ancestors, Sukra Koya, went to consult Deur (God):

> Deur asked him, 'Do women have a flow of blood every month?'
>
> 'No,' he said, 'I have never heard of that.'
>
> Deur plucked a leaf and gave it to Sukra: 'Pound up this leaf and put it in the place where people fetch

159. Otto Dempwolff, 'Märchen der Zalamo und Hehe in Deutsch Ost-Afrika' in *Anthropophyteia* (9) 1904:396-397.

> water. All the unmarried girls will get a flow of blood. It will frighten them at first, but you must explain things to them and teach them how to bathe at the end of their time and boil their clothes in a new pot.'
>
> Moreover, Deur said, 'On the third day after the first bath, tell the girls to make a doll of grass. They must blacken the doll with charcoal and then take it with a hen's egg to a crossroads. There they must sacrifice a fowl in my name and bury the doll and the egg.'[160]

The Koya did as Deur had advised, and from then on all ended well as far as healthy progeny was concerned. In other Koya stories a fruit or vegetable provokes the first menstruation among the first foremothers.[161] The message is simply that menstruation is part of a healthy life.

Other traditions have a different view of the matter, and the first menstruation is presented as a punishment for a woman's first grave infringement in the early days of mankind: 'Abuse came from your mouth, blood will flow from your vulva.' [...] Since that day women have had a period of blood-flowing every month. (Bondo, India)[162]

In Judaism, Christianity and Islam, stories and comments abound presenting menstruation as a well-deserved punishment. In various rabbinic stories Eve menstruates for the first time after she has slept with the archangel of death Samael or the Serpent, who opened the source, 'and this is how the flood of impurity and the monthly female illness have come into the world.'[163]

160. Elwin 1954:475-476.

161. Ibid.

162. Elwin 1949:274.

163. Eisenmenger, *Natursagen*, (1711) 1907:211.

Satan smartly turns God's commandment upside down in a Javanese Islamic story: he fools Eve by telling her that she will only be chased from paradise if she does not eat the forbidden *khuldi* fruit. Since there are only two such fruits, Eve immediately swallows one. It gives her such immense pleasure that she falls down and faints. Then right away she starts bleeding, and because 'she did not remember the divine prohibition of eating the *khuldi* fruit, all women lose blood during the monthly periods.'[164]

Neither in the Genesis story in the Bible nor in the Quran is there any reference to menstruation as a punishment for Eve eating the forbidden fruit, but various interpreters reinforce the hierarchical relations between men and women by imposing punitive sanctions on male contact with an 'unclean' woman. The belief that menstruation was impure resulted in detailed prescriptions in the Hebrew Bible: 'When a woman has a discharge, and the discharge in her body is blood, she shall be in her menstrual impurity for seven days, and whoever touches her shall be unclean until the evening' (Leviticus 15:19).

The Quran (2:222) also advises men to stay away from women as long as they are 'impure', without making a connection between menstruation and the violation of God's commandment. But Quran scholar Tabari (839-923) considers Eve's first menstruation as a punishment for making the tree in paradise bleed by eating its fruit. The work of Sahih al-Bukhari, considered by Islamic scholars as the most authentic book after the Quran, associates lack of intelligence, a female lack since Eve, with menstruation:

> Once Allah's Apostle [...] passed by [a group of] women and said, 'O women! Give alms, as I have seen that the majority of the dwellers of Hell-fire were you (women).'

---

164. Steenbrink: 118.

> They asked, 'Why is it so, O Allah's Apostle?' He replied, 'You curse frequently and are ungrateful to your husbands. I have not seen anyone more deficient in intelligence and religion than you. A cautious sensible man could be led astray by some of you.' The women asked, 'O Allah's Apostle! What is deficient in our intelligence and religion?' He said, 'Is not the evidence of two women equal to the witness of one man?' They replied in the affirmative. He said, 'This is the deficiency in her intelligence. Isn't it true that a woman can neither pray nor fast during her menses?' The women replied in the affirmative. He said, 'This is the deficiency in your religion.'[165]

In the Quran there is no association between menstruation and intelligence, and nor did I find it elsewhere.

In Christianity the presumed uncleanness of the first foremother (and all women after her) formed a stark contrast with the 'unstained purity' of the Virgin Mary. The Catholic Church still sticks to the doctrine that Mary was a lifelong virgin with an intact hymen in spite of giving birth, and never menstruated.[166]

Oral stories go into the details of the first people's bodily changes after the eating of the forbidden fruit—in which Adam gets a better deal than Eve. In the Igala story quoted at the start of this chapter, and in various other traditions, Eve swallowed the fruit in a hurry and began to bleed, whereas Adam reacted hesitantly and the forbidden fruit got stuck in his throat, and that's where man's Adam's apple comes from.

Some Islamic variants of the Adam and Eve story still serve as proof of Eve's hypersensitivity to Satan's arguments. In Turkish

165. Sahih al-Bukhari Book 6, Hadith 304.

166. Ranke-Heinemann: 21.

rural communities, the eating of the forbidden fruit is explained as a sign of women's moral weakness, the very reason why women must be supervised by men. Girls are taught that the female body is repulsive and needs to be carefully hidden. Even though men may sometimes lose blood—while hunting, in a war or in an accident—for them the loss of blood is incidental. Men are independent, they master their blood and their sperm, while women leak blood and milk from their bodies uncontrollably.[167] Such reasoning converts physical differences into justification of a hierarchical order.

Monthly magic

A disadvantage can be turned into an advantage, as we learn from a note written by Pliny the Elder (23 or 24-79 AD), who believed that a naked menstruating woman would suppress whirlwinds, hailstorms and lightning. If, in her monthly state, she walked around a field, caterpillars, beetles and other vermin would spontaneously fall from the ears of corn.[168]

This does not prevent many cultures from associating contact with a menstruating woman with entirely negative connotations. Her bleeding would weaken hunters and warriors, kill young plants, sour wines, putrefy meat, curdle milk, and the horse's back on which she sat would break. In many communities she was forced to pass her 'unclean' days in isolation.[169] This tendency

---

167. Carol Delaney, 'Mortal Flow: Menstruation in Turkish Village Society' in *Blood Magic*, 1988:79 and 82.

168. As explained in the work of his nephew Pliny the Younger, *Historia Naturalis*, xxviii. Chapter 23, in John Bostock's *Pliny the Elder* web edition.

169. Peggy Reeves Sanday, *Female Power and Male Dominance: On the Origin of Sexual Inequality*, 1988, Chapter 5; Eloïse Mozzani, *Le Livre des Superstitions: Mythes, Croyances et Légendes*, 1995:512ff. For the search of a cultural balance during the mighty flowing of blood, see the work Mary Douglas.

towards negative thinking about menstruation might well have been increased by widespread mistrust of the daughter-in-law, the 'stranger' intruding on the family to live as the son's wife.

Numerous rules have been invented to limit the perceived damage. In the ultra-orthodox Jewish tradition, the appearance of a menstruating woman in public would cause disasters: her blood prevents bread from rising and damages the harvest. And according to medieval Jewish mystic sources, 'God abandons menstruants because God cannot suffer impurity.'[170] The ancient Greeks believed that menstruating women would make the land barren, the mirrors they looked in turned opaque, and sex during a period made them pregnant with snakes. In parts of Japan and among some Amerindian peoples, women were obliged to stay away from cattle, and were not allowed to touch people's food. A North Siberian belief held that during menstruation women should not look up at the sky, since the sky represents purity. In Europe, a stubborn rumour circulated that sex with a menstruating woman would cause male impotence or other disasters such as baldness. As soon as an Australian Aboriginal discovered that his menstruating wife had been lying on his blanket, he killed her on the spot, and within a fortnight he himself died of sheer terror.[171]

Among the Ila in Zambia there was a belief that a man would lose his manhood by eating with a menstruating woman. She was not allowed to touch pots and pans, and had to stay away from the common cooking fire. In some cultures, women were set apart in a menstruation hut and not allowed to eat food that had been declared taboo for them—usually the most appreciated and healthiest dishes such as meat or fish. In Winnebago belief, sacred

170. Sharon Faye Koren, *Forsaken: The Menstruant in Medieval Jewish Mysticism*. Lebanon: Brandeis University Press, 2011.

171. Briffault's examples (1927) are referred to in Lederer, Chapter 4.

objects would lose their power in contact with a menstruating woman, and even ghosts would not survive contact. So many rules have been invented worldwide to combat women's monthly bleeding that Briffault in his three-volume book *The Mothers* (1927) devoted twenty-five pages to the topic, with the modest mention that his elaborate list was far from complete.

Briefly summarised, the most frequent restrictions on women during their periods, are:

1) sex is not allowed;
2) menstruating women must take into consideration limitations regarding dress, eating, movement and contact with things or people;
3) they are not permitted to touch male ritual equipment or weaponry;
4) they are not allowed to prepare or cook food;
5) they are set apart in special huts.[172]

Such rules turned out differently in practice than originally intended. There is no single or absolute menstrual taboo, and taboos surrounding the menstrual cycle may well have restricted the behaviour of other people more than the menstruating woman herself. Women certainly made smart use of the rules by shifting blame for family disasters on menstruating co-wives or by frightening a husband to death with the threat of mixing drops of menstrual blood in his food. Anxiety and negative attention to female periods from women as well as men have promoted hierarchical relationships and apartheid of the sexes.

Menstrual blood was believed to be dangerously powerful, and menstruation was one of the most baffling enigmas for people

---

172. Briffault in Lederer, ibid.; Robert H. Lowie, *Primitive Religion*, 1925:211ff; Reeves Sanday 1988:104.

to explain. In many cultures women themselves internalised the importance of their monthly seclusion. They would never risk exposing the family and the community to its negative effects, even to the point of perceiving themselves as seriously harmful and dangerous during menstruation. As we have seen, in some Amerindian cultures, women exploited the authority that menstrual bleeding afforded them, arguing that this was 'the time when we are powerful and the men are afraid'.[173]

Women's blood and sex

In southern Portugal women derived special powers from menstruation, even though they believed (late 1970s) that these powers were beyond their own control: plants withered away and objects started moving as soon as a menstruating woman came close. In that region women tell a story about São Bras (Saint Blaise or Blasius), the only male saint to be carried around on a local holy day. In churches he is depicted with striking red hands, which he sustained as a result of indiscreet behaviour long before he was canonised. Driven by sexual passion in his youth, he had groped a young menstruating woman, and when he took his hands away from under her skirts, they were covered in blood. Since then, São Bras devoted his life to good works, but his hands remained blood-red to remind him and others of this reprehensible behaviour in his youth. This Blasius story is a local version of the life story of the Armenian physician, bishop and canonised martyr.[174]

In Greek and Roman antiquity as well as in the Jewish tradition there was a taboo on sex with menstruating women.

---

173. Mary Douglas 1975:62-63; Marta Weigle 1982:171-173.

174. Denise L. Lawrence, 'Menstrual Politics: Women and Pigs in Rural Portugal' in *Blood Magic*: 117-136

Roman natural scientist Pliny the Elder, and many scholars after him, insisted that sex with a menstruating woman was dangerous. In the first century, Jewish-Greek scholar Philo of Alexandria banned sex with menstruating women because menstrual blood would keep the womb moist and thereby damage the vitality of male seed. Sex was only meant to produce offspring, according to the reasoning of that time. It was already known that during monthly periods nothing could be begotten, so what was the point anyway? Christianity adopted the existing prohibition without critical reflection.

Jews and Christians alike quoted threateningly from the book of Leviticus (20: 18): 'If a man lies with a woman having her sickness, and uncovers her nakedness, and she has uncovered the fountain of her blood; both of them shall be cut off from among their people.' Some translations upgrade 'cut off' to 'exterminated'. An explanation for this merciless punishment might be that religious Jews as well as many non-Jews were convinced that menstrual blood was toxic.[175]

The dangers were increasingly depicted as a threat. Whether or not under classical influence, some church fathers were certain that children born sick or disabled were the result of sex during menstruation. The most frequently mentioned diseases or abnormalities were leprosy, hydrocephalus, epilepsy, paralysis, crossed eyes, crooked legs, a hump or insanity. From the fifteenth century, the idea that disabled babies were born due to conceiving during menstruation lost its persuasiveness. Still some Christian theologians kept those frightening ideas in play for their believers through the ages—here and there even into the twentieth century.[176]

175. Ranke-Heinemann 1990:21.

176. For detailed clerical Catholic ideas about menstruation, cf. Ranke-Heinemann, part II.

Initially, the early church distinguished itself from surrounding cultures by asserting equality between men and women, but sooner or later, male church scholars excluded women from the liturgy and the holy altar on the basis of 'monthly impurity'. And in the Catholic Church women are still not allowed to be priests.

In various traditions menophobia, the fear of menstrual blood, is still deployed to keep women away from certain positions. Fear of the polluting presence of menstruating women was and is strongest in societies where men feel that their authority is at risk: they feel compelled to avoid women's blood and other dangerous female substances as much as possible. In the event of contamination, they desperately try to eliminate the harmful effect by any means.

Male menstruation

The widespread belief in the dangers of menstrual blood continued to intrigue those who did not have the experience, so it is not altogether surprising that according to some myths, in the beginning menstruation was a man's business:

> Long ago things were different from now: the women had beards and moustaches and the men had something small inside their bodies, it looked like a shell and it contained a living creature. Every month that creature caused them to bleed. Their wives had no such flow of blood, but for the men this was very inconvenient. For some days every month they had to stop carrying out chores such as cutting wood or working in the fields. It was too risky for them to go outside at the time of blood, because the tigers smelled it and ate them immediately.
>
> One day there was a marriage and everyone prepared to go to the wedding festivities. A young wife said to her

> husband, 'Why don't you take my beard and moustache for a change and give me your little shell? I would love to see what it feels like to have blood flowing from me.' He agreed and so it happened that the girl stuck her beard and moustache on her husband's face and she fitted his shell with the living creature into her own body.
>
> After the wedding they tried to return the things they had exchanged, but the hair had stuck to the man's face and the shell could not be removed from the girl's inside. 'It is not too bad,' the girl said. 'I can now get plenty of cloth, because I need at least seven layers to cover my parts. And also, my husband looks very handsome with that beard.' She went out and when the other women touched her, they too began to bleed and from then on, all women have a monthly period.[177] (Halba, India)

Here, again, the bleeding is not a matter of guilt or punishment at all. Various Eastern European stories also imagine how, in the beginning, God imposed the menstrual period on Adam and the male gender. So in ancient times men had blood flowing from their knees every month—or from a body part that went unnamed for reasons of prudishness—but they did not know how to deal with menstruation or with other 'women's issues' such as cleaning, cooking or giving birth, so God reversed the roles. Such stories are told by women with great enthusiasm to confirm that men are unable to cope with traditional female roles.

In a number of cultures, initiation rites of boys during puberty served to reverse the malignant effect of female blood that contaminated all men during their birth from the mother's body. A boy receives an incision in the tongue at the start of

177. Elwin, 1949:240.

puberty—an operation that causes bleeding, just like a girl's first menstrual period. The tongue is deemed to have been seriously polluted by the mother's milk he drank from the day of his birth. With the incision, he is safely released from all the pernicious female elements and influences he gulped down during his childhood.[178]

In Melanesian and Australian cultures, the belief in and fear of the malignant influence of female menstrual and birth blood developed from the fact that men and women were considered interdependent. Both sexes were weakened by the 'contaminating' effect of sex, but the woman has an advantage because her monthly bleeding relieves her of the contagion, whereas recurrent contact with women weakens men further and further.

In his book *The Island of Menstruating Men*, Ian Hogbin describes the reasoning that the people of Wogeo (an island off the north coast of Papua New Guinea) developed about female uncleanness in their society: women are naturally inferior but can be dangerous during menstruation. A Wogeo man has the right to beat his wife, but in doing so he takes a risk: at her next period, she can touch his food and cause him a fatal illness.

When a Wogeo boy starts having sex, he must initiate his own 'period'. He first catches a lobster and removes one of the claws, which he keeps with ginger in a leaf until the day set for the bleeding, on which day he fasts. He undresses on a lonely beach, wades into the water up to his knees, sets his legs apart and as soon as he gets an erection, pushes the foreskin back and cuts the glans with the lobster claw, first on the left and then on the right. When the wound begins to dry up and the seawater no longer turns red, he walks back to the beach where he wraps his penis in leaves. He is not allowed to have sex until the next new moon.

---

178. More examples and details in Bettelheim, 1954:167ff.

For those who believe in it, this operation has the desired effect: after the bleeding the boy's body glows with energy and self-confidence. It is also the custom for warriors to take a bleeding before they go on a raid; for traders, before carving out a canoe for an overseas trip; and for hunters, before weaving a new net to catch wild pigs. So the men have created their own successful menstrual rituals to deflect from the harmful influences of female blood.[179]

Of the worldwide list of disasters caused by menstruating women, we may hope that most have now been reduced to footnotes in local cultural history. An old family anecdote from the southern United States provides a simple recipe for women who worry that their loved one might run away—just put 'a spoonful of your "time of the month" in his coffee regularly,' and he'll never leave you. The proof is delivered at the end of the story: 'Your uncle died in your aunt's arms and loved her to his last breath.'[180]

Ideas about blood and blood loss are culture-bound, but apparently many ancestors were so wary of menstrual blood that they undertook strict measures to make their world liveable. Gradually, menstruation has given rise to effective means for degrading women and keeping them out of the public space. Nonetheless, women's bleeding remains awe-inspiring: they bleed every month, but it suddenly stops when in the darkness of that inscrutable womb a new life begins to stir.

---

179. Ian Hogbin, *The Island of Menstruating Men*, 1970:96ff.

180. Matthew Kirksey, quoted in *Blood Magic*: 35.

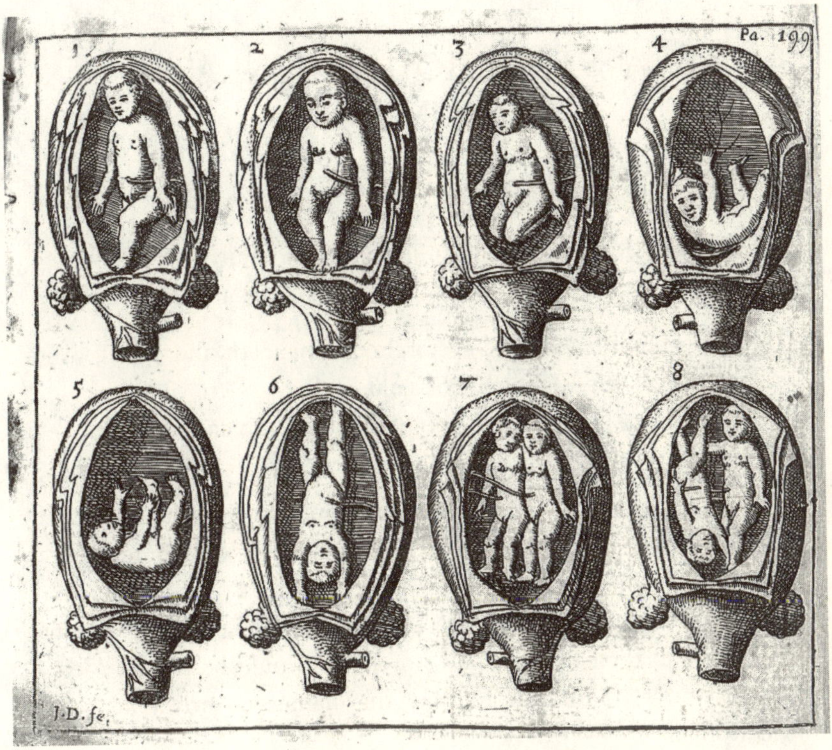

Foetuses in various positions. Jane Sharp, *The Midwives Book*, 1671.

6. A STOREHOUSE BENEATH THE NAVEL

> She who leaves a child behind, lives eternally.
>
> (Chagga, Tanzania)

> The woman who has a storehouse beneath the navel, will never die of hunger or cold.
>
> (Sephardic, Spain/Portugal)

In Congo, I asked my all-male first-year students to write an essay about 'the purpose of life'. They agreed almost unanimously that having children was far and away the most important part of life. During our discussions it turned out that their biggest fear was that their future wife's storehouse would be locked. Men can of course be infertile too, but the blame was firmly laid on the women.

Fertility and pregnancy are praised in all cultures. In proverbs, a childless woman is harshly compared to a tent without tent pegs (Ladino), a day without sun (Czech), a cow without a bell (German), a tree without birds (Thai), a solitary flower on a mountain top (Vietnamese), and so forth.

In stories, childless women desperately look for a solution to their disastrous lack:

> [They] fell pregnant as soon as they were in the vicinity of certain places: rocks, caves, trees or rivers. The infant

> souls entered their bodies and they fell pregnant. Whether these infant souls were the souls of ancestors or not, one thing was certain: they had been waiting all this time to become human, hidden in crevices or cavities, in pools or forests. They had already led some kind of embryonic life in the womb of their real Mother, the Earth.[181]

The Earth was where children came from, which is why nineteenth-century Europeans believed children were brought by aquatic animals—fish or frogs—or by birds, especially storks.

Miraculous pregnancy

Miraculous conceptions are of all times and cultures. Storytellers explore human anatomy and life-creating powers with curiosity. A Baniwa story from Brazil has the first woman falling pregnant when she gently pressed a stick against her cheek. In their desire to fall pregnant, some women look for help in extraordinary places, others in certain drinks or food. Or they meet a spirit or an angel, before a child comes to life inside them. Unusual conceptions reflect the enduring human wonder at the coming into existence of new life.[182]

Sometimes the stars are invoked, or the sun or the moon, the wind or lightning, ancestors or symbols of power. Offerings are made to a wide range of entities. Sometimes it's a question of coming into contact with a special footprint in stone or rock, supposedly from Adam or Buddha, from Ali (Muhammad's son-in-law) or the Christian Saint Thomas.

A Chinese woman who saw a huge human footprint wanted a son of the same impressive proportions:

181. Mircea Eliade, *Myths, Dreams and Mysteries*, 1960:164-165.

182. Weigle: 86ff.

> The woman stood still where the Supreme God had left an imprint of his big toe and at that moment, at that spot, she felt how her core was seized and—filled with deep religious wonderment—she realised she was pregnant.[183]

There are innumerable stories about people connecting with the powers of stone: stones are solid, they do not die, whereas mankind is mortal. No wonder young women let their bodies slide over stones or must jump over a whole row of fertility stones to fall pregnant. In the French city of Rennes there are stones known as *pierres des épousées* or *pierres marieuses* that are sought out by brides-to-be for their powers of marital bliss. Near Verdun there is a rock known as the 'Armchair of Saint Lucie', where the saint was said to have left an imprint of her body, and women who wish to become pregnant should simply sit on the chair.

Amongst Muslims a similar idea is found near Tunis, at the famous tomb of Sidi Fethalla. Childless women go there, risking their lives as the climb is steep and slippery. Some even do so repeatedly. On Saturday, this holy man's day, they first invoke him and then rub a flat stone on their belly.

As well as stones enhancing fertility, there are rivers, lakes and springs endowed with the same effect. You can drink their special water or immerse yourself in it. A spring can make women fall pregnant after a benevolent god has added a few drops of sperm to its waters.[184]

The importance of fertility is magnified in impressive shrines, for example, in Hindu culture. Infertile women pray mostly to Shiva, the god of creative power and fertility. His emblem is the lingam, which can be found on street corners or in temples,

---

183. P. Saintyves, *Les vierges mères*, 1908:22ff.

184. Many examples in Mircea Eliade, *Naissances Mystiques*.

in the form of a standing stone. In the southern Indian city of Thanjavur, a famous temple dedicated to Shiva, more than a thousand years old, boasts an 8.7-metre-high lingam, one of the largest in the world. Lingams come in all sizes, they are rubbed with special oil, covered with flowers and perfume, offered sacrifices, and people prostrate themselves in front of them. Infertile women spend a night in the temple in a special room reserved for them. There, in the dark, they are visited by Shiva. The inner part of the temple, the holy of holies, is called *karuvarai*, the Tamil word for 'womb room', with *karu* meaning foetus.[185] In many rituals a simple touch suffices. In short, there are a striking number of stories about pregnancy in which men play no role at all.

In several origin stories there were just women at the beginning of time, or countries where only women lived and managed fine without men, and we are told how pregnancy came about in these communities. In India and Taiwan, it is said that the women were fertilised by hornets or by the bulging navels some women had, or they pleasured themselves or each other with wooden organs.

The wind was also believed to be a powerful fertiliser, although some variants specify that only a storm could have the desired effect. It happened this way—the woman who wanted to fall pregnant climbed a mountain or stood on a roof, bent over, lifted her skirt, and the wind blew around her vulva, causing a child to spontaneously grow in her belly.

Prevailing male perspectives commented with clear disapproval on such imaginary female communities. Their accounts are tinged with fear—not least of being superfluous to the impregnation process. These women were said to be man-haters, they wept whenever a baby boy was born instead of a girl; or they would immediately kill all male babies they gave birth to. Those poor

185. More examples in Saintyves.

little boys were torn apart or had boiling water poured over them. And these are just a few of many more dreadful scenarios.[186]

Male apprehension about such stories is expressed in contradictory ways. First, in a warning against unconstrained female power aimed at destroying men—just look how they exterminate baby boys! Second, in a boundless need to belittle women—of course, they cannot survive all by themselves, without men; the girls they give birth to are degenerate and worthless, and these women are unfit to give birth to a healthy baby boy; women who masturbate with a wooden penis will only produce children without bones, who won't survive for more than a few days. No, sturdy male offspring require real male potency. There is an unstable balance between female birth-giving and male attainment and assumptions of power. It is quite human to debunk a fearful obsession by inventing a more reassuring version of events.

Male input

The idea that only the mother produced a child is probably the oldest, but over time the male contribution has been greatly magnified, in line with the emergence of patriarchal societies. This development is reflected in both myths and in literary texts. The *Eumenides* (451 BC) was the final part of a trilogy of tragedies called the *Oresteia* and written by the Greek playwright Aeschylus. They were performed together during the annual Dionysos Festival in Athens. In the *Eumenides*, Orestes is being chased by the Furies or revenge goddesses after he kills his mother Clytemnestra, but Apollo stands up for him:

> The mother of what is called her child, is no parent of it, but nurse only of the young life that is sown in her.

186. E.g. Lederer: 105.

> [...] The parent is the male, and she but the stranger, a friend, who, if fate spares his plant, preserves it till it puts forth.[187]

This belief is of Egyptian origin, according to historian Diodorus of Sicily (*c.* 90-30 BC) who observed that the 'Egyptians hold the father alone to be the author of generation, and the mother only to provide a nest and nourishment for the foetus.'[188]

It is relevant here to go back for a moment to the world of the Greek gods, a divine world where female anatomy was not needed for procreation. In his work on the origin of the gods, the writer Hesiod (mid-eighth century BC) called the supreme god Zeus' first wife Metis wiser than all other gods and humans. However, after the prophecy that the king of the gods would lose his power to her second child, Earth and Heaven advised Zeus to swallow his pregnant wife: only then would his power remain superior to all immortal gods. Fearing the loss of his lightning-hurling superiority, Zeus grasped his pregnant partner with both hands and wolfed her down.

From within his belly Metis could continue to generously provide him with wise advice, and in due course he himself gave birth to a daughter—bright-eyed Athena. The blacksmith Hephaestus cleaved Zeus' skull and from her father's head leaped the proud goddess, fully armed, or in Hesiod's words:

> [...] the awful, the strife-stirring, the host-leader, the unwearying, the queen, who delights in tumults and wars and battles [...] a fearsome queen who brings the sound of war and, tirelessly, leads the host.[189]

---

187. Aeschylos, *Eumenides*, lines 657-661, quoted in Needham: 25.

188. Ibid.

189. Hesiod, *Theogony*: 925-926.

Eileithyia, goddess of childbirth, assisting Zeus at the birth of Athena from his head. Painted amphora, 550-525 BC. Musée du Louvre, Paris.

The story of pregnant Metis literally disappearing from sight and leaving the birth of her child to her husband, is reminiscent of the creation myth in which the mother of all humans, Eve, appeared from Adam's body. Zeus was a god and Adam a human, but in both myths childbirth was undertaken by a male character.

Some stories play with this role change or make jokes about it. For example, the Hittite god Kumarbi falls pregnant when he inadvertently swallows a drop of an opponent's sperm while hitting him hard in the belly. The previously mentioned Japanese god Susanoo and his sister Amaterasu compete in producing new gods by exchanging objects and shattering his sabre and her jewels. Divine offspring pops out of their mouths—she produces three girls and he, five boys. She claims the boys and leaves the girls to him, because the boys were produced with her jewels and the girls with Susanoo's sabre.[190]

Men's armpits sometimes serve as an alternative womb, or the hollow of the knee, as in the case of the Yami in Taiwan, where one first man was created from a stone and another from a bamboo stalk.

> [They] had very long penises attached to their knee joints. Their knee joints swelled up and itched, and after a while they started to give birth. A boy burst out of the son of bamboo's right knee and a girl out of his left knee. A boy burst out of the son of stone's right knee and a girl out of his left knee. These children grew up and married each other.[191]

Inuit stories opt for a shamanic solution. After a global disaster that destroyed everything and everyone, two grown male shamans rise up from two mounds of earth. They live together and soon one of them becomes pregnant. The non-pregnant man sings a magic power song for his pregnant partner:

> A human being here
> A penis here.
> May its opening be wide
> And roomy.
> Opening, opening, opening![192]

The male anatomy got in the way of childbirth, and a change of sex was unavoidable. Hence the pregnant man's penis had to

190. Hesiod in Baring and Cashford: 333ff; Pierre Lévêque: 31ff.

191. Arundel Del Rei, *Creation Myths of the Formosan Natives*. Tokyo: The Hokuseido Press, 1951:39-41. The Yami are Indonesian-related people. See also Baumann: 221-224.

192. Iglulik Inuit, Canada. Knud Rasmussen, *The Netsiluk Eskimos*, 1931:209.

split wide open and transform into a gateway of life, before he could give birth.

Those without birth-giving capacity nonetheless monopolised reproduction in societies where they were in charge. The emotions and tensions evoked by the womb are not only reflected in creation myths and religious views, but also in a global wealth of proverbs. Container metaphors are rife: pots, vases, bags, gourds, rice pans and many other objects are provided with lids and locks to protect the womb and shield it against dangers from outside.

Myths confirmed the respective roles of men and women in the process of childbirth, while supporting proverbs sustained the prevailing morality with powerful images drawn from uncertainty about the desirable answer to two crucial questions, the first regarding whose child was in the womb. Many proverbs set out that a woman should mate only with her own husband:

> Two male hippopotamuses cannot live in one pool. (Mandinka, Mali)
> There can only be one tiger in each cave. (Spanish, El Salvador)
> Two male bears don't hibernate in one den. (Yakutsk, Russia)
> You don't cook two large bones in the same pot. (Ovambo)
> The eye of the needle can't hold two threads. (Arabic)

The chosen metaphors for male and female anatomy conjure the danger of female uncontrollability and insist that a monogamous relationship is a must for women. Cheating men and male desire are met with greater understanding in sayings such as, 'A thief cannot be blamed if he finds the gate open' (Colombia). Or justified by arguing that his nature cannot be helped, especially in stressful times: 'In stormy weather every hole seems like a harbour,' according to wisdom from Mexico. 'Women and money tempt even Brahma the creator,' goes a Telugu saying from India. How could a man resist, if even the gods can't? The point that civilisation cannot function without self-control seems to be lacking in such arguments.[193]

The second crucial question correlates with the first—how much do male and female elements contribute to the new life budding in the womb? As this question does not have a simple answer, proverbs rarely go into the matter. It is mostly philosophers and scholars who have tried to crack the case.

Throughout history secular power and religious ideas have bent science to their interests via subjective appreciations of physical characteristics, with blood and sperm the most striking ingredients: male fluids were clearly rated higher than female ones. In a Jewish story, undoubtedly influenced by Aristotle, God commands the soul to enter the sperm before conception takes place. The soul does not wish to descend into that 'impure' sperm, but God forces it there. Cloaked in the male reproductive cell, the soul—the superior (because life-bringing) element—arrives in the womb where the new human being will take shape.[194]

According to Islam only God has the power to create life. In the Quran both parents generate semen that fuses in the womb to create life, a vision drawn from another Greek role model, Hippocrates. This two-sperm model goes against Aristotle's idea that it is men who deliver the breath of life or 'soul' to the womb. In the Middle Ages Muslim scholars preferred the version in which women's contribution to the process is diminished, whereas men's role is emphasised in intriguing ways:

> Men's knowledge and expertise of the maternal body take precedence over women's experience, and, to some extent, God's omniscience. In contrast to the Quran, medical

193. See 'Messages of Metaphors', Chapter 5 of *Never Marry a Woman with Big Feet* (in the original Yale edition, 2004).

194. Ginsberg, *The Legends of the Jews*, Vol. I: 56-57; Steenbrink: 44.

> writings insert themselves between God and the womb in order to ensure an intimate and mysterious partnership previously inaccessible to them.[195]

They also extensively discussed the puzzling issue as to why a child takes after one parent more than the other. Due to paternal insecurities, they were inclined to conclude that the father determines the genetic features of the child. Do phenotypic similarities then prove that a woman has not committed adultery? And if the child resembled neither of the parents, does it follow that she had been unfaithful? This problematic and distrustful reasoning also goes against the Quranic requirement that four witnesses are required to prove infidelity.

Could it be that the child would resemble the parent who was first to orgasm? To have children resemble their father, some argued, the man had to come before the woman, and with more powerful orgasms. But then, why would one sperm cell be more powerful than another? It was all quite confusing. One thing, however, was agreed: 'powerful' sperm produced a son who looks like his father, and considerably increased a man's status, while daughters diminished the father's masculinity (more in Chapter 10).

Following the same line of thought, children who took after their mother (or neither parent) had to be the outcome of weak male semen unable to dominate the female contribution. To avoid such an unwanted interpretation, Islamic medical scholars preferred the hierarchical view in which the male contribution was superior, whilst the female body was a passive and dependent container controlled and dominated by men who embody 'the deity's elusive, ineffable efforts to produce life', with children who resemble their fathers (instead of their mother or someone else) equated with the life that God commands:

---

195. Kueny: 73.

> In order to appease paternal anxieties, male physicians see the need to de-emphasise the reproductive role of the mother, who becomes a passive recipient of prevailing male seed that must engender a child who resembles the father who sired it [...]. Such views contradict the Quran where God displays total control over the womb and its contents, or invites women to participate along with him in the production of life. In the context of the revelation, children can look like mothers, fathers, grandfathers, or no one at all. In the everyday world, however, a man must work to establish the dominant connection with his child, even if it means suppressing a woman's reproductive capacity, accusing her of adultery, or rejecting his own progeny on the basis of this similarity.[196]

In the Quran only God has unlimited power over the womb and its contents, but in earthly discussions on heredity, the man is put forward as a close second. The realistion that men could not produce offspring themselves led to interpretations reducing the uterus to a passive repository for the life-bringing sperm of men. In all three monotheistic religions, one finds theological statements plainly ignoring Eve or her contribution to the process, while eagerly confirming that all humans originate from Adam's loins (meaning: his sperm) or that his spine contained 'the great reservoir of the human race'.[197] The one who was created first assumes power over the one created later. Jewish, Christian and Islamic theologians continued to repeat this adage on the basis of a common interpretation of a story in which Eve originated from one of Adam's ribs or directly from Adam's body.

---

196. Kueny, 2013:52ff. For a wealth of information on medieval Islamic ideas, see 'Mapping the Maternal Body', Chapter 2 of her wonderful book *Conceiving Identities*.

197. See also Robert McElvaine, *Eve´s Seed*, 2001.

Not only in Adam and Eve stories, but also elsewhere, the desired hierarchical make-up of society was confirmed in a number of ways. The female body was reduced to a carrier of the mini-human, which the man implanted into her ready-made. Without the seed, no pregnancy. In extreme cases an animal vessel could even take over the function of the womb. In an Indian story the first man is extremely lonely after the first woman passes away. The only things he has are his cow and a thin blanket. One night he loses his seed in a dream and the next morning, he spreads out his blanket to dry on the roof. The cow pulls the blanket from the roof, eats it and becomes pregnant. She then gives birth to a boy and a girl who become the first Gadaba ancestors.[198]

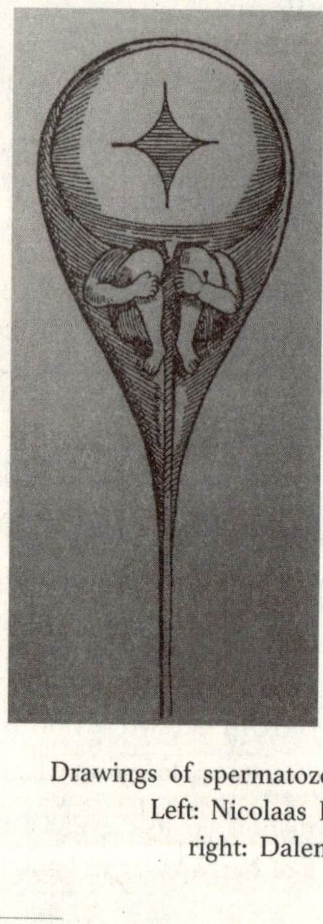

Drawings of spermatozoa with a little human inside.
Left: Nicolaas Hartsoeker (1656-1725);
right: Dalempatius (1670-1741).

198. Elwin, 1949:35.

Influenced by ancestral stories and common societal values, science also held onto certain fixed ideas. Up until the seventeenth century, respected Western scholars clung to the Aristotlean view that it is the man who deposits human life into the womb—or the complete unborn child. Into the eighteenth century, various scientists continued to claim that under the microscope they had seen extremely small humans in the crawling sperm, complete with arms, legs and heads.[199] There are even drawings to 'prove' it.

The Dutch scientist Antoni van Leeuwenhoek (1632-1723) put his own sperm under a microscope and saw it move. His Delft colleague Reinier de Graaf (1641-73) carefully studied an ectopic pregnancy and noted the existence of *bollekes* ('little balls') in the female reproductive organs, leading his successors to the discovery of human egg cells. Finally, it became undeniable that both male and female reproductive cells contribute to conception and pregnancy. But still, nervous scholarly discussion was provoked as to whether a sperm cell ultimately contributed more to the emerging embryo than the female egg.

In her informative two-volume *Masculin/Féminin*, anthropologist Françoise Héritier investigates the origin of the difference in appreciation of men and women. She acknowledges great differences between cultures, but also notes that everywhere power was based—and often still is—on 'the managing of reproduction, and therefore of female fertility and, in particular, of the female capacity to bear sons for men unable to do that themselves.'[200] Throughout history this unfathomable need for predominance and control has prevented interested parties from doing unprejudiced and unbiased research.

---

199. Needham: 183ff.

200. Françoise Héritier, *Masculin/Féminin II : Dissoudre la Hiérarchie*, 2002:288.

Courtship and its consequences

In most creation myths there is a lack of interest in the pleasure of sex, the dominant message being the need for reproduction. This message has often been confirmed in proverbs: 'Women and goats, choose them for their breed' (Spanish, Latin America) or 'If you are impatient to have a child, you marry a pregnant woman' (Fulfulde, West Africa).

The first people had to multiply and become many, as stated in the Book of Genesis—understandable when your starting point is an almost empty world. Sometimes there are references to sexual appeal between people. A story of the Pima (or Akimel O'odham) people of Mexico and Arizona tells how the magician who made the world shaped two humans who 'were rather like himself and identical with each other in every part.' Suddenly, he realised that they had no genitals and would therefore be unable to reproduce. He corrected his mistake:

> So he pulled a little between the legs of one image, saying: 'Ah, that's much better.' With his fingernail he made a crack in the other image. He put some pleasant feeling in them somewhere. 'Ah, now it's good. Now they'll be able to do all the necessary things.'[201]

With or without pleasure, the consequences of sex tend to turn out differently for women than for men. 'A woman hides the penis, she won't hide her swelling belly,' goes a Mamprusi observation from Burkina Faso. Myths usually don't go into the different outcomes for the sexes, but proverbs all over the world warn girls in colourful metaphors. A man may deny his involvement, but women can hide their pregnancies no better than they can

201. Richard Erdoes and Alfonso Ortiz, *American Indian Myths and Legends*, 1984:46 (on the basis of fragments from the 1880s).

conceal their love, a cough, a hunchback or riding a camel. Here are a few more:

> The cow receives the bull in secret but gives birth in public. (Kurdish)
> The tongue shows what it has eaten. (Lunda)
> A fire and a girl's pregnancy cannot be kept secret. (Rwanda)
> Love, pregnancy and going up a mountain cannot be hidden. (Arabic, Egypt)

Production within the human womb is relatively limited. In Uganda, women are sometimes compared to a field where now and then you harvest just one or two potatoes. More common is the metaphor of a jar, bowl or bag filled by the rightful owner—and emptied at specific times. But then, who is the owner, and whose are the children after birth? 'A girl is like a peanut seed, she increases the clan,' according to the Congolese Woyo tradition. She is invaluable for the production of future generations and her children belong to the whole community. That idea is losing its value in times of growing individualism.

In Dar es Salaam, I was listening to a discussion between African colleagues about who ought to own the children after a divorce. One of the men said, 'They will go to the man, of course, because he is on top when they are being made.' Everyone laughed, but when I asked him if he was serious, he said, 'Yes, in my tradition the children always go to the man.' When I lived in Congo, I also often saw this put into practice.

Until recently in the Western world, based on the traditional male earner and female carer model, children were generally assigned to the mother in the case of a divorce, but this is no longer set in stone. In societies where traditional gender divisions are questioned and 'house husbands' are not uncommon; judges now tend to appoint the children to the parent who over the years has visibly been the primary carer.

The hen and the rooster

Obligatory female virginity remains an inexorable requirement for marriage and motherhood in many societies. The trick was to convince the woman that female chastity equated to good motherhood, to make her believe that the status of her offspring depended on her 'virtue', as Sarah Blaffer Hrdy explains in *Mother Nature*.

That message is emphasised in the universal metaphor of hens and roosters. Desired female traits are projected onto the hen, and supposedly common male traits onto the rooster. Roosters who cheat on their hens are met with sympathy for their natural promiscuity. Old or young, it is argued, they are all the same—though he may refuse a hen who eats with him while laying another rooster's egg. Hens should only mate with their own rooster, content with their position as one of his many partners. As surviving without him is out of the question, a sensible hen avoids quarrelling and adopts an attitude of submissiveness. Her motherly love is expressed in metaphors of warm feathers and wings for all her chicks. Roosters should do the crowing and hens stay silent, because the reverse would cause the house to 'collapse' (Japanese) and the family to be 'doomed' (Chinese). What is wisdom? 'The hen knows when it is morning, but she looks at the mouth of the rooster,' as an Ashanti proverb puts it. In other words, let him carry the conversation, while she looks after their brood. God help the pitiful coop where the hens are crowing while the rooster is mothering the chicks!

Rigid patterns in male and female behaviour are reinforced in contemporary nature documentaries. About mating, a voiceover tells us that the male tries to remove a rival's sperm before implanting his own, while the no less interesting sex life of the female goes without comment. 'We encounter, with monotonous regularity, the "dominant" male defending his "territory"; the hierarchies between males in their access to females; the existence of harems. We hear of females (and young males) assuming submissive postures. And we hear endless examples of home-making and parental provision.'[202]

Where human relationships are ordered on the basis of instincts from the animal world, sex is reduced to the production of offspring—without a word of criticism about 'natural' dominance, aggression and the claiming of the other as property.

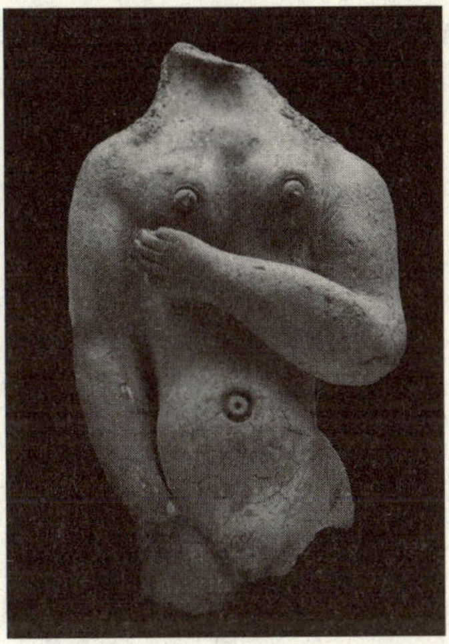

Roman terracotta votive of a pregnant woman, c. 100 BC-200 AD, Suffolk, England. Wellcome Collection, London.

Dangerous childbirth—and safe contraception

Pregnancy and delivery have always been a significant cause of death for women and babies. Today childbirth remains a risky activity. Globally, an estimated 295,000 women die each year due to complications in childbirth according to the WHO. In

202. Rosalind Coward, *Female Desire*, 1984:212ff.

Europe and North America there are ten and eighteen maternal deaths respectively per 100,000 births; in sub-Saharan Africa that number rises to 542. The global infant mortality rate has decreased from an estimated sixty-five deaths per 1,000 live births in 1990 to twenty-nine deaths per 1,000 live births in 2018—which still equates to four million deaths a year.[203]

Thousands of years ago the Sumerians already voiced concerns about the precarious fate of a woman frequently in labour: 'A mother who gave birth to eight sons, lies down in weakness.' No wonder such a productive woman is scared of another pregnancy. The Haya in Tanzania also voice disapproval at the eighth birth: 'The woman who said, "How well and easily I give birth," died with the birth of her ninth child.' Indeed, 'Pregnant women have one foot in the grave,' according to a German saying; a Vietnamese warning similarly observes: 'A pregnant woman stands at the brink of the graveyard;' and Papiamentu-speaking people of the West Indies used to worry that 'The last child kills its mother.' Even though most women and men want children, their wish is not limitless, and it's questionable whether the following sayings are positive:

> Two can make ten. (Mongolian)
> Under bad stars woman give birth to two babies a year. (Pashto, Afghanistan)
> Every year a child and in nine years, twelve. (Bulgarian).

Nonetheless, there are plenty of boasts about men who produce many offspring. And men are not at risk at the moment they become fathers. On the contrary, 'He who fathers offspring, never

203. More information: https://www.who.int/reproductivehealth/publications/maternal-mortality-2000-2017/en/ and https://www.who.int/data/gho/data/themes/topics/indicator-groups/indicator-group-details/GHO/infant-mortality.

Plate 1. Niki de Saint Phalle, *She–A Cathedral*, 1966.

Plate 2. Peter Paul Rubens, *Birth of the Milky Way*, 1636-1637.

Plate 3. Xiwangmu, Golden Mother/First Ruler/Queen Mother of the West. Eastern Han Dynasty. Ceramics, second century.

Plate 4. Statue Xiwangmu in West China, honoured with rainbow-coloured fireworks on Mother's Day 2011. Xining rural area.

Plate 5. Coatlicue, the Aztek Earth Goddess—'our grandmother'. National Anthropological Museum, Mexico City, *ca.* 1500.

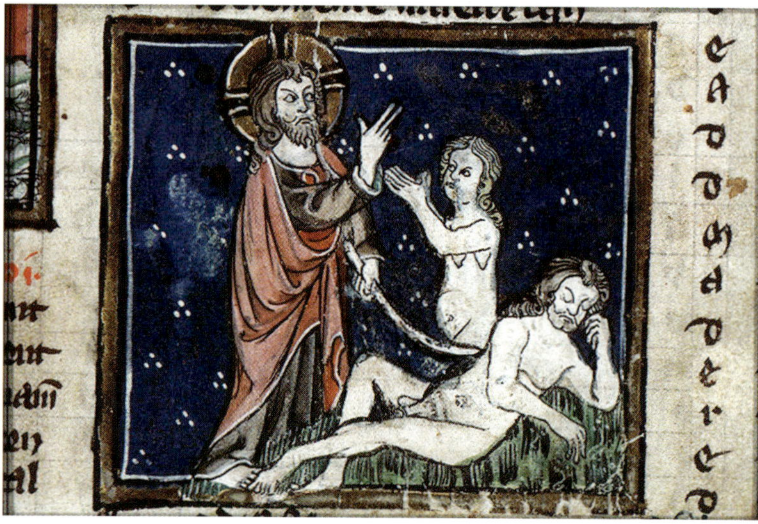

Plate 6. *God Builds Eve on Adam's Rib.* Illustration from Jacob van Maerlant's *Spieghel Historiael, ca.* 1325-1335.

Plate 7. Bartolo di Fredi, *God Assisting Adam Giving Birth to Eve.* San Gimignano, fourteenth century.

Plate 8. Hindu goddess Parvati. Tamil Nadu, bronze. Eleventh century.

Plate 9. Bas-relief of Shiva and Parvati. Mount Kailash, late sixth century.

Plate 10 a. (Above): *Androgynous Christ in the Grave*. Anonymous, sixteenth century
Plate 10 b. (Below): Enlarged cut out from *Androgynous Christ in the Grave*.

Plate 11. *Saint Mary Nursing Jesus, Surrounded by Angels.* Crete, second half of fifteenth century.

Plate 12. Black Virgin, Island of Gorée, Senegal.

Plate 13. Piero di Cosimo, *Portrait of Simonetta Vespucci as Cleopatra*. Genua, 1490.

Plate 14. 'Frying pan', ceramics with marked vulva and double rows of ornamental fertility triangles. Death gift, Syros, 2800-2300 BC.

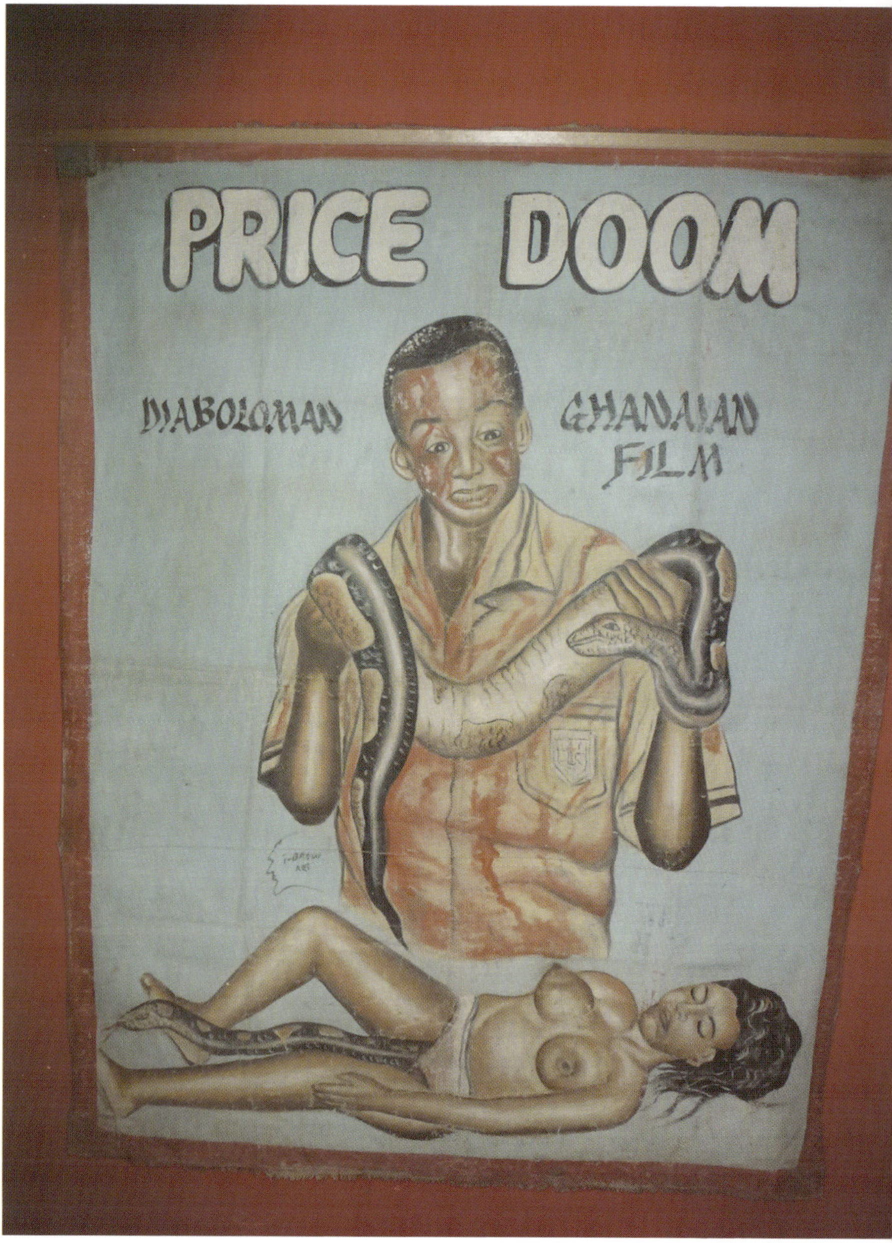

Plate 15. Ghanaian film poster.

Plate 16. Priest deflowering a bride. Outside, the groom is waiting for his turn. Persian manuscript of Al-Qazwini (1203-1283).

Plate 17. Goat servi
as a wet-nurse.
Cuba, 1903.

Plate 18. François Clouet, *La Dame au Bain* (Two Kinds of Breasts), 1571.

Plate 19. Exemplary Chinese daughter-in-law breastfeeding her old mother-in-law. Ivory.

Plate 20. (Above): Peter Paul Rubens, *Daughter Breastfeeding her Father in Prison*, 16

Plate 21. (Below): Cornelis Cornelisz van Haarlem, *The Miracle of Haarlem*, 1591.

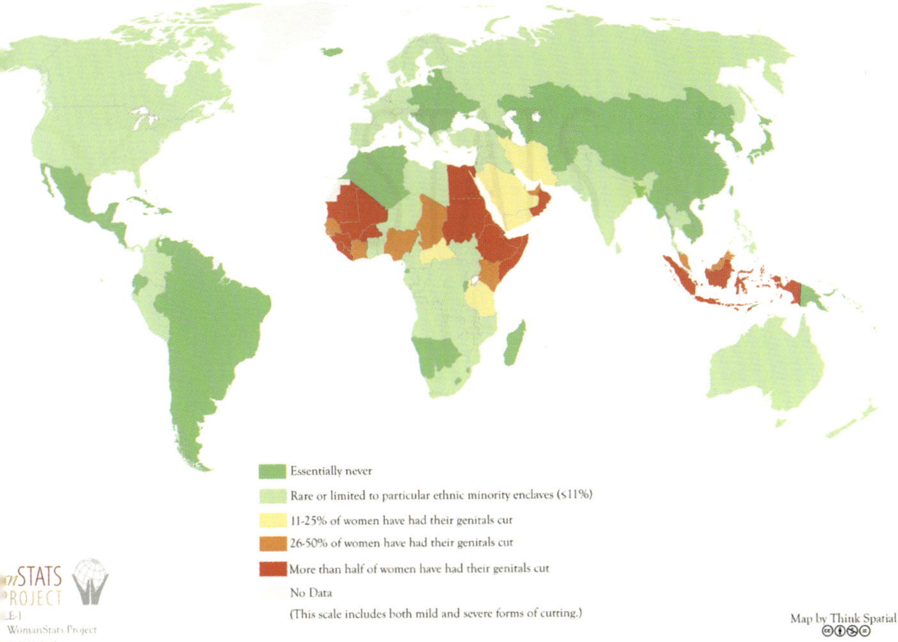

Plate 22. (Above): World Map: Prevalence of Female Genital Cutting, 2015.

Plate 23. (Below): World Map: Laws Concerning Property Rights for Women, 2017.

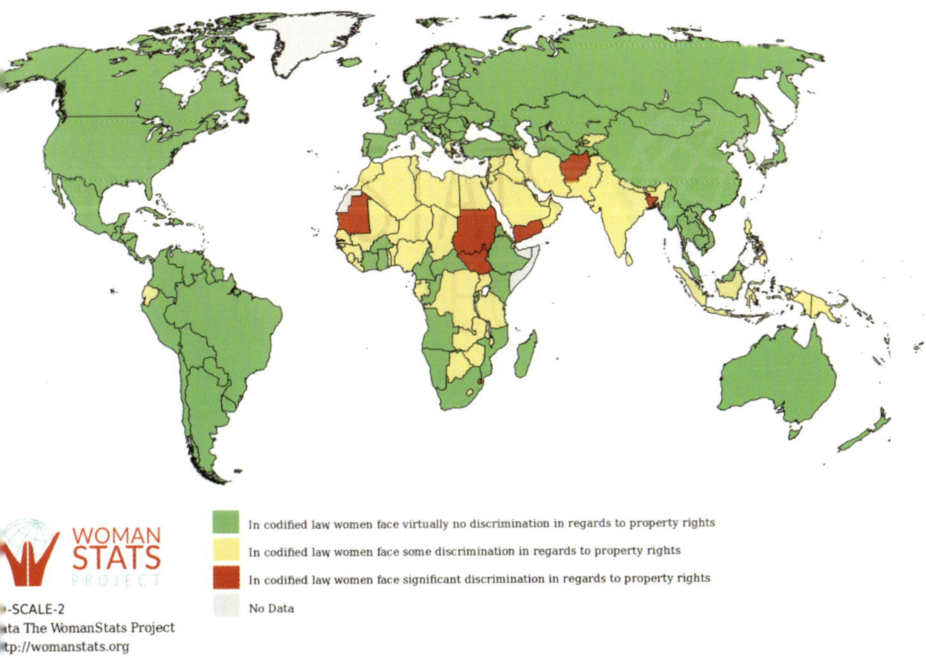

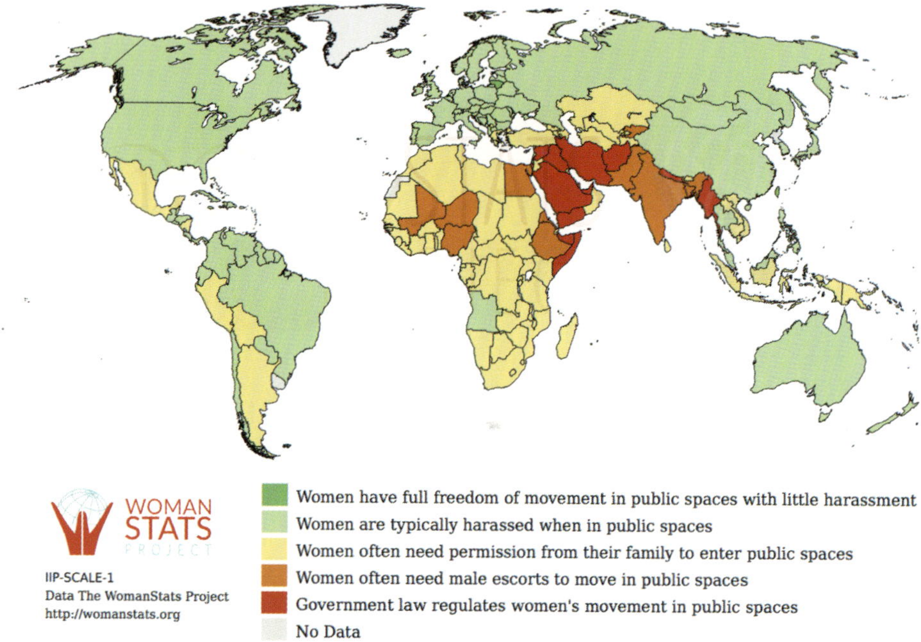

Plate 24. (Above): World Map: Women's Mobility Scale, 2017.

Plate 25. (Below): World Map: Physical Security of Women, 2014.

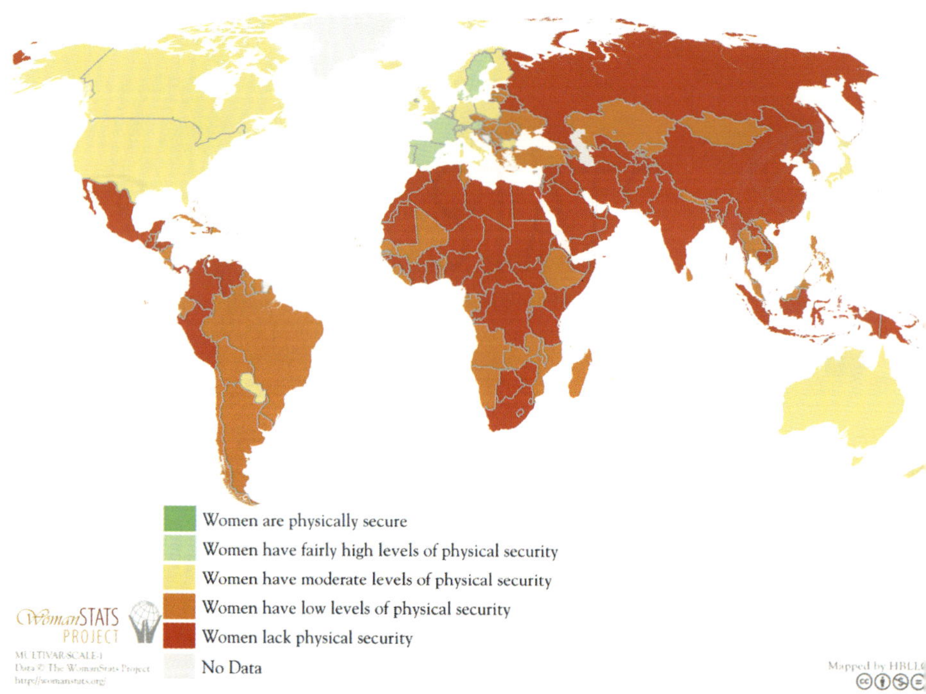

dies,' is a triumphant statement in Arabic. A unique example in the field of male immortality was Moroccan sultan Moulay Ismail Ibn Sharif (1646-1727), who fathered forty sons in a period of three months, and the impressive total of 888 children via his many wives and concubines. After his death, a beautiful mausoleum was built in his honour in Meknes. But perhaps the absolute fathering champion was the Mongolian ruler Genghis Khan who is said to have sired more than a thousand children. Whichever of them was the biggest daddy, one thing is absolutely certain: the matter of producing heirs only rarely causes a man's death—and then it's more likely at conception than at birth.

The history of the womb is riddled with desire, insecurities, distrust, scepticism, prestige, unforeseen surprises and unwanted risks determining the lives of women and their legal or illicit partners—until the invention of the contraception pill in the mid-twentieth century. The hormone-suppressing pill was first prescribed in the US in the late 1950s as a cure for menstruation disorders, with the side effect of temporary infertility. That side effect turned out to be so appealing that an astonishing number of women knocked on the door of their GPs with menstrual problems. The pill was first approved for contraceptive use in the US in 1960, and today 1.1 billion out of 1.9 billion women of reproductive age worldwide use some form of contraception (including traditional methods).[204]

This doesn't mean that male control of female sexuality is no longer on the agenda. Slightly embarrassed, a Turkish restaurant owner in London shared with me his father's favourite saying: 'A stick on the back and a child in the womb'—whilst beseeching me to believe that he did not share his father's opinion at all.

---

204. United Nations Department of Social and Economic Affairs: *Contraceptive Use by Method*, 2019.

He went on to explain that in the past, in his country of birth, men believed this was the only way to control women. The men supporting that statement must have been really afraid of female power. And, possibly, they still are, because similar traditional ideas haven't disappeared and may even still be quite popular, at least among supporters of President Erdoğan.

In 2014, the Turkish president told women they were not equal to men, and that they ought to have at least three children. In a nationally televised speech he gave at an educational foundation in 2016, he again urged women to have more children. Muslim families should not practise contraception, 'I say this openly: We will increase our descendants; we will increase our population. Family planning, birth control, no Muslim family can practise such an understanding.' In spite of his proclamations, one-fifth of married women in Turkey practise birth control.[205]

Prominent Catholic clergy also ban contraception—without asking men or women whether it is in their best interest. Why do the guardians of dogmas from a distant past turn a blind eye to the worries and dilemmas of today's believers? Safe contraception makes it possible for people to determine the size of their family, prevents teenage pregnancies, death in childbirth and millions of unwanted children. Affectionate lovemaking without risk of pregnancy brings personal freedoms, while reinforcing care, attention and better chances in life for wanted children. Finally human sex can be unhinged from its biological purpose. The command to be fruitful and multiply has after all been amply fulfilled.

---

205. https://www.independent.co.uk/news/world/europe/turkish-president-recep-tayyip-erdogan-says-no-muslim-family-should-use-contraception-a7056816.html.

Statuette of a nourishing mother,
Phemba fertility cult, Kingdom of Kongo
(Mayombe, DR Congo), *c.* 1880.
Wellcome Collection, London.

7. THE MAGIC OF THE NOURISHING NIPPLE

Whatever you sucked from the tit, will be spilt over your grave.

(Spanish, Bolivia)

The milk of mother goddesses and the Virgin Mary is widely perceived as possessing miraculous powers. But in various cultures, the breast milk of ordinary women is also believed to have magical effects. The belief that 'Mothers' milk is holy,' as a Mongolian proverb has it, probably goes too far, but ideas of breastfeeding passing on good (and bad) qualities is widespread.

From the nipple to the grave

In ancient Rome, slave women were used as nurses, but there were also professional wet- nurses for rent at a spot called *Columna Lactaria* (Milk Pillar or Column). These women were proud of their profession and able to negotiate a good salary. Greek nurses were in especially high demand among Roman civilians, in the belief that the baby would suck up the language of the nurse via their milk so that in addition to Latin, the child would speak fluent Greek.

The seventeenth-century Dutch poet Jacob Cats thought that a child who suckled a stranger's milk would acquire a dubious character; a true mother would never trust someone else to do her maternal duty:

> Employ O young wife, your precious gifts
> There is nothing an upright man would rather see
> Than his dear wife bid the child to the teat
> This bosom that you carry, so swollen up with life
> So finely wrought, as if it were ivory orbs.[206]

Cats was far from alone in the opinion that breast milk affected a child's psyche. In nineteenth-century France, there was even a bill preventing mothers of bad moral reputation from nursing their own babies.

Among Muslims there is a traditional fear of Jewish, Christian or worse, *kafir* milk, the milk of an unbeliever, that would sway the baby's faith. When an Islamic mother is unable to breastfeed her own baby, the wet-nurse must meet other requirements too. The Prophet Muhammad instructed Muslims to protect their children against drinking the milk of 'adulteresses and madwomen'.[207]

Milk has to be halal, is the reasoning, and no modern milk bank can fully guarantee that milk is of Islamic origin. In Turkey, using donor milk is relatively common, and thought to considerably lower the death rate of children in rural areas, but the question of whether a child that has been nursed by an atheist is doomed to grow up to be an unbeliever, is still a matter of debate between Islamic scholars and medical doctors.

---

206. Jacob Cats, *Moeder, Houwelijck*, (Simon Schama's translation) quoted in Hufton, *The Prospect Before Her*, 1996:200.

207. Ulfat Shaikh and Omar Ahmed, 'Islam and Infant Feeding' in *Breastfeeding Medicine*, 2006:164.

At the breast of an animal or an animal at the breast

The Swedish scientist Carl Linnaeus's view was that a child breastfed by a lioness would imbibe great courage. It is unclear as to whether this observation was based on scientific research. Of all the stories about human babies breastfed by a wild animal, that of Romulus and Remus is one of the best-known. In Roman culture Diva Rumina was the patron goddess of nursing human and animal mothers. Her temple was located near the fig tree under which, according to the story, the two boys had been nursed. The founders of Rome had been abandoned by their mother after a pregnancy due to rape, and the two babies were close to dying of hunger when a she-wolf took care of them.

Romulus, Remus and the she-wolf. Bronze, twelfth century.
Capitoline Museums, Rome.

The Jewish Talmud allowed babies to be fed by a female animal if the wellbeing of the child depended on it. The Islamic tradition discouraged the feeding of babies with animal milk, out of fear that the child would gain animal characteristics. In Christian circles the topic was much less discussed. In a late-nineteenth-century French drawing, two women each hold a drinking baby under the belly of a female donkey, while a woman with a third baby is waiting her turn. Thanks to the milk of she-donkeys a charitable orphanage kept the abandoned babies alive.[208]

Orphan babies being nursed by she-donkeys. French engraving, 1895.

In the eighteenth and nineteenth centuries goats became more and more popular as wet-nurses (see Plate 17). In 1816 a German writer even published a book with the title *The Goat as the Best and Most Agreeable Wet-Nurse*. Not only was she a lot cheaper than a hired wet-nurse, but also a lot safer during times of syphilis and other deadly diseases.

---

208. Osborn, M.S. 'The Rent Breasts: A Brief History of Wet-nursing' in *Midwife, Health Visitor & Community Nurse*, 1979; 15(8): 302-306; Samuel X. Radbill, 'The Role of Animals in Infant Feeding' in Wayland D. Hand, *American Folk Medicine: A Symposium*. University of California Press, 1976.

There are also instances where women would lovingly breastfeed baby animals: fawns, monkeys, puppies or piglets, either to help the animal survive (for religious or commercial reasons) or for pure affection. In Central America, Western travellers came across women of different cultures breastfeeding various kinds of young animals such as squirrels, possums, wild cats and boars.[209] Among some people in Papua New Guinea it is not uncommon to put your own baby on one breast and a piglet on the other. 'The pig is our heart,' is the explanation.

Putting a small animal on the breast also served to harden the nipples of inexperienced mothers or relieve engorged breasts, but Westerners seem to have forgotten these old customs and remedies. Instead, the very idea provokes shocked reactions, as recently happened in Ireland, where emotions ran high at a picture on a dog calendar of a famous model breastfeeding a little dog. In another example in the United States, people were shocked by the cover of the album *Boys for Pele*, depicting the singer Tori Amos breastfeeding a piglet. Such reactions reflect a need for concrete boundaries between humans and animals, or between culture and nature.

Two kinds of breasts

During the European Renaissance wealthy women refused to breastfeed their own children. 'In a century where the erotic potential of the breast began to obscure its maternal function, many ladies were simply not willing to devote themselves fully to their babies, at the expense of their relations with their husbands, not to mention their lovers,' writes Marilyn Yalom, and so they

---

209. Karin Brulliard, 'Why Goats Used to Breastfeed Human Babies', *Washington Post*, 25 February 2016; https://en.wikipedia.org/wiki/Human-animal_breastfeeding.

happily hired wet-nurses. But they were also put under serious pressure:

> The practice of sending babies away to rural wet-nurses was roundly condemned by medical doctors, humanists, priests, preachers and other moralists throughout Europe. A body of literature sprang up during the Renaissance declaring that it was a mother's duty to breastfeed and that the use of a wet-nurse was a risky substitute for the biological mother. [...] Some moral arbiters went so far as to call the refusal to breastfeed one's own child a sin, especially in countries like Germany and England, where Protestant reformers were calling for a more stringent morality.[210]

Nonetheless, out of the fear of sagging breasts, many women were sending their babies to the countryside for as long as twenty-four months. In upper-class families a wet-nurse came to live in the home. François Clouet's famous painting *La Dame au Bain* (1571) reflects not only the class differences of his time, but also the contrast between erotic and nursing breasts. In the foreground, between draped red curtains, stands a chestnut bathtub in which an unknown lady sits—possibly a young Mary Queen of Scots. She wears a diadem in her hair and a pearl on her forehead, and she has striking, relatively small, bare breasts, which have managed to maintain their youthful shape due to the hired wet-nurse behind her. The wet-nurse has a swaddled baby at her ample breast, while in the background a servant girl warms water for the lady's bath. The breasts of the woman in the bath are meant to please, those of the wet-nurse to work for her daily bread (see Plate 18).

210. Yalom: 70-71.

Being a wet-nurse was usually a labour of love, but with rising demand the value of the job went up, allowing many women to earn a good living by their breast milk. The wealthier the infant's parents, the more influential the wet-nurse:

> Those who found themselves at the very highest levels, such as the wet-nurses attached to the family of the pharaoh, were the equivalent of the great court ladies presiding over significant networks of power. The wet-nurses to the queens of France were entitled to any number of perks, including the name 'Madame Poitrine' (Mrs Breast), which was worn like a badge of honour in certain French families long after the monarchy had disappeared.[211]

Gabrielle Palmer, author of *The Politics of Breastfeeding* (2009), discovered that being a wet- nurse in seventeenth- and eighteenth-century England was a great job that could provide a woman with a higher salary than her husband. As a Royal wet-nurse one was honoured 'for life'. In England, legendary wet-nurse Judith Waterford was able in her prime to effortlessly produce almost two litres [four pints] of milk a day, and on her eighty-first birthday in 1831 was still producing breast milk.[212]

The profession of wet-nurse dates back to ancient times. In Mesopotamia a wet-nurse was hired for two to three years and could be paid in kind in barley, oil, wool or even silver. An old Sumerian saying even proclaims that wet-nurses determined the fate of kings in the women's quarters. This may seem exaggerated, but it does show that these women had huge responsibilities. If a baby died, whilst in the care of a wet-nurse, it was immediately assumed that she had taken on a second baby without the consent

---

211. Yalom: 160.

212. Viv Groskop: 'Not Your Mother's Milk', *Guardian Health*, 5 January 2007.

of the parents. Such a serious accusation had to be proved, but in the case of Hammurabi's law (*c.* 1780 BC) the punishment was harsh: 'cut off the breasts'.[213]

A similar wet-nurse tradition existed in China. The last Chinese emperor Pu Yi (1906-67) felt extremely unhappy when he was suddenly ceremonially crowned while still a child. His wet-nurse Wen-Chao Wang was the only one who could comfort him. He developed a close connection with her and she probably breastfed him till his teenage years. During the Cultural Revolution Mao abolished this 'decadence', but after a long political prohibition the old custom returned to Chinese society. No doubt recent bottle-milk scandals in China have contributed to a new legion of highly paid wet-nurses. Once again, wealthy Chinese families go in search of healthy pregnant village women who, right after delivering their own baby, are willing to breastfeed the baby of a well-off city woman. Their own children stay behind with the grandparents in the village, who try to find a cheap local wet-nurse for the remaining newborn. This sacrifice is made up for by the lucrative salaries super-rich families are willing to pay.

The demand for wet-nurses is also rising among Hollywood celebrities, many of whom are either unwilling to breastfeed or unable to because of breast implants. But a license is needed, because outsourced breastfeeding can be construed as child abuse. There was a case in Oklahoma in 2003 where a woman breastfed someone else's baby without consent, and faced a fine of five hundred dollars and a jail sentence of up to a year for having bad morals.[214]

213. Marten Stol, *Women in the Ancient Near East*, 2016.

214. Groskop, ibid.

Charitable nursing

There's no end of stories about selfless nursing nipples that give the woman who own them extra lustre. The Prophet Muhammad had several successive wet-nurses, according to tradition. The first was Halima who, during a disastrous drought and driven by need, went with other women to Mecca, searching for a wet-nurse job even though she could hardly feed her own child. When the women reached Mecca, they were one after the other offered the Prophet as an infant to be nursed. They all declined, because Muhammad's father Abdullah had died six months prior to the Prophet's birth, and to raise an orphan would only result in more hardship. Not finding any other baby to suckle, Halima went back and decided to take him. As soon as she put him on her breast, 'the milk started flowing miraculously'. She nursed the Prophet on one breast and her own son on the other, and both babies were fully satisfied. Moreover, her female camel, who on the road hadn't given a single drop of milk, suddenly had a full udder again. For sure, Halima had 'a blessed soul' at her breast.[215]

The all-sacrificing love of daughters for parents or in-laws is an important theme in many stories. The exemplary daughter-in-law nursing her illustrious mother-in-law has been portrayed as an example of pure harmony in China (see Plate 19)—an ideal that goes against widespread proverbial wisdom about the relationship of a young wife and her mother-in-law. The breastfeeding of a needy relative was considered an act of the highest charity in many traditions globally.[216]

---

215. Kueny, Chapter 4 and http://www.islamweb.net/prophet/index.php?page=showarticle&id=174579.

216. http://www.theepochtimes.com/n3/2043878-filial-piety-touches-heaven-stories-of-virtuous-daughters-in-law/. With thanks to colleague and sinologist Wilt Idema for clarifying information about the image.

The ambience shifts when the parent in need is of the other sex. In Rome, the story of Cimon and Pero was presented as an exemplary act of piety and honour. Cimon is an old man, imprisoned and condemned to starvation. Visitors are allowed, but bringing food is forbidden. To keep him alive, his daughter Pero visits and breastfeeds her father every day. When he is still alive after a month, a jailer spies on them and catches them in the act. The judges to whom he reports are so moved by this great parental love, that the daughter is not punished for her offence and the old man is released.

In the Western world, this story became a valid theme in the arts, partly due to the tension between charity and the erotic, incestuous implications of a father drinking from his daughter's youthful breast. There is less room for erotic associations when the artist zooms in on the imminent death of a declining man with ageing features and untidy grey hair, or on the rusty irons that confine him to his cheerless cell (Peter Paul Rubens: *Roman Charity*, c. 1612; see Plate 20).

In some paintings the daughter's sleeping baby lies on the cell floor (Rubens) or she feeds her father from outside, through the bars that separate them, as in Caravaggio's *The Seven Works of Mercy* (1607). The Turkish artist Ferhad Özgür was also inspired by this dramatic situation to make a short film—which impressed many viewers, but not those (presumably unfamiliar with the ancient story) who condemned it as 'sick porn'.[217]

The history of a renowned painting in the Frans Hals Museum in Haarlem reflects how people's views change when they have more information about a story or image's cultural background. The artwork, painted in 1591 by Cornelis Cornelisz of Haarlem, entitled *A Monk and a Nun* (see Plate 21), was also recorded in museum records as *The Miracle of Haarlem*.

---

217. https://www.youtube.com/watch?v=c33499mGtAk.

> According to legend a nun was accused of having become pregnant. To verify this a monk had to squeeze her breast and if it produced milk, she was guilty. But instead of milk she produced wine—the reason for the wine glass on the table. Instead of proving the nun's guilt the miracle was witness to her faith. Yet the legend may not have been the real subject of the painting. Pictures of amorous monks and nuns were a popular genre in the late sixteenth century. This may in fact be a satire on the immorality of the cloisters and the Catholic Church.[218]

Or perhaps the artist's intentions were playfully ambiguous.

Unpredictable mothers

From the breasts of the respectfully invoked Yoruba mother goddess Jemaya spring all streams fertilising the land, but male fascination with divine nourishing breasts invariably comes with mixed feelings. She deserves respect, but the divine mother remains a fickle creature to be approached with care. An old Yoruba song full of underlying anxieties refers to the powers of 'the Mothers', a collective term acknowledging the special powers of women, elderly, ancestral or deified:

> Honour, honour today, oooooo.
> Honour to my mother [...].
> Mother whose vagina causes fear to all.
> Mother whose pubic hair bundles up in knots.
> Mother who sets a trap, sets a trap...[219]

---

218. https://www.franshalsmuseum.nl/en/art/a-monk-and-a-nun/.

219. A.B. Ellis, *The Yoruba-speaking Peoples*, 1894:43-44; Drewal in *African Arts* 7 (2), 1974:60.

The primal gateway as a curse (and its resolution) in times of crisis that we saw in Chapter 5 is alive and well in the Yoruba tradition.

Freud connected the mother goddess with the earliest stages of development—the child experiences the mother as a source of both gratification and abstinence, through which the greediness of a libido is sometimes expressed via aggressive and sadistic wishes and actions in later life.

Melanie Klein rewrote some of Freud's ideas about the breast and ego development in young children. For her, the breast is the first important experience in a child's life and thereby marginalises the role of the father. In the very beginning, a mother is nothing more than two breasts for an infant: breasts that appear and disappear at intervals beyond the child's control. According to Klein, the child's first mental activity consists of fantasies projected onto the breast, from which it is relevant to carefully analyse feelings of envy and hatred that can arise. Taken off the breast, a baby develops an early fear, as does any early physically or psychologically frustrating experience that stands in the way of gratification. Klein distinguishes between the generous 'good' breast and the refusing 'bad' breast that keeps the milk to itself:

> Now, what one might call the 'good' breasts become the prototype of what is felt throughout life to be good and beneficent, while the 'bad' breasts stand for everything evil and persecuting. The reason for this can be explained by the fact that, when the child turns his hatred against the denying or 'bad' breast, he attributes to the breast itself all his own active hatred against it—a process which is termed *projection*.[220]

---

220. Melanie Klein in Simon Richter, *Missing the Breast*, 2006:61.

If in his earliest fantasy the frustrated infant wants to devour his mother's breast, does he imagine that he is destroying his mother? By turning his own hostility against her, he is at the same time terrified that she might devour him. A hungry baby that lingers in the desire for the lost paradise of unification with the mother breast will never get over the anxious feeling that he cannot do without her while she can without him.

If stories about male creators, male divine breasts and pregnancies represent repressed birth-giving and breastfeeding wishes, then the good news is that fulfilment of those wishes is getting closer. For now, only transgender people who were born female are able to conceive, but sooner or later, men and women really could share all birth-giving, breastfeeding and other care duties. In the 1990s physiologist and evolutionary biologist Jared Diamond predicted that the human species is 'a leading candidate for male lactation', because in combination with hormonal injections, manual stimulation of a father's nipples will stimulate the dormant but present potential to produce milk.[221]

Breastfeeding fatherhood promises a new balance, the beginning of the end of the ancient injustice that disrupted harmony between the sexes. In May 2016, a flash mob of young men in China began practising: clasping fake babies to their bare male breasts, for the time being only in honour of Mother's Day.

221. Jared Diamond quoted in Richter: 8-9.

Artemis of Ephesus, the 'Great Mother Goddess'.
Roman copy, marble and bronze, second century BC.
Capitoline Museums, Rome.

8. MAMMALIA

To the river that took him, the old man screamed: 'Mamma!'
(Adyghe)

Linnaeus derived his classification of humans and other lactating animals as *mammalia* from the Latin word *mamma* meaning not only 'breast', but also 'mother' or 'nurse'. The intimate relationship between mother and child starts at the breast, and words connecting breast and milk exist in various languages. The Chinese word for milk is *ru*, and the breast is referred to as *rŭfáng,* literally meaning 'milk house'. In the Amerindian language, Quechua, the word for the motherly breast, *ñuñu,* comes together with the verb 'to drink breast milk'. In Africa too the words for breast and milk often coincide, for example, in Swahili *ziwa* means 'breast' and *maziwa* 'milk'. The same holds for the Austronesian languages in the South Sea, Madagascar and most islands of Southeast Asia: two ancient forms (*susu* and *nunuh*) come up in one form or another. Both mean 'breast', and often also have the meaning of milk, mother and feeding. In many languages the word mother or mama means literally 'the woman who gave me breast milk'.[222] There are no erotic connotations in any of those meanings.

---

222. With thanks to culture and language specialists: Sander Adelaar (Melbourne); Willem Adelaar (Leiden); Willem van der Molen (Jakarta); Aldin Mutembei (Dar es Salaam) and Kristofer Schipper (Fuzhou).

Mamma

Lactation developed in the mid- to late-Triassic period about 200 million years ago as a form of nutrition and protection against infections. Before family planning, the breasts of our foremothers produced milk for about half the time between puberty and menopause. All in all, a woman spent ten years of her life nursing, and during her fertile life produced about 1,350 litres of milk.[223]

In many cultures there was a taboo on having sex with women nursing a child. Women fed their babies for at least a year or two; those who didn't were pregnant again within a few months. Breastfeeding is no safe means of birth control, but when the baby sucks on the breast, hormones are released (prolactin and oxytocin) that reduce the growth of the egg cell and obstruct the build-up of the womb lining. Gradually the child will drink less often or at greater intervals, and the chance of conception increases.

Even in medical circles, breast milk was understood to be 'adapted blood'. Since women did not menstruate during their pregnancies, it was believed that women transformed blood into food for their babies. The process of nursing mothers turning blood into milk would be endangered by having sex: it would disrupt the flow of milk, and might even kill the newly-formed foetus. Thanks to that common misunderstanding, women were granted a brief period of relief with a child or two on the breast before the next pregnancy announced itself.[224]

Unlike humans, other mammals' nipples hang beneath the body and out of sight: they only have a nursing function and become flat again after the nursing period. Since our ancestors

---

223. Geoffrey Miller, *The Mating Mind*, 2001:242-243.

224. Thomas Laqueur, *Making Sex: Body and Gender from the Greeks to Freud*, 1990:36; Yalom: 70.

Sitting mother goddess breastfeeding two children. Second century AD. Valkhof Museum, Nijmegen.

started walking upright, male genitals and female breasts came into direct view. It remains guesswork as to what time in human evolution female breasts gained their full shape, even when not graced with milk. But for *Homo erectus*, breasts became a sign of health and fertility, and a selection criterion for partner choice.

Gradually breasts have become part of changeable ideals of beauty and fashion. As Naomi Wolf forcefully argues in her bestseller *The Beauty Myth*, 'sexy' breasts gave and give women, as long as they are young, limited power unattainable to them in most other fields. But an obsession with breasts in advertising and the media goes against the best interests of women and the development of their talents.

Multiple breasts

One of the Seven Wonders of the Ancient World, the sanctuary of the Greek goddess Artemis, was located in Ephesus in present-day Turkey. Due to the many round bulges protruding from the front of various Artemis statues, the Greeks gave her the nickname 'many-breasted one'. Multiple breasts also occur in humans. In the medical world the phenomenon is called polymastia. But during puberty usually only two mammary glands develop into breasts:

> If we were rats or pigs, our twin milk strips would develop into a total of eight teats, to meet the demands of large litters. Mammals such as elephants, cows, goats and primates, which give birth to only one or two offspring at a time, require only two mammary glands, and so the bulk of the milk strip regresses during fetal development.[225]

Extra mammary glands usually don't develop into fully-formed breasts, but after birth-giving they may produce milk. In 1886, a case was reported in Europe of a twenty-three-year-old woman with six additional breasts. After her first delivery nothing special happened, but after her second, all eight started leaking milk.

All kinds of stories have been told about polymastia. Women with more than two breasts were seen as monsters and put on show. Medical doctor and philosopher Fortunio Liceti wrote a book about this phenomenon, published and popularised in Amsterdam in 1665, eight years after his death. Anne Boleyn, the unhappy wife of Henry VIII, who was persecuted as an adultress, was said

---

225. Nathalie Angier, *Woman: An Intimate Geography*, 1999:141-142.

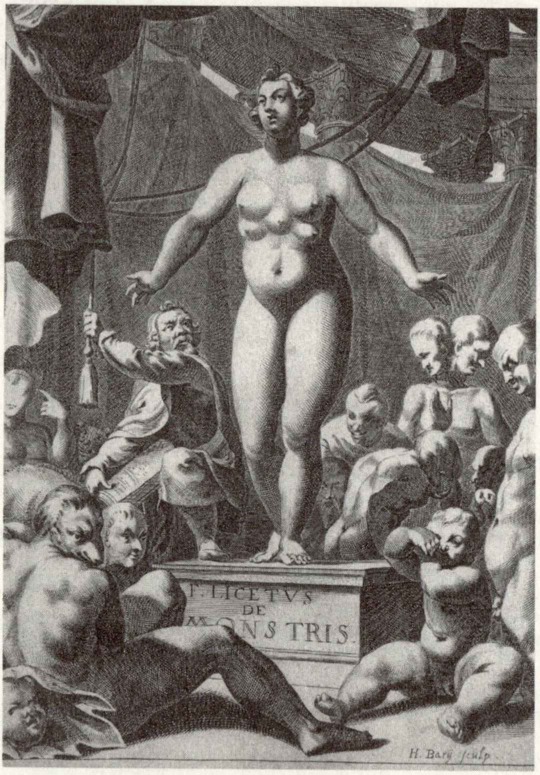

Illustration from the 1665 edition of Fortunio Liceti's *De Monstris*. Leiden University Libraries.

to have a third breast, a story that undoubtedly contributed to her discredit. Women with more than two nipples risked being accused of witchcraft in earlier centuries:

> Witch-hunters often had their suspects stripped and publically examined for signs of an unsightly blemish that witches were said to receive upon making their pact with Satan. [...] Prosecutors might also search for the 'witches' teat', an extra nipple allegedly used to suckle the witch's helper animals. In both cases, it was easy for even the

most minor physical imperfections to be labeled as the work of the devil himself. Moles, scars, birthmarks, sores, supernumerary nipples and tattoos could all qualify, so examiners rarely came up empty-handed.[226]

Pupazza frascatana, c. 1960.
Musée des Civilisations de l´Europe et de la Méditerranée (MUCEM), Marseille.

In the town of Frascati in Italy, biscuits known as *pupazze frascatana* are baked in the shape of a woman with three breasts, and are seen in every baker's window. The caption of one I found one in Marseille's MUCEM gives her name as Gina, in sweet memory of former movie star Gina Lollobrigida. Legend has it

226. https://www.history.com/news/7-bizarre-witch-trial-tests; *Cultural Encyclopedia of the Breast*, 2014:264ff.

that two breasts produced milk and the third, wine. According to some the tradition goes back to ancient bacchanalia, whilst others believe it was a brilliant invention of wet-nurses in the Renaissance: a fake breast filled with wine would soothe children into sleep in no time.

Milk ties as a ban on sex

Modern-day developments burden traditional believers with dilemmas, and bring forth juridical advice from religious authorities or spiritual leaders that is not always easy to obey in practice.

On the basis of the Islamic prohibition of sexual relations between a man and the woman who once nursed him, in 2007 an Islamic scholar issued a fatwa that decreed breastfeeding to be the perfect solution for the growing problem of undesirable interactions between men and women in the workplace, instructing women to breastfeed their male colleagues. After five feeds, 'milk ties' are extablished, preventing any sexual relations. Thus the religious ban on mixed company could be lifted without violating Islamic law. Women would even be allowed to have their hair uncovered in the presence of the men they had nursed.[227]

The initiator, Dr Izzat Atiya, a specialist on the Prophet Muhammad's statements at Cairo's prestigious Al-Azhar University, based this fatwa on medieval interpretations of a minority point of view insisting on the strict separation of sexes—when a man and a woman meet who are not direct relatives, Satan will be the third party present, and that always means trouble. The fatwa caused uproar and was ridiculed in the media, and soon withdrawn by an Al-Azhar committee that disapproved of the fatwa because it contradicted the principles of Islam and morality.[228]

---

227. Sam Shamoun, 'Islam and the Nursing of Adults': https://www.answering-islam.org/Shamoun/nursing-of-adults.htm

228. BBC News, 22 May 2007: http://news.bbc.co.uk/1/hi/world/middle_east/6681511.stm.

Modern Muslims hardly ever seem troubled by the thought that Satan is present during work-related meetings with a colleague of the opposite sex, but ultra-orthodox scholars keep pressuring each other and other believers to hold on to real or supposed statements by the Prophet Mohammed.[229] The extremely diverse comments on this fatwa make clear that the motherly and sexual function of breasts are easily mixed up and get in each other's way.

On Islamic websites believers often ask whether or not a man can drink his wife's breast milk. Is it only halal if you spit it out at once? The answers of Muslim clergy contradict each other. On the one hand, a husband is allowed to 'enjoy his wife in whatever way he wants, such as kissing, touching, looking, etc. [...] if he sucks on her nipples, this comes under the heading of the intimacy that is permissible.' According to some imams, however, it is better that a man avoids drinking his wife's breast milk, even though it has 'no effect'. To be safe, they always add that 'Allah knows everything the best.'[230]

Examples of traditional 'milk tie' relations are widespread. From Afghanistan and India to North Africa and the Balkans, breast milk, that unique nourishment, fulfils special needs.[231] The creation of such a bond can, for example, save a relationship about to break:

> In Georgia, if a husband thought his wife unfaithful, he called the suspected paramour to his house, bared his

229. Extensive information on the withdrawn fatwa about obligatory breastfeeding to male adults at work can be found in *Naked or Covered*: 179ff.; https://islamqa.info/en/2864; https://islamqa.info/en/47721.

230. https://islamqa.info/en/answers/47721/the-limits-within-which-a-married-couple-may-enjoy-intimacy-with-one-another-and-the-ruling-on-a-man-suckling-from-his-wife.

231. Jeremy MacClancy, 'The Milk Tie' in *Anthropology of Food*, 2 September 2003:229; https://journals.openedition.org/aof/339.

> wife's right breast, put salt on it, and asked the man to kiss it. The suspect had no option: if he kissed it, he would be milk-tied to the woman for life and so could not, under threat of punitive retribution, have sex with her; if he did not kiss it, he incriminated himself and faced punitive retribution. Once the deed was done, the husband would address the couple: 'Man, behold your mother. Woman, behold your son.' He could now rest assured; his wife and new milk son-in-law could meet openly without fear of raising any suspicion, for incest was out of the question.[232]

In another example, a Palestinian woman publicly pushed her breast into a male stranger's mouth with the words, 'You are my son in the Book of God, you have drunk from my breast.' The reasoning behind this ritual adoption was that a woman on the road for some time with a man not belonging to her close family was thus able to protect her respectability.[233]

Erotic lactation

The verb 'to nipple' does not seem to exist in the English, but I for one would champion it. In Dutch, it was in the dictionary until the nineteenth century, meaning 'intensely fondling a woman's breasts out of lewd passion.' *Nippelen* originates from *nijpen*, meaning 'to pinch', but nippling is doing it nicely without hurting. Joost van den Vondel, for example, used it in his play *Samson, or Holy Revenge* (1660), when referring to Samson passionately caressing Delilah.[234] Apparently this was the perfectly right term for the

232. Ibid. 25.

233. Granqvist in MacClancy: 23.

234. http://www.collignon.tv/nippelen.htm; *Nieuw woordenboek der Nederlandsche taal*, 1864:12-24;

affectionate sucking, petting and pinching of the nipples. The term may have disappeared, but the practice has not.

Fervent fondling, kneading and massaging stimulates milk production. A woman of sixty-five, the mother of adult children, went to see a gynecologist in Amsterdam because milk was flowing from her breasts. She thought she had cancer, but after being questioned by the gynecologist, the origin of this innocent phenomenon was that her husband couldn't get enough of nippling her. Due to his loving attention, lactation had spontaneously got going again. A woman doesn't even need to have been pregnant to produce milk.

Natural breastfeeding for babies may develop into a nostalgic breastfeeding relationship between adults. Where does motherly nursing end and erotic lactation begin? From research in 2005 carried out amongst 1,700 British men it appeared that more than 30 per cent not only enthusiastically fondled their partner, but also happily drank from the breast along with the baby. The main reason provided was 'emotional need'.[235] The research doesn't mention whether these men hadn't had enough breastfeeding as babies.

The oldest profession has been modulated to meet this emotional need among adult men, which is referred to as lactophilia or milk fetishism or, with obvious disdain, as infantilism—especially when a man wants to crawl back into the baby-on-the-breast role, and is willing to pay for being given a treat by mommy (sometimes even with a nappy on), as if to play out incestuous desires. Instances of 'lactation prostitution' can be found all over the world.[236]

---

235. Lois Rogers, 'Earth Dads Give Breast Milk a Try'. *The Sunday Times*, 13 March, 2005; https://wikipedia.ory/wiki/Erotic-lactation.

236. Ibid.

In 1903, the German philosopher Carl Buttenstedt warmly recommended erotic lactation as both a natural form of birth control and a source of sexual pleasure. His book was well received, but critics also warned against the danger of pathological arousal of sexual feelings in both partners. In 1938 it was forbidden by the Nazis as harmful.[237]

Serving breast milk to adults was once considered an act of charity towards needy elders and prisoners (see p.118). In England there are mentions of breastfeeding used as medicine as early as in 1655, recommended as a treatment for adults suffering from eye diseases and tuberculosis.[238]

Over the last couple of years, the benefits of breastfeeding for adults have been rediscovered in China. On various websites the service of wet-nurses is offered for ailing adults as well as infants. Customers can choose whether they want to drink the milk directly from the breast or from a glass. Pictures of young mothers are provided for men to choose from, clearly to tempt some who are not seeking medical assistance. By taking a subscription to Mother Nature's smoothie, customers can always return to their favourite breasts. From time to time, a group of women is arrested for online sales of their milk, as disapprovingly reported in various newspapers:

> The crooks allegedly hired mothers with newborn babies to breastfeed adults and, according to the newspaper report, the women fed their babies powdered milk to concentrate on selling breast milk for business. China's Ministry of Public Security coordinated with police to break up two gangs involved in the business, the report said. The police

237. Carl Buttenstedt was the author of *Die Glücks-Ehe: die Offenbarung im Weibe, eine Naturstudie* ('The Happy Marriage').

238. Ibid.; Mary Prior, *Women in English Society, 1500-1800*, 1991:6.

> said more than 200 people from across the country paid for the breastfeeding and prostitution services advertised on websites. According to a local newspaper, there were several websites that offered to provide young mothers to breastfeed adults for a fee.[239]

Is breastfeeding a new way to show how wealthy you are in China? In Shenzhen, adults who can afford it are hiring wet-nurses for the special nutritional value of breast milk. Those with a demanding job, poor personal health and a high income can take on a wet-nurse for daily personal use—at a salary of 12,000 to 20,000 yuan a month.[240]

A woman who had been in the business herself mentioned that there are two types of customers: those who wanted only the milk, the so-called clean service, and those who wanted more, referred to as the dirty service. A number of mothers only got regular customers if they were also willing to offer sexual services, according to the *Beijing News*.[241]

The majority of Chinese internet users reacted to the story with indignation: ethical values were being violated, and women treated as consumer goods.[242] All at a time when the Chinese government had made every effort to promote breastfeeding amongst young mothers—especially since a couple of serious bottle-milk scandals led to the tragic deaths of babies.

In Japan the Bonyu Bar (Mother's Milk Bar) in Tokyo hires women for the service of its customers. Their work consists of

---

239. https://www.indiatoday.in/world/story/chinese-women-gang-sells-own-milk-to-men-with-breastfeeding-fetish-233686-2015-01-01.

240. https://qz.com.com/103834/in-china-whealthy-adults-drink-breast-milk-while-millions-of-infants-stick-with-formula.

241. https://ww.indiatoday.in/world/story/chinese-women-gang-sells-own-milk-to-men-with-breastfeeding-fetish-2336860-2015-01-01.

242. https://wikipedia.ory/wiki/Erotic-lactation.

pouring and serving a glass of breast milk for the equivalent of about fifteen euros or offering the milk directly from the breast to the client for two or three times as much. In the latter case women are also prepared to ruffle the hair and whisper their name and sweet words of comfort into the ear of the customer sucking on the nipple. Most customers are between thirty and forty years old.[243]

The examples from China and Japan are not the only paid-for transactions. Men in other parts of the world also seem to like to be cuddled by a nursing mother. A Nigerian man confessed that he had once tried it out with his ex-girlfriend and it turned out to be an intimate and beneficial experience. He sought out the woman again and now pays for the service. Even though he admits the relationship looks sexually loaded, it does not mean sexual pleasure to him, but intimacy. Another man found his wife nursing their first baby so erotic that 'her breasts dripping with milk turned him on.'[244]

A long article in the Nigerian *New Telegraph Online* discussed the fundamental question: to whom do breasts belong, the husband or the baby? It collected a number of comments on fathers' envy of babies taking over and claiming the breasts they considered their property. The discussion flared up during World Breastfeeding Week (first week of August) after the Lagos State Commissioner for Information had seriously advised fathers to stop competing with their babies for ownership of breasts:

> Rather than compete with the infants, men should encourage their wives to engage in exclusive breastfeeding which is vital for infants especially during their first six

---

243. Https://www.atlantico.fr/antlantico-light/japon-prendrez-biern-verre-lait-maternel-1974264.html#9m3mpYQ4xxmSZqB6.99.

244. https://allafrica.com/stories/201601201337.html.

> months. His statement, however, generated a lot of mixed reactions from men; many objecting vehemently to what he said with some even arguing that their wife's breasts are their exclusive property and not for their babies.[245]

Summarising the mainly humorous reactions, they avow that it's the man who is the rightful owner: 'I need those breasts more than the baby, because they belong to me and are part of the price that I paid dowry for.' Or: 'The baby may have leased them for a time, but they are mine!' And: 'Their perfect roundness and warmth are the reason why I suck on the breasts of my wife, whether or not she is feeding a baby.' The majority openly insist that 'breasts belong exclusively to the man' or, in the carefully considered words of one businessman: 'The man is the full custodian of the breast, but must take backstage when the baby is on the show. Both man and baby need the breast; while one needs it for nutrition and that is for a season, the other needs it for satisfaction and for keeps. [...] The baby owns the milk but I own the breast.'

In another newspaper, *The Nation*, the topic is dealt with from a women's perspective, and they seem to agree with the men. One example:

> My husband has the right of first refusal. My view is that the man owns the breast, not the baby. When a woman is breastfeeding, the baby can claim ownership of the breast, (But) after the breastfeeding period, the breast goes back to the husband until the woman conceives again. So, it's only during breastfeeding that a child can lay claim to the breast. If not, the husband owns the breast.[246]

---

245. https://www.newtelegraphng.com/2017/08/breastfeeding-wives-breasts-not-babies-nigerian-men/ (no longer online, alas).

246. Precious Dikehowa: 'Should Men Stay off Wives' Breasts?', *The Nation*, 23 October 2015.

The idea of a woman as the owner of her own body and body parts is entirely absent.

Breast milk remains an intriguing phenomenon in many respects. It has even been experimented with in dishes. Some websites advertise recipes for breast milk ice cream, butter, cheese and yoghurt; muffins, bread and cake; breast milk risotto with mushrooms; breast milk lasagne and breast milk fruit shakes. Initiatives using breast milk as an ingredient for production and sale tend to have a short life. A cheese was produced by New York restaurant owner Daniel Angerer with milk from his own wife, which he served as a complimentary canapé with figs and Hungarian pepper. The restaurant was immediately given a warning by the New York City Health Department that prohibited further production and sales.[247] The same fate awaited a dessert served in a London restaurant called Baby Gaga Breast Milk Ice Cream. In spite of having been prepared from carefully selected milk made available by mothers approved by the National Health Service as blood donors, this special ice cream was confiscated within a few hours and its sale curtailed. Moreover, Lady Gaga started a court case because the product's name was too similar to her own.[248]

Before that, a New York art gallery offered visitors cheese made from the breast milk of three women. The Lady Cheese Shop was a four-day art installation by Miriam Simun, meant to raise ethical questions about modern biotechnologies. She hoped that her cheese would make people think twice about the various ways in which the human body has been used as a factory in which blood, hair, sperm, eggs and organs are produced to be harvested by others.[249]

247. https://www.theguardian.com/world/richard-adams-blog/2010/mar/09/breast-milk-cheese-new-york.

248. *Cultural Encyclopedia of the Breast*: 65-66.

249. https://www.huffingtonpost.co.uk/entry/breast-milk-lady-cheese-shop_n_866075

Such questions are no less relevant when talking about other animals—which brings us back to the *mammalia* that Linnaeus classified the human species as being part of. Of course, it takes the mammal with the biggest brain to come up with the idea of letting adults suck on female breasts for payment.

PART III

POWER AND POWERLESSNESS

Saint Agatha of Sicily being tortured. Royal Library, The Hague.
Medieval manuscript, *c.* 1390-1400.

9. SHE WILL KNOW WHY

Oh, Saint Agatha,
who withstood the unwelcome advances from unwanted suitors,
and suffered pain and torture
for your devotion to Our Lord,
we celebrate your faith, dignity and martyrdom.
Protect us against rape and other violations,
guard us against breast cancer
and other afflictions of women,
and inspire us to overcome adversity.

(Prayer to Saint Agatha)

Male violence against women appears to exist everywhere around the world as a result of presumed female unfaithfulness or men's fear of being abandoned. We have also seen how fear of women's uncontrollable sexuality and birth-giving capacity gives rise to the male urge to have control over the womb—because without male intervention the world would be in chaos.

The devouring mother

Different origin myths have the first ancestors breaking out from a vessel, gourd, bottle, pot or egg. In each version, the womb metaphor refers to both fertile fullness and greedy threat. In her beautiful book *La mère dévorante*, Denise Paulme analyses African story variants on the topic of an uncontrollable gourd, which swallows everything and everyone until a ram succeeds in cleaving the gluttonous monster with a powerful headbutt and frees all the living from being locked up inside. The alarming gluttony of the gourd can only be annihilated by a redeeming male element—a virile ram or muscular lumberjack.[250]

In a positive sense, the gourd symbolises the ideal mother, but the female pregnancy experience also gives rise to male need for compensation. Male superiority is mainly displayed outside the home 'in the domain of public life from which women are preferably excluded.' Such stories are full of incidents or dramas in which male order overcomes chaos blamed on women.[251]

Those who want to keep the birth-giving privilege in check apply the usual mechanisms: on the one hand, belittling women wherever possible; on the other hand, warning against destructive female power. The great similarities between men and women are ignored because the emphasis on sexual differences keeps the hierarchy intact.

The devouring gourd reflects the fear of unbridled wives and voracious wombs that also emerges in psychoanalytical practice. The need to contain female power leads to aggressive comments about successful women and, unfortunately, to extreme physical violence.[252]

Behind the front door

The human weakness of violence against women stems from the fact that men were usually physically stronger and developed

250. Denise Paulme, *La mère dévorante*, 1975.

251. Paulme: 282; Héritier II:131-132.

252. Jean Cournut, *Pourquoi les hommes ont peur des femmes. Essai sur le féminin érotico-maternel*, 2015; Lederer, ibid.

more muscle strength through hunting, while women, pregnant or surrounded by children, depended on a 'protector'. Why has this violence not stopped in less unsafe societies? Evolutionary psychology, looking for an answer to this question, came to the conclusion that a combination of obsessive sexual behaviour and aggression produces a dangerous cocktail:

> The risk of physical and even fatal violence increases proportionally to a woman's partner value: young and attractive women are much more likely to be abused by their partner than older or unattractive women. This is especially true if the woman is much younger than her partner, because her age makes it easy for her to find a more attractive partner [...]. The pattern of those acts of violence and the general fact that young men worldwide are particularly aggressive and commit most violent crimes [...] fit sexual selection theory like a glove.[253]

Traditionally, fertile women have been restricted in many ways, whereas women after menopause had more freedom and were sometimes allowed to 'drink beer like a man', as a Ganda proverb used to define the difference. Despite different cultural and religious backgrounds, quite similar restrictions have been imposed on women throughout history, as aptly summarised by Griet Vandermassen:

> Phenomena such as the veil and the headscarf, purdah, imprisonment, infibulation, clitoridectomy, the chaperoning of women, the high appreciation—or requirement—of female chastity, the concept of women as property and of adultery or rape as property violation,

253. Griet Vandermassen, *Darwin voor dames*, 2005:168-169.

> looking down on prostitutes, equating 'the protection of women' with 'protecting them from sexual contact' and laws that justify male violence if it was provoked by 'dissolute' behaviour of their spouse, daughter or sister.[254]

Old and recent examples illustrate how wives and mistresses were often automatically regarded as the property of the husbands. In the Chinese Ming Dynasty (1368-1644), some experienced heads of families compiled secret documents in which they noted their thoughts about sexual life within the family. A fragment from one of those books has been preserved, in which the anonymous writer notes that every human being has shortcomings, including women. They all must be reprimanded, but a woman who does not improve her life deserves a beating: she must lie down on her stomach on a couch, her pants are unbuttoned and she will receive five or six blows to her buttocks, according to the rules—not on her back or thighs:

> Occasionally, however, there are men who when administering punishment to a concubine will strip her naked and bind her to a pillar with ropes and whip her indiscriminately till the flesh bursts and she is covered with blood. This will not only harm the woman but also the man himself, and thus one's women's quarters are degraded to a torture chamber as that of the tribunal. This should by all means be avoided.[255]

'Beat your wife regularly, if you don't know why, she will know why' is still a popular proverb in West Africa. I heard it for the first time jokingly quoted in Dakar where my Wolof spokesman

254. Ibid.

255. Van Gulik: 269.

assured me it was of Arab origin. A similar European example is the Iberian message: 'To keep your wife on the rails, hit her, and if she derails, hit her.' Introduced to America long ago by Spanish settlers, it smoothly transitioned into Puerto Rico's oral tradition. Violence against women has been unabashedly promoted in proverbs from almost everywhere:

> For whom beats up his wife, God improves the food. (Russian)
> Women and cutlets, the more you beat them, the more succulent. (German)
> A woman, a dog and a walnut tree, the more you beat them, the better they be. (Western Europe and United States)
> Clubbing produces virtuous wives. (Chinese)
> A beaten woman is going to be a better wife. (Korean)
> The nails of a cart and the head of a woman only work when they are hit hard. (Rajasthani, India)[256]

Such harsh statements may look like tough talk or bravado to impress friends, but physical violence has never been just a matter of male boasting. Violence against women was part of the way in which a man, as the legal owner of wives and daughters, was taught to exercise his authority. Proverbs about aggression against women—especially wives—reflect the logic of that 'traditional' mentality without reticence or embarrassment. Many women are still beaten by men, mainly by intimate partners or close relatives, as various UN studies confirm.[257]

---

256. For proverbial violence, see Chapter 4 in *Never Marry a Woman with Big Feet*. For worldwide proverbs about violence, see: www.womeninproverbsworldwide.com.

257. http://www.unwomen.org/en/what-we-do/ending-violence-against-women/facts-and-figures.

Factors associated with sexual violence against women include:

- lower levels of education;
- a history of exposure to child maltreatment;
- witnessing family violence;
- antisocial personality disorder;
- harmful use of alcohol;
- community norms that privilege or ascribe higher status to men and lower status to women;
- low levels of women's access to paid employment;
- low level of gender equality;
- past history of exposure to violence;
- marital discord and dissatisfaction;
- difficulties in communicating between partners;
- male controlling behaviours towards their partners;
- beliefs in family honour and sexual purity;
- ideologies of male sexual entitlement; and
- weak legal sanctions for sexual violence.[258]

A multitude of proverbs confirm that violence against women is a tradition that has been passed down since time immemorial. It is certainly not 'the bitter fruit of sexual liberation in the late 1960s', as Spanish bishops claimed in 2005 when the Spanish government finally began to work on reducing the notorious macho violence in the country. Following the same line of thought, a Spanish archbishop stated in 2016 that domestic violence was caused by women seeking divorce—a statement he felt obliged to make after a forty-three-year-old woman had been strangled by her forty-one-year-old husband.[259]

---

258. https://www.who.int/news-room/fact-sheets/detail/violence-against-women, updated March 2021.

259. https://www.huffingtonpost.com/entry/archbishop-domestic-violence-spain_us_568bc89ee4b06fa6888374d8.

Fortunately, there are other religious comments as well. After pastors had openly condemned violence against women in the 1990s, the US Conference of Catholic Bishops officially spoke out against it in 2002: 'We state as clearly and strongly as we can that violence against women, inside or outside the home, is *never* justified. Violence in any form—physical, sexual, psychological, or verbal—is sinful; often, it is a crime as well. We have called for a moral revolution to replace a culture of violence. We acknowledge that violence has many forms, many causes, and many victims—men as well as women. The Catholic Church teaches that violence against another person in any form fails to treat that person as someone worthy of love. Instead, it treats the person as an object to be used. [...] While violence can be directed towards men, it tends to harm women and children more.'[260]

Such official statements by clergymen are also of great importance in Islam, where 'disciplining' women is still locally recommended and justified as a tradition. Orthodox views tend to refer to Ahadith texts in which the Prophet Muhammad is claimed to have said, 'Do not beat your wife as you would thrash your slave girl.' So, contemporary believers wonder, what is allowed and what isn't? And why? Here is an ultra-orthodox answer:

> In view of her weaker understanding and obstinate nature, Islam has under special circumstances and as a matter of expediency, permitted admonition, even light corporal punishment in extreme cases. And this is the last resort that one may have recourse to, when other measures have failed to put her on the right track. [...] Experience shows that woman is irritable by nature and is easily agitated.

260. https://www.usccb.org/topics/marriage-and-family-life-ministries/when-i-call-help-pastoral-response-domestic-violence; https://en.wikipedia.org/wiki/United_States_Conference_of_Catholic_Bishops.

> She is so constituted that her feelings are easily injured and as against this, man has greater intellect and can put up with a lot of irritation.[261]

In several Islamic books and on many websites the warning is that 'woman was not created to be ill-treated and beaten.' However, orthodox messages are apparently in favour of traditional hierarchy, insisting that, in the directions given by the Prophet, men have been granted precedence over women: 'If both of them have the same footing, the equality of status in authority will result in the breaking up of the household.' As there cannot be two kings in one realm, the man has to be the king in the home and, if necessary, he is allowed to beat his wife, be it only 'lightly' and 'in such a way that the skin is not injured.' And he does not have to answer for this to anybody. As narrated by Umar ibn al-Khattab: 'The Prophet (peace be upon him) said: "A man will not be asked as to why he beat his wife."'[262]

In the meantime, the changes for women's good thanks to Islam are emphasised in the light of the pre-Islamic Arabian context:

> [...] where women enjoyed no higher status than that of the beasts of burden and chapel, the man used to ill-treat them as much as they liked, and beating them and inflicting other physical injuries on them were in the day's work. But with the above command, gone all forms of tyranny and oppression [...] and women were very much relieved.[263]

---

261. Mufti Zafeeruddin Miftahi, *Modesty and Chastity in Islam*, 1993:143.

262. Ibid. 141-145. *Kitab Al-Nikah*, Book 11, Number 2139-42 in http://www.answering-christianity.com/beating_yes.htm.

263. Ibid. 147.

Of course, there's no end to improving the situation of women. Arguing that the position of the man as king in his own home must remain unaffected, orthodox Islamic clerics keep going back to ancient traditions, but more than ever before contemporary believers consult imams with critical questions regarding these cherished ideas. Searching for allies, some orthodox interpreters even combed through the Bible for texts justifying violence against women from a Christian perspective, without finding convincing support for corporal punishment of women.[264]

The orthodox reasoning that everything must remain as it was in the Prophet Muhammad's time maintains the husband's Islamic right to physically punish his wife or wives. Fortunately, there are now countries, such as Tunisia, where the Quran remains a source of inspiration, but is no longer understood as a literal blueprint for modern society. One thing is certain—every powerful contemporary plea by Muslims and other influential clergy against taking old recommendations of violence against women literally, will contribute to the protection of modern women who are burdened by aggression from their partner or end up as deadly victims.

Echoes of brutal and unrestrained violence against women continue to resonate all over the world. Until the second half of the last century, there were not even laws in most countries to combat domestic violence. It was considered normal and people looked the other way, because: 'When husband and wife quarrel, keep your distance' (an old saying in the Netherlands). The fundamental difference is that not only does legislation against violence now exist in many countries, the issue is being discussed more openly than ever before.

---

264. http://islamiat101.blogspot.nl/2012/12/wife-beating-in-bible-and-christianity.html; http://www.answering-christianity.com/beating.htm.

Breast rippers and other instruments of torture

Male aggression is often directed at parts of the body that men themselves don't possess, as can be concluded from a rather sad litany of information about mutilation and rape. In *De Vrouw in Natuur- en Volkenkunde* (*The Woman in Physics and Ethnology*, published at the beginning of the twentieth century), the authors depict gruesome traditions of breast mutilation—unfortunately without explaining the underlying motives:

> In Australia, the nipples of young girls are pulled out to make suckling impossible. Even in the last century there was a horrific mutilation in the Christian sect of

Coptic girl, about twenty years old, with mutilated breasts. Engraving, late nineteenth century.[265]

265. In Ploss and Bartels, 1912.

> the Copts in Russia [in which] the nipples of ten-, nine- and even seven-year-old girls were cut off; and when the case came to court, these children obstinately persisted, that they had inflicted this mutilation on themselves [...]. Apparently, the sacrament played a major role in their religion. Instead of the host, they were given a small piece of bleeding girl's breast.

This may look unbelievable, but the book includes illustrations.

In Christian legends about saints, 'pagan' rulers assault beautiful and pious girls who end up as devout martyrs. An early example is provided in multiple stories about Saint Agatha (*c.* 231-251), whose martyrdom was popularised by Saint Jerome and others in the sixth century. Agatha was born in Catania or Palermo in Sicily and became one of the first canonised Christians. After this exemplary virgin of noble descent rejected the advances of the Roman governor and refused to marry him, he tortured her to death:

> During these tortures she prayed: 'For love of chastity I am made to hang from a rack. Help me, O Lord my God, as they knife my breasts.' Agatha rebuked the governor for his barbarity: 'Godless, cruel, infamous tyrant, are you not ashamed to despoil a woman of that by which your own mother nursed you?'[266]

Agatha died from the consequences of her torments. The patron saint of breast cancer patients, rape victims and wet-nurses, women in desperate situations still call on her in prayer. The main symbols of Saint Agatha are breasts on a dish—drawings and paintings depict her bearing her own severed breasts on a silver platter

266. https://www.catholicculture.org/culture/liturgicalyear/calendar/day.cfm?date=2016-02-05.

or holding in one hand the pincers gripping one of her breasts. An illustration in a medieval manuscript shows two men each ripping off a breast from her frail body.

On 5 February, Saint Agatha's feast day, a procession carries her life-size statue ornamented with a wealth of jewellery through the streets of Catania, surrounded by thousands of crying and moaning people invoking her; and Sicilians indulge in a traditional sweet spongy pastry in the shape of a virginal breast covered with a crunchy icing and topped with a candied red cherry—to keep the memory of St Agatha's cruel fate fresh in the mind. Originally made by nuns, these *minni di virgini* are now available at the confectioner's.

Cassatella di sant'Agata or *minni di virgini*,
Cantania, Sicily. (Stefano Mortello).

Iron instruments of torture in museums make clear that putting someone on the rack does not only happen in stories.

In Europe in the Middle Ages some instruments were especially invented for breasts or wombs. The Breast Ripper, consisting of iron pincers with claws, was either used cold or red-hot to brand the exposed breasts of an unmarried mother or to put pressure on a female suspect accused of blasphemy, heresy, adultery or carrying out an abortion:

> Used as a way to punish women, the breast ripper was a painful and cruel way to mutilate a woman's breasts. [...] A common variant of the breast ripper is often referred to as 'The Spider', which is a similar instrument attached to a wall. The victim's breasts were fixed to the claws and the woman was pulled by the torturer away from the wall; successfully removing them.[267]

A woman forced to undergo this torture was horribly disfigured for the rest of her life, if she didn't expire on the spot.

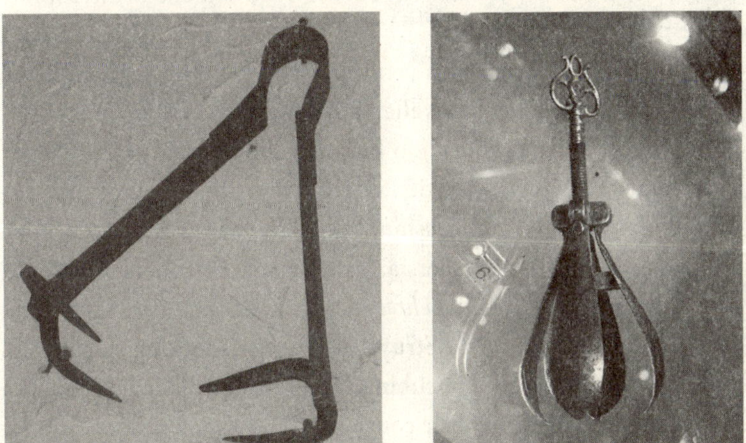

Medieval instruments to torture women.
Left: Breast Ripper. Foltermuseum, Freiburg; right: Pear of anguish. Fortress Museum, Salzburg.

267. http://www.medievality.com/breast-ripper.html.

Another instrument was the 'pear of anguish'. A small version was applied to the mouth or anus of men; a larger model was pushed through a woman's vagina into her womb. From the outside, a screw was tightened further and further, as a result of which the sharp blades of this pear-shaped instrument swung open internally. Torture with the pear irremediably maimed the affected cavity—almost always with a fatal outcome.

Aggression against breasts, wombs and genitals still occurs, and not only in porn fantasies. In areas of Syria and Iraq where IS prevailed until recently, Christian and Yezidi girls were raped and tortured by their so-called owners, who treated them as sex slaves. According to their interpretation of the Quran, raping a slave was not a sin. Sometimes breasts and other sensitive body parts were cut off as punishment. Contemporary IS views are in line with traditional cultural or religious views of woman as just one big pubic region: no one but her legal owner should see her body and women who disobeyed the requirement of invisibility were punished.[268]

An extreme seventeenth-century example of this mentality was recorded by the Dutch traveller Jan Janszoon Struys. This sailor from North Holland had a job building the Russian tsar's fleet in Astrakhan. One day, that city was besieged by Cossacks and he ended up as a slave in Dagestan. There an Islamic Khan prevailed as vassal of the Shah of Persia. In his book *Drie Aanmerkelijke en seer Rampspoedige Reysen* (*Three Considerable and Very Disastrous Travels*, Amsterdam, 1676) Struys reported a shocking incident in the region—the Polish concubine of a Persian trader had found a way to escape to the Polish consulate. The Khan gave the trader permission to get the girl back and 'do with her whatever he wanted.' He chose to skin her tarnished body alive and draped

268. http://shoebat.com/2014/09/16/muslims-take-christian-girls-cut-breasts/.

her stripped skin on the wall of a separate room as a warning to all his other concubines.

In 1673, Struys returned to the Netherlands as a free man and commented on this tragic event in his travel story: 'Even though they are the dirtiest, most horny and unfaithful men, they still want their wives to be honest, chaste, and faithful.' A lifelike engraving of the woman's horrific torture was included in his book. On the right of the image, the woman is tied down in preparation for the skinning; being stripped off; her clothes and slippers strewn on the floor. In the room next door, the Persian trader explains to his assembled concubines that a similar fate awaits them should they ever take it into their heads to attempt such an escape.[269]

From Jan Janszoon Struys' *Drie Aanmerkelijke en seer Rampspoedige Reysen.* Copper engraving, 1676. Leiden University Libraries.

269. Jan Janszoon Struys, *Drie Aanmerkelijke en seer Rampspoedige Reysen.* Amsterdam: 1676; re-issue: 2014. With thanks to Arnoud Vrolijk, curator Eastern Manuscripts, Leiden University Libraries.

In the same period, no less gruesome tortures were occurring across Europe. The breasts of women accused of witchcraft were frequently cut off before they were burned at the stake. An ill-famed case is the history of the Bavarian Pappenheimer family, itinerant latrine cleaners. Before mother Anna was burned as a witch, executioners cut off her breasts and stuffed them first in her own mouth and then in those of her two sons to ridicule her role as mother.

Everywhere in the world mothers of adolescent girls worry about lustful men who cannot be trusted to keep their hands off these innocent youngsters. Concerned about the wellbeing of their daughters, they sometimes carry out disastrous security measures to prevent worse scenarios. One of those measures is the tradition of 'breast ironing', which occurs in rural areas of Cameroon and some other African countries:

> Breast ironing is a breast-flattening practice performed on adolescent girls by applying a firm pressure massage with hot objects, such as stones, coconut shells, pestles, spoons, and even hammers. Application of hot fruit peels and tight chest binding to make the girl's chest look flat usually follow the massage.[270]

As with infibulation and clitoridectomy, mothers, aunts or grandmothers take control over the bodies of the girls in their families in matters of breast ironing. The intentions are good—by means of breast mutilation the mothers try to make their daughters less sexuallly attractive to protect them against assault and rape, HIV infection and unwanted pregnancy, in the hope that they will stay longer in school and be able to take care of themselves and their children in future life. Nevertheless, this practice produces

270. *Cultural Encyclopedia of the Breast*: 68ff.

mainly negative effects, from painful blisters and infections to abscesses, from damage to the mammary glands and unsightly scars to post-traumatic stress.[271] In some areas, more than half the girls undergo this dangerous treatment. Campaigns for abolition are carried out intermittently, but there is still no law prohibiting this harmful tradition. Laws are a good first step, without being a watertight guarantee of the abolition of degrading practices.

Sexual aggression in times of war

Rape is a constant in history, just like the unequal treatment of men and women before the law. In most cases the victim has to give more accountability than the perpetrator. Some see rape as a male strategy to control women. For women, the psychic scars of rape turn out to be more painful than scars of 'normal' physical abuse. All the previously outlined examples of aggression affecting girls and women took place in situations outside of armed conflicts. In wartime, insecurity is dramatically magnified and rape is turned into a weapon. In military conflicts, women and children have always been easy prey for objectionable sexual behaviour. In the former Roman settlement of Cornelia on the Neckar in present-day Germany, the Huns under the command of Attila (406-453) killed all the men, then raped the women before cutting off their breasts. The town later became known as Wimpfen, a corruption of the German word *Weiberpein* meaning 'women's pain'.

Such offences have also occured in more recent history. Towards the end of World War II, soldiers of the Red Army raped one hundred thousand women en route to Berlin. Serial rape is a disastrous weapon that deeply humiliates not only the victims but also their families. Convinced that they had lost their honour, the girls were encouraged (often by their own fathers)

271. https://newint.org/features/2013/05/01/tales-of-taboo/.

to commit suicide; and hundreds did. Men whose wives were victims sometimes killed their entire family and then themselves. A raped woman was seen as a tarnished woman.[272]

Until recently, this offence was not taken seriously and was not considered a war crime. From time to time, eyewitnesses from war zones lift the edge of the thick veil that still covers most sexual offences. Three examples from different parts of the world:

> A Rwandan victim acts as a witness in the Rwanda Tribunal: 'If you now listen to the radio and hear about war in other countries where rape is used as a weapon, we know that silence kills you slowly, but when you talk about it, the wound cures gradually.' [273]

Nadia Murad, a victim of sex slavery in Iraq, is determined to inform the world about all the IS horrors she was submitted to: 'I am willing to testify and tell the court what he has done to me and to all other Yezidi girls.' In 2016, Murad became the first UN Goodwill Ambassador for the Dignity of Survivors of Human Traficking, and in 2018 was awarded the Nobel Peace Prize (with Denis Mukwege) 'for their efforts to end the use of sexual violence as a weapon of war and armed conflict.'

Mumtaz Begum, Rohingya, a victim of brutal Burmese military violence, also refuses to remain silent: 'I want to tell the world everything the soldiers have done...They raped us and killed us. We want justice.'[274]

All recent conflicts, from the Bosnian War to the wars in Syria,

---

272. Jolande Withuis in *Trouw*, 25 November 2017.

273. https://www.theguardian.com/film/2015/oct/09/rwanda-genocide-documentary-uncondemned-filmmaker-death.

274. http://www.independent.co.uk/news/world/asia/rohingya-crisis-women-rape-muslims-burma-military-soldiers-ethnic-cleansing-genocide-a8103441.html.

Iraq and Congo, show that rape is still used as a weapon. The continuing civil war in South Sudan has seen not only opposition groups and criminal gangs hunt women and girls, but the soldiers of the South Sudanese army too—with permission from those high up in the military—to make up for unpaid salary.

Most women choose to remain silent about sexual violence because they know that previous victims were abandoned by their husbands and expelled from the community as soon as the shaming news became known. Thus they are punished twice.[275]

Dieudo Hamadi's beautiful documentary *Mama Colonel* (2017) breaks the taboo, showcasing the challenges faced by Congolese head of police Colonel Honorine Manyole as she is trasferred to Kisangani. She goes to the market with a megaphone and addresses the traumatised market women in public: 'Don't stay stuck in yourself, come and talk about what has happened to you.' The camera glides past eyes that have seen unimaginable war horrors, and faces ravaged by ungraspable grief. Thanks to the patiently listening ear of this senior police officer, these women meet for the first time a person who understands to what extent the horrors of sexual violence completely destroyed their lives. That someone takes their blood-curdling war stories seriously is crucial to each of them personally, but making such abuses public can be liberating for an entire community.

Throughout history, rulers large and small have always considered the bodies and labour of their subjects to be at their disposal. They do not seem to think of those belonging to the

275. OHCHR and UNMISS, 'Violations and abuses of international human rights law and violations of international humanitarian rights law in the context of the fighting in Juba, South Sudan in July 2016' (January 2017); https://www.theguardian.com/global-development/2016/jul/29/women-south-sudan-raped-un-compound-juba-kill-me-instead; http://www.independent.co.uk/topic/south-sudan.

underlying group, class, race or gender as fellow human beings. Excesses in wartime are extreme examples of this. In his book *The Power Paradox* (2017), American psychologist Dacher Keltner argues that power makes people less empathetic. In an interview with a newspaper in the Netherlands, he cited the behaviour of Donald Trump as an example: 'His focus is primarily on maintaining power. He makes impulsive decisions, disrespectful comments and tells self-glorifying stories—all signs of abuse of power, which evoke stress and anxiety in others. Stress is a pre-eminent characteristic of powerlessness.'[276]

In the course of history, dominant positions are usually occupied by men. If women have naturally more empathy than men, have they mainly developed that talent because they had little or no power? It would be nice for women at the top to continue to nurture and propagate empathy in positions of power and not let this talent wither away as their power increases—but no human inclination is alien to women. They too abuse positions of power, as American female soldiers demonstrated, for example, in their behaviour towards male prisoners in Iraq and Guantanamo Bay. In the army, women continue to be specially trained in interrogation techniques that are humiliating for men from Islamic traditions. [277] No, power is not conditioned by male genitals and, yes, every person walks through life with a good dose of aggression. This does not alter the fact that so far men have raped considerably more women than the other way around.

Rape culture is an outgrowth of age-old traditions of inequality, but popular culture, media, gaming, porn and advertising images continue to respond to sex and sexual violence by presenting women as physical commodities up for grabs. Male sexual anxiety

276. *NRC-Handelsblad*, 9-10 December 2017.

277. Coco Fusco, *A Field Guide for Female Interrogators*, 2008.

and helplessness can turn into contempt and violence, because frustration is more easily vented on those over whom you have power. In many cases, family members, grandparents and mothers cooperate in child marriages, genital mutilation of girls and other kinds of violence due to unwavering traditions and family honour. Or they encourage or even force girls into prostitution because the rest of the family is in danger of starvation.

Looking back, there is one noticeable difference with the past—more victims of violence speak out today and their voices, formerly smothered in the cover-up of history, are less often ignored, ridiculed, shrugged off or looked at with indifference or disbelief. A sign of hope.

Hoped-for male progeny: embryo on an imaginary umbilical cord inside a female body. Etching of a painted and carved door, New Guinea.[278]

278. In de Clercq and Schmelz, 1893.

10. GENDER IMBALANCE

> A whole night of labour and then only a daughter.
>
> (Spanish proverb)

> The elder Sister said: 'We have really lost nothing, for we remember it all. Let them have that small part. For aren't we still sacred? [...] We still have our wombs, don't we?' And the younger Sister agreed with her.
>
> (Wulamba origin myth)

The chaos of life involves ambivalent us-them relationships, in which differences are more often emphasised than similarities—differences in gender, language, culture, colour, class, religion, and so on. To limit ourselves to gender differences: young girls and boys already mutually compare their differences and are sometimes envious of each other. Or they wonder why they can't have both a penis and a womb. Thanks to Freud, penis envy has become a popular concept, but the existence of womb envy has also been demonstrated again and again.

Oh no, it's a girl

The image from New Guinea that opens this chapter reflects the widespread traditional view that a baby boy is more welcome than a baby girl, a view probably as old as patriarchy. Some four thousand years ago that view was already popular, as evidenced in auspicious and inauspicious omens preserved in cuneiform script on Mesopotamian clay tablets:

> If a man's penis is long and thick, he will have sons.
> If a woman's nose is symmetrical, [she will give birth to] sons.
> If a man has sex with a woman on fallow land, she will give birth to a daughter; if he sleeps with her in a field or garden [on cultivated land], then she will give birth to a son.[279]

For various reasons, the birth of a son has often been greeted with considerably more enthusiasm than that of a daughter. Preference for children of a specific gender is not only related to the structure of society and traditional access to sources of income, but also to obstinate ideas (whether religiously inspired or not) putting men 'naturally' on a higher plane than women. In many cultures, such a literally expressed love for sons came to be passed on over the generations and centuries, so that globally many mothers still derive their highest achievable social prestige from giving birth to boys. No wonder women themselves went along with that preference, brainwashed as they must have been by that wish-for-a-son mentality, as expressed and confirmed openly and loud in proverbs, for example, in Europe:

> He who leaves a boy behind is not really dead. (Danish)
> Many sons, many blessings of God; many daughters, many calamities. (German)
> When a girl is born, even the roofs cry. (Bulgarian)
> When a wife gives birth to a boy, even the walls of the house rejoice. (Armenian)

279. With thanks for personal information to Assyriologist Marten Stol.

In other parts of the world, people have also been taught to cry at the cradle of a daughter and cheer at the birth of a son. The disadvantages of a daughter are widely measured: she is 'a lost child' (Bengali), 'nobody's relative' (Mongo) 'cigarettes' ashes' (Arabic), and so on.[280] The following statements are still popular in the Arab world:

> When a daughter is born, the threshold weeps for forty days.
> Every daughter is a handful of trouble.
> Let's pray to the Prophet until the boy comes.

As we have seen, although according to the Quran men and women both contribute to the emergence of life, medieval Muslim theologians and doctors were inclined to present the mother as the passive partner in which the privileged male seed is planted. The Persian Muslim scholar Ibn Sina (980-1037), known as Avicenna in the West, compares male and female genitals and concludes that one set is 'complete and extends outward, while the other is incomplete and held back on the inside, as if it were an inverted male organ.'[281] In various traditions, fathers still experience the birth of a girl as a shameful loss of face to other men in their own community. In Asia, female babies are often commented upon in extremely negative ways, for example, in China:

> Rather one son with a hump than eighteen golden daughters.
> A stupid son is better than a crafty daughter.
> It is a blessing to bear a son, a calamity to bear a daughter.

Or in India:

> Virtuous is the girl who suffers and dies without a sound.
> (Bengali)

---

280. For details: *Never Marry a Woman with Big Feet*, Chapter 2:93ff.

281. Quoted in Kueny: 51; see Laqueur 1990 for similar ideas among Western scholars.

> Those who lie, give birth to daughters. (Telugu)
> When a girl is born, don't take care of her, she will grow like a cactus; when a boy is born, take good care of him, as you would with a rose tree. (Rajasthani)

The latter proverb reflects a mentality that is common in many other Indian states, especially in the conservative north where many people have little or no school education and patriarchal culture is dominant.

Contemporary birth statistics reflect the disastrous consequences of constant negative messages about daughters. The deep-rooted Indian preference for a son over a daughter has not only led to selective abortions, but also to higher mortality among little girls. According to a UN report, India is among the few countries in the world where, in 2018, the infant mortality of girls exceeded that of boys.[282] Around 22 per cent of deaths among girls under five in India can be attributed to sex discrimination through neglect, according to researchers. Based on data from 2000 to 2005, 40 per cent more girls than boys die before the age of five, because they do not receive medical care or food. The excess female death rate amounts to 18.5 per thousand girls, equating to an estimated 239,000 excess deaths per year as a 2018 study in *The Lancet Global Health* showed:

> The considerable effect of gender bias on mortality in India highlights the need for more proactive engagement with the issue of postnatal sex discrimination and a focus on the northern districts. Notably, these regions are not

282. https://www.thehindu.com/news/national/indias-under-5-mortality-of-girls-exceeds-that-of-boys-unlike-global-trend-says-report/article30550394.ece; https://www.un.org/development/desa/pd/news/levels-and-trends-child-mortality-2020-report.

the same as those most affected by skewed sex ratio at birth.[283]

In large Asian countries the male/female ratio is severely disrupted: for a thousand boys in India, you find around 930 girls and, in some regions, a hundred fewer. The appreciation of sons over daughters regularly goes so far that a girl does not even get the chance to start her life.

In rural areas the suffocating of a baby girl right after her first breath—an operation called 'the wet towel' for which the midwife was allowed to charge a modest extra fee—is fortunately now a lot less common. But other methods include crushing the baby's neck, drowning or poisoning her (assistance at the birth of a boy is rewarded with a double rate). In the informative 2013 documentary *It's a Girl*, midwives in some states of India admit in interviews that they were paid to kill about half of the baby girls they helped to bring into the world.[284]

In India, more than one million sex-selected abortions take place annually. This traditional preference for sons, in combination since the 1980s with the increasingly widespread application of pregnancy ultrasound scans to find out early on whether the foetus is a boy or girl, has led to a dramatic lack of women throughout Asia—an alarming development first raised in 1990 by Indian economist and Nobel Prize winner Amartya Sen in an essay in *The New York Review of Books* entitled 'More Than One Hundred Million Women are Gone'. UN researchers estimate that over two hundred million have 'disappeared' in the meantime—eliminated by selective abortion, infanticide, inferior nutrition and neglect in childhood.

---

283. https://www.thelancet.com/journals/langlo/article/PIIS2214-109X(18)30184-0/fulltext.

284. https://www.youtube.com/watch?v=upnpD3ZByM4.

In India, laws that prohibit sex-selective feticide and infanticide have been passed. Giving and receiving dowry was technically prohibited back in 1961 with the intent to reduce emotional abuse of and physical violence against women. However, the political will to actually apply these laws is often lacking. Doctors still take ultrasounds; the police and courts are bribed. One of the main reasons for the preference for sons is of a religious nature—in Hinduism only a male descendant can ignite a funeral pyre to release the soul and ensure reincarnation.

Despite increased medical knowledge, the 'blame' for giving birth to a female child is often still placed on the woman. As a result, under pressure from family and community, men in South Asia sometimes abandon their wives and start a new family hoping for a son. Many Indians in Western countries, who are highly educated and prosperous, continue to favour sons over daughters. In practice, this irrational preference has resulted in a serious imbalance of the male-female ratio. The surplus of bachelors leads to violent behaviour, and in areas where the ratio is most disturbed, the crime rate is increasing.

This problem also exists in China—on average, twelve hundred boys to a thousand girls are born, and in some regions the ratio is even thirteen hundred to a thousand. In the Western China province of Xinghai a few years ago, students told me that according to calculations, by 2020 there would be forty million more men than women. The prediction pretty much bore fruit.[285] These young men were very concerned: would they ever be able to find a wife? Life is increasingly difficult for unskilled men who are referred to as 'bare branches' in China—they have a

285. In 2020, the sex ratio of the total population in China is 105.302 males per 100 females—an estimated 738.25 million males to 701.08 million females. In India, males outnumber females by fifty-four million. https://population.un.org/wpp/Download/Standard/Population/.

shorter life expectancy, many of them becoming depressed and sometimes aggressive.

Meanwhile, trafficking in women and sex slavery are growing all over the world. Girls are kidnapped, seduced or sold as prostitutes. In some cases, poor families buy one girl to serve as a bride for all the men in a household. The more unequal the male/female ratio, the more men start looking for younger and younger brides. It means that girls curtail their schooling, can't find work, and are forced to give birth before their bodies are ready. Among young women this course of events results in a high percentage of suicides. [286]

What is the solution? Negative opinions about girls and daughters can change. In South Korea where the balance between the numbers of boys and girls was also disturbed, the government has made a major effort to adjust social thinking patterns and cultural traditions. The situation there has now improved considerably. By questioning the preference for sons, by constantly paying attention to the problem in the media and in education, a new generation is growing up with a different mentality. Such government action shows that patient discussion about the origins and consequences of traditions contributes successfully to the adjustment of centuries-old patterns.[287]

Lack

Perfection in the form of androgyny must be a long-standing human wish, or there would not be so many stories in which first ancestors were blessed with both sexes. Myths about world

286. Lakshmi Vijayakumar, 'Suicide in Women', *Indian Journal of Psychiatry*, July 2015, pp.233-238.

287. 'Son Preference and Sex Ratio' infogram at http://www.womanstats.org/maps.html.

parents, in various iterations of bisexual unity, represent the universe as having a male and a female component, as a divine being with characteristics of both human sexes, such as the Hindu god Brahma:

> In the beginning, there was nothing but the Great Self, Brahman. That is to say, nothing but Brahman existed. [...] Now Brahman looked around himself and saw nothing. He felt fear. [...] Brahman was lonely [and] took the form of Brahma, the Creator. Brahma felt no delight; lonely people never do. He yearned for someone to keep him company and his thoughts split the temporary body he was using into two parts, like the halves of a clam shell coming apart. One of the two parts was male and the other female. They looked on each other as husband and wife. To this day, a happily married couple are like two parts of one being with Brahma in both of them.[288]
> (Hindu, India)

My neighbour in Lubumbashi, the Congolese writer and scholar Clémentine Faïk Nzuji, told me another story about the human loss of bisexual perfection. In her Luba culture, the first ancestor, Mvidi Mukulu, is 'a great hermaphrodite being' and lived happily in a beautiful garden where there was a wonderful palm tree in a light open space. Only one thing was not permitted here—walking a whole circle around the shady palm tree in the middle of the garden would disturb the perfect harmony. Unavoidably, this ban led to an obsession:

> Our perfectly happy first ancestor wanted just one thing: to walk full circle around the palm tree, and one day this

288. This old myth originates from the *Brihadaranyaka Upanishad*, probably dating back to about 1500 BC; the quoted passage is from *Parallel Myths*, 1994:39-40.

> first human being began to walk around the motionless tree. Arrived at the starting point again, our ancestor fell apart in two halves. One half became man, the other half became woman. Ever since that time, men and women have been longing for the lost unity, a paradise they sometimes find briefly back in one another. (Luba, DR Congo)

It is thanks to that primal experience of completeness that men and women keep feeling attraction to each other.

In Plato's *Symposium*, written around 385 BC, the conversation at a dinner is also devoted to the topic of bisexuality, love and mutual sexual attraction in a story explaining why men and women keep looking for their lost perfection. Here, ideal love either bridges the gap between a man and a woman or between people of the same sex.

In times of crisis, cultures often appeal to rituals in which men dress or behave like women or vice versa, believing that male and female potencies combined in one person will increase society's life force, arguing that one plus one results in considerably more than two, and opens doors that would otherwise remain locked. To get access to that power, elements of both sexes are ritually brought together in one person—such as putting male seed on female breasts or rubbing menstrual blood onto young boys, or someone of the opposite sex eating a cut clitoris, believing that androgynous powers generate extra vitality.[289]

Almost every society is inclined to force children's hormonal processes in the direction of one sex or the other. Initiation rituals to turn boys into men are often more extensive than initiation rituals for girls, whose menstrual periods visibly mark the beginning of adolescence.

289. For a detailed study of androgyny, see Baumann.

A lack of the characteristics of the other sex can be experienced as especially harrowing in societies where one sex is more valued or enjoys more privileges than the other. So jealousy of the dominant sex is more commonplace than jealousy of the less-valued sex. Undoubtedly girls are (or have been) envious of the self-evident privileges of boys who are allowed more freedoms and more opportunities: more education, being able to travel alone without being disgraced or losing their honour, and access to a number of domains deemed inaccessible to girls. The WomanStats Project world maps are crystal-clear testimonies of the global consequences of that age-old emphasis on sex differences (see Plates 22-25).

In their morning prayer, orthodox Jewish men openly express their gratitude: 'Blessed are you, Lord our God, Ruler of the Universe, who has not made me a woman.' A common Kurdish saying observes that 'it is better to be a man for one day than a woman for ten days.' A woman I interviewed from Bhutan agrees: 'Being born a woman means a wasted life', and 'I won't come back female' is an old Ashanti saying in southern Ghana, reflecting women's hopes for a better position in a next life. Most oral traditions reflect a gender hierarchy in which it is self-evident who are to be the speakers and who are the silent ones, the keepers of knowledge and the ignorant, the travellers and those staying at home—as if this were the irreversible natural order of things.

It is quite understandable that most researchers have paid less attention to male envy of women and female bodily functions than the other way around. Until well into the last century most anthropologists were men, and it is likely that they had a blind spot for male envy of women. [290] Yet that envy exists, and one of the most common devices to provide adolescents with a way of overriding it and to establish the required roles in society was to introduce initiation rites.

---

290. See, for example, *Perceiving Women*, 1981.

The circumcision of boys exists in so many cultures around the world, usually around puberty, that this custom seems to meet a deep-seated need. Initiation rites sometimes serve as 'proof' that the men thereby give birth to their sons without any female interference: the initiated boy is 'dying of his childhood' and is only now really born for the first time, thanks to his father.[291] This form of wishful thinking puts medieval scholar Paolo Certaldo's previously cited statement about the son who has to obey his father who gave birth to him, 'even though his mother provided practical aid'—in a wider context. It remains surprising that such reasonings have rarely been interpreted as womb envy.

Male initiation is almost everywhere more extensive than female, and usually takes place during puberty, the period in which girls have their first monthly bleeding. It is not without significance that a little blood is released when the foreskin is cut away. In this process female 'birthing behaviour' is sometimes literally imitated. Among the Iatmul in Papua New Guinea, boys even had a huge symbolic vulva thrown over their heads during their initiation. Emphasis on masculinity, (re-)birth as a 'real man' or male birth-giving in circumcision rituals frequently go along with explicit negative feelings towards women.[292]

In the Western world too, there has been a tendency to think that the birth of girls was due to a lack of virility—thanks in part to the lasting influence of reliable old sexist Aristotle. In his famous work on animals, written between 347 and 322 BC, the philosopher provided the world with powerful statements about the huge differences between men and women:

291. Bettelheim, *Symbolic Wounds*: 104ff. Of course, jealousy is not the only motive for male initiation rites; they are also connected with fertility and the care for all the living.

292. Sierksma, *Religie, Sexualiteit en Agressie*, 1979:105 and 57; Bettelheim: 111ff.

> For females are weaker and colder in nature [than males], and we must look upon the female character as being a sort of natural deficiency. Accordingly, while it is within the mother it develops slowly because of its coldness (for development is concoction, and it is heat that concocts, and what is hotter is easily concocted); but after birth it quickly arrives at maturity and old age on account of its weakness, for all inferior things come sooner to their perfection or end, and as this is true of works of art so it is of what is formed by Nature.[293]

Whether or not inspired by this or other Greek philosophers, Western physicians and other scholars continued to conduct empirical research, with perspectives often demonstrably clouded by their own bias. Thanks to traditionally cherished ideas, the female body was portrayed as a deviation from the 'norm', or as a less perfect or inferior variant of the male. It looks as if, subconsciously, male envy led to ever stronger belief in the male seed as the essential contribution to the life of a child. The contribution of women in pregnancy and birth-giving was considered less important or even negligible.

Studying myths and other commentaries on the female body transmitted around the world, one cannot ignore the legacies brought forth by womb envy. They make understandable why men invented and imposed rules excluding women from religious and other professional practices. The usual explanation was (and in some traditions still is) that only men had the brains needed for those roles, for the very reason that they were men. Authors such as Françoise Héritier in her important two-volume work *Masculin/Féminin* and Robert McElvaine in *Eve's Seed* argue the

293. Aristotle, *On the Generation of Animals*, Book Four, 6. Translation from the Greek: Ebooks University of Adelaide, Australia.

very opposite: those patterns of thinking ensue from what men were physically unable to do—giving birth to and suckling society's children.

The two sexes have been provided with different tools, but why can't people be dissimilar and still treat each other as equals? Freud continued to emphasise sexual differences and reaffirmed centuries of influential reasoning that women are 'inferior' to men. His emphasis on female penis envy and his claim that girls blame their mothers for having sent them 'so pathetically incomplete' into the world might well stem from his own subconscious womb envy.[294]

In their practice, psychiatrists and psychotherapists come across men who are jealous of women. At children's dressing-up parties, boys sometimes put pillows under their jerseys to imitate breasts or pregnant bellies. There are those who openly admit that they envy girls who will have children later: 'They hate them for it, and dream of violence; cutting off breasts, pulling out vaginas.' They feel frustrated by women not responding to their advances or simply for not being allowed to touch those breasts.[295]

There has undoubtedly been an irresistible need for the message that men are superior to women and that it makes sense for men to be in power.

The theft of women's secret

In many societies, domination is based on special knowledge or a secret society of members sharing a specific bond. During puberty rituals, youngsters become partakers of this secret knowledge for the first time.

A secret impresses as long as it remains hidden from outsiders.

---

294. McElvaine, Chapter 12.

295. Oral information and literature, e.g. in Lederer: 55-56, 153; Bettelheim: 39ff.

Stories say that 'once, long ago' women were in charge because they possessed a special secret, until the men managed to steal it from them. Since then, men have been in power, and they will be as long as they succeed in carefully guarding the secret among themselves and make sure it never falls back into the hands of women ever again. No easy task, of course.

In some traditions, women are threatened that just accidentally seeing or touching the secret object(s) will make them drop dead on the spot, and knowing the secret or even having a vague conjecture about it will be enough reason for their being murdered. Usually, the secret takes the concrete form of material objects such as ancestral masks, trumpets, flutes or bullroarers[296], raffia skirts, wooden or stone artefacts with special powers, a ritual hut or sacred bags. According to the stories, originally such objects or power symbols were women's property; women had conceived, invented and made them. Sometimes the secret is not even a tangible object, but consists of a ritual or sacred songs. In some cases, the secret makes direct reference to the tyrannical power of women, cleverly overhauled by brave men after much male suffering, as we saw in the Gikuyu story from Kenya in which the men gained power by making all the women pregnant at the same time.

The Wulamba origin myth of the Australian Aboriginals tells of a similar theft in the Dreamtime, the time when the Djanggawul—the first ancestors—a brother and two sisters, are travelling together through the otherwise uninhabited land. On the way, lots of offspring constantly come forth from the wombs of the

296. An ancient ritual wind instrument dating back to the Paleolithic period for communicating over great distances. It has been found in Europe, Asia, the Indian sub-continent, Africa, the Americas, and Australia: https://en.wikipedia.org/wiki/Bullroarer.

exceptionally fertile sisters, and it is the brother who takes care of laying these babies down on the grass: children born in each place are the first ancestors of the clans living there ever since.

No further news follows about female descendants, as the story focuses on a group of sons born from the wombs of the two sisters, joining their primal ancestor the Djanggawul brother. As men among each other, they complain about having 'nothing', not even symbols of their own, whereas the women have 'everything'. That is why they decide to take the *ngainmara* (folded mats representing the womb), containing the *rangga* (sacral poles, symbols of the penis). One day, in search of food, the two sisters leave these mighty symbols of their unstinting fertility and creativity unattended in the camp, and the brother and his companions swoop in to steal them.

When the women discover the theft, they run to the place where their brother is sitting with the other men. As soon as they see the women coming, the men begin to sing the sacred songs. Doing so, they prove that from now on, by stealing the fertility symbols, they have also taken from the sisters the authority to execute the sacred ritual that had been exclusively female. The younger sister anxiously wonders what to do now that they have lost their sacred symbols and power, but according to the older sister, this was not disastrous at all:

> We know everything. We have really lost nothing, for we remember it all, and we can let them have that small part. For aren't we still sacred, even if we have lost the bags? Haven't we still our uteri? And the younger Sister agreed with her.[297]

297. This is a concise summary of the long and detailed Aboriginal story transcribed in Ronald M. Berndt, *Djanggawul: An Aboriginal Religious Cult of North-Eastern Arnhem Land*, 1952; the text is on pp.40-41; the image on p.25.

This comment reveals what it's all about: life-giving power. They certainly haven't lost it, but the symbolic theft marks an essential reversal in male/female relationships as well as in the division of labour. The men had always collected the food for the women and ground the nuts to knead bread. They had also taken care of the children, but from now on all this became women's work. Significantly, the reversal of roles was only possible due to the theft of the sacred power that from that point on belongs to the men. And there is more.

A crucial detail in the story is that the brother 'takes over' the bodies of the two sisters by considerably shortening their clitorises. Traditionally, the brother had an exceptionally long penis, while the sisters had no less spectacularly elongated clitorises. Like their brother with his penis, the sisters also left traces of their remarkable genitals in the sand wherever they walked.

From that moment on things radically change. The brother first cuts off the elder sister's clitoris until there is only a small piece left that does not extend beyond her thigh. Then he applies the same surgical intervention to the body of the younger sister:

> 'Ah,' said the Brother, 'Now you look more like proper women and it is easier for me to see the slit of your vulvae. Let me try them out.' First he copulated with the younger Sister. 'That feels nice,' he said. Then, turning to the elder Sister, he copulated with her too. 'That's very enjoyable,' he told her. 'I can feel the short end of the clitoris touching my penis, as I couldn't before.'[298]

The story does not report whether the women with their truncated clitorises appreciated or enjoyed the brother's performances. The brother argues that from now on the women have nothing to hide

298. Ibid.

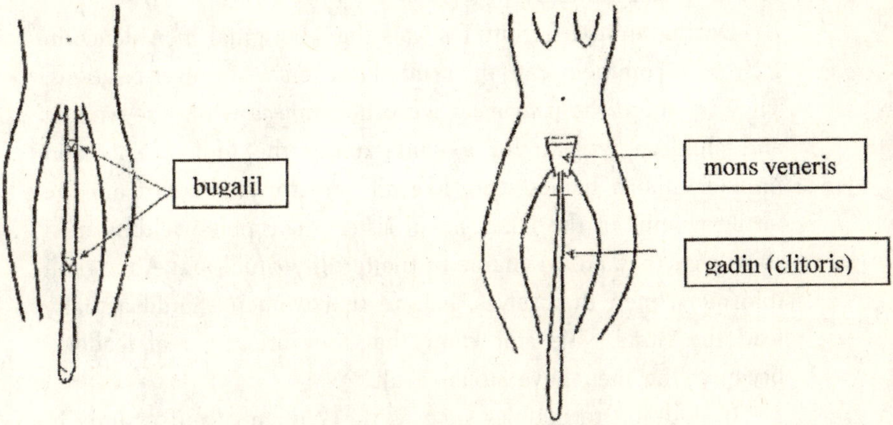

The impressive genitals of the Djanggawul brother and elder sister.
Drawings by Aboriginal informants, c. 1950.

anymore and the man has free access to the vulva. Interestingly, the long clitorises cut off by the brother were the equivalent of and looked exactly like the poles (symbolising the phallus) in the sacred bags or mats, and are now lost forever to women. This robs the women of their 'masculinity'—according to the reasoning that a woman with a clitoris is a woman with a phallus. The Djanggawul brother still has his own long penis: en route he swings it over his shoulder and wraps it around his neck, just as before. The Wulamba story seems to confirm a new status quo, but appearances deceive, as fear has not been overcome:

> In the myth the women catch fish by sitting in the water with their legs spread apart and by catching their victims in this unmistakable trap [...]. In daily life a copulating woman is referred to as the one catching a fish. A similar symbol is the whale, from whose mouth a small fish barely escapes.

Such references are reminiscent of the frightful devouring mother or the '*vagina dentata*'.[299]

During annual fertility festivals the Aboriginal men dance in a circle to commemorate the symbolic reversal of power relations. They bombard the *ngainmara* with their *rangga* while the women and children wriggle for a while under the folded mats and imitate unborn babies who, like all ancestors, emerge from the fertile wombs of the Djanggawul sisters. The pole-wielding men show that they are in charge of the fertility ritual, but Aboriginal informers, men themselves, believe that women should actually lead the ritual: 'We still know that they are the real leaders,' because 'the men have stolen it all.'[300]

In addition to peoples such as the Wulamba and Aranda in Australia, the theme of stolen sacred objects also occurs in West Africa, Papua New Guinea and in Central and South America. The myths share common topics and ultimately the message below, summarised from South American myths, amounts to the same result everywhere:

> First, the sacred objects belonging to men (masks, trumpets, ritual lodges, songs, and the like) originally were invented by women and owned by them; or, if they originated with the men, their secrets were discovered by women, who contaminated their sacredness by viewing or touching them [...] Spying on the sacred instruments was a death warrant for all violators of the prohibition.
>
> A second theme running through these myths is that a position of authority adheres to the possessors of tribal secrets, and that those who sit in authority, whether females or males, may also enjoy a life of relative leisure.

---

299. Sierksma 1979:180. My translation.

300. See Berndt: 2-3 and 40.

> The trumpets and lodges are the badge of this authority, permitting one sex to dominate the other. However begun, the myths invariably conclude with the men in power. Either the men have taken from the women the symbols of authority and have installed themselves as the rightful owners of the ceremony and its paraphernalia, or they invoke violent sanctions against the women whom have dared to challenge male authority. In no version do the women win the battle for power. Instead, they remain for ever the subjects of male terrorism, hidden in their huts, fearing to look out on masked spirits and trumpeting ancestors.[301]

In many cultures, children and women were instilled with paranoid fear, believing that the sight of these power symbols was deadly. Men who wear ancestor masks represent the powerful spirits of those ancestors. It is only at their initiation that boys are taught that these dancing spirits are ordinary men.

In his novel *Things Fall Apart*, the Nigerian writer Chinua Achebe refers to this traditional ritual in his own Igbo society, where the masked dancers are called *egwugwu*:

> The drums sounded again and a flute blew. The *egwugwu* house was now a pandemonium of quavering voices [filling] the air as the spirits of the ancestors, just emerged from the earth, greeted themselves in their esoteric language. The *egwugwu* house into which they emerged faced the Forest, away from the crowd [...]
>
> And then the *egwugwu* appeared. The women and children sent up a great shout and took to their heels. It was instinctive. A woman fled as soon as an *egwugwu*

301. Bamberger quoted in Weigle: 281.

> came in sight. And when, as on that day, nine of the greatest masked spirits in the clan came out together. It was a terrifying spectacle.[302]

Sometimes the men's protection of their secret knowledge against female outsiders takes excessive forms. In *Le Cru et le Cuit*, Lévi-Strauss describes a horrific Chamacoco story (Paraguay/Brazil) in which, unexpectedly, the secret of the mask-wearing men falls back into the hands of women. The Chamacoco woman who finds out the mighty secret is a mother who had shortly before been raped by her own son:

> A young man was laying sick in his hammock when he briefly saw his mother's vulva. She had climbed the roof of the cabin to fix the covering. Desire flashing into him, he waited until she came down again and raped her.[303]

Right after the rape, the son has a moment of weakness that the mother aptly makes use of by stealing the secret of the masks—knowledge taboo to women, and meant to be told among men only: 'Since the myth itself contained the secret of the masks, to share it with the opposite sex would have endangered the male-dominated society that men evidently felt to be always on the brink of collapse.' [304]

As soon as the men realise that this mother knows their secret and has also shared it with the other women, they are so deeply shocked that there seems to be no other solution than to kill all women. One woman succeeds in escaping the slaughter, but that is of course not the end of the story.

One day, the only surviving woman attracts the attention of a man walking under the tree in which she's hiding. The man

302. Achebe: 62-63.

303. In Lévi-Strauss, *Le Cru et le Cuit*, 1964:120.

304. Bierhorst, 2002:137.

gets such an erection that he is unable to climb up to her and the other men rushing in fail as well. Eventually, they catch the woman, rape her and cut her into pieces that end up soaked in the sperm under the tree. All the men choose a piece of that seed-soaked flesh and take it back to the village, each of them puts it inside his own home. Then they leave again to go fishing together. On their return, they find that a complete woman has sprouted from each body part of the murdered and sliced-up woman—the breasts, abdomen and thighs have turned into fat women, while the thin ones remind us that they had once been fingers and toes.

This is how new life originated from the last surviving life-producing woman even after she had been killed, the only one left who knew the men's secret and thereby caused terrifying panic. The story is directly inspired by and connected with the oldest agriculture. A multitude of new lives is being created by cutting up the dead body into pieces, in exactly the same way as women divided their tubers and tucked them into the ground to grow new crops.

Breadwinners

Hunting is older than agriculture, and the usual division of labour was that men hunted and women gathered food. The first steps towards growing crops was something unprecedented. The discovery that by sowing seeds close to home, placing banana cuttings and tubers into the ground, you can grow new banana trees and yield new tubers, was a real milestone in cultural history. Sierksma and others consider agriculture as women's invention. Or, in the words of an Indian informant in the Orinoco area: 'The women who give birth to the children also know best how the plants can be multiplied.'[305]

---

305. Sierksma 1962:144.

As men often returned from the hunt empty-handed, the women took care of the larger share of the food supply via the proceeds from their own piece of land, and relationships between the sexes changed:

> The invention of agriculture meant the emancipation of women, and men in these old equatorial cultures found it as difficult to cope with as their twentieth-century peers. Hence, in areas around the equator, agriculture began to become more important than hunting, and men sometimes resented women who had crushed their sense of indispensability.[306]

Hunters who had felt superior as breadwinners in households and communities that until then had depended solely or mainly on them, must have experienced the food input of women as threatening. This led to the establishment of male-only secret societies as a psychologically indispensable counter-offensive to restore superiority. With a prestigious secret, the men could renew their assumed right to authority and all the privileges derived from it, enabling them to get women and children to do unpleasant work for them.

Sooner or later in all story variants, men succeed in stealing women's secrets. By retelling the myth that there was chaos before men were in charge, existing power relationships were confirmed again and again. Thanks to their binding function, many myths magnified the differences between the sexes and accordingly invented rules in which all tasks were hierarchically divided by gender, age and class.

During their initiation, boys, strongly influenced by their mothers and other women in the community in childhood, received

306. Ibid. 145.

the news that female influence and authority must no longer play a role in their lives. Among the Selknam in Tierra del Fuego, boys were even told during their initiation that they should never let their wives share in their intimate thoughts, 'for if you do, they might regain the power they had in the past.'[307] To be a man, boys had to break free from the shackles of maternal care and learn not to be women.

One of the ways to deal with that confusing change in adolescence was to develop toughness and a contemptuous attitude toward women. The need to verbally 'destroy' women is strikingly visible in popular wisdom. To counter it, a Spanish proverb warns: 'When you talk about women, think of your mother.' And several studies show that this problem decreases or even disappears when men play a more active role in the early stages of their sons' lives.[308]

Several scholars explain aggression and dominance among men as a psychodynamic reaction to male awareness of female power. The institutional arrangements that embody male dominance and the cultural justification of it are not only confirmed by creation and origin myths, but also by popular culture in general and the many contemptuous proverbs about threatening female power. Of course, the impact of continuous negative messages over the centuries has been enormous. Their echoes still resound all over the world, and a majority of contemporary women still believe that a woman is unfit for a leadership position.

Why the male need for stories securing secrets and power from women, and why the long-standing tendency to exclude

---

307. Bierhorst: 162.

308. J. and B. Whiting, *Children of Six Cultures: A Psycho-Cultural Analysis*, 1979:193; Peggy Reeves Sanday, *Female Power and Male Dominance*; Jean Stockard and Miriam M. Johnson, 1979:210.

women from the public space? The argument in the Wulamba myth was that women had 'everything'. What they meant was that in addition to their 'small penis', they had wombs producing all human offspring. That imbalance, experienced as a great injustice, had to be made up for by ruling out female performance in any other domain. Their own 'lack' has encouraged men to curb the power of women via authoritative myths and stories, scholarly theories, comments, religious regulations, jokes and social taboos, decrying 'undesirable' female qualities, and making male performances appear superior by any means.

From leading to lagging behind

A Chukchi myth clearly manifests male unease about the inequality of creation capacity. The male creator, Raven, sees his wife first swell and then give birth to two children she calls people, and she seems intensely satisfied in a strange way. Her life-giving activity upsets him so much he feels a deep urge to create something himself, all the more since his wife presses him to produce a place on which their children can live. Raven gravely doubts he will be able to do so and the children laugh at him. In the end he solves his problem by shitting and peeing with all his might until his body is completely wasted. And that's how mountains and valleys, rivers, oceans and lakes came into being—a world fit for the first humans.[309]

Origin myths develop from prevailing interests. The creative mother goddess, once presented as an autonomous life-creating body, gradually disappeared from view almost everywhere, and in the monotheistic religions was replaced as the creator of all life by an autonomous, masculine god.

---

309. In his essay, 'Earth Diver: Creation of the Mythopoeic Male', Alan Dundes refers to the ideas of Erich Fromm and other psychoanalysts, 1980:279.

Wouldn't life have been a lot more manageable for a man if he were in control of all reproduction? All kinds of stories ponder this—often between the lines—but some writers openly admit this need for control. In ancient Greek philosophy, the idea of the innate inferiority of women was so common that the Greek poet and thinker Hesiod (mid-eighth century BC) called the 'race of women...an evil to mortal men, with a nature to do evil.' He found it extremely regrettable that a man could not reproduce his own kind without a woman's intervention.[310]

The fact that women give birth to sons and daughters can be read as a variation on the principle identified by historian Jan Romein as an 'inhibiting lead'.[311] Female ownership of procreation encouraged men to go beyond birth-giving capacity in as many other areas as possible—economics, politics, science, art and culture, to name a few. Exclusion of women in all these areas has been perpetuated through the ages. Partly thanks to the unwavering cement of myths, a world order was created that raised one gender above the other out of an immense need for compensation.

Despite being held back, women sometimes exercised more power than they thought possible—small-scale power as mothers or wives or mistresses, with men as unwilling prey or defenceless victims. But male fear of female power always pops up in popular culture, as a contemporary joke demonstrates:

> After death, men must knock at one of the two heavenly gates intended for them. One gate is for men who have been oppressed by women in their lifetime, and the other for those who haven't. Saint Peter inspects the newly arrived. He first peeps through a crack in one gate where a huge

310. Hesiod 7-9 and Semonides in Lloyd/Jones, Hugh. *Females of the Species*, 1975:18ff.

311. Jan Romein in *De dialektiek van de vooruitgang*, 1937:9-64.

line of men is patiently waiting, all of whom have been oppressed by their wives. Peter closes the door and takes a look at the other gate, where just one scraggy man is patiently standing and waiting.

'Hey, what are you doing here?' Peter asks, somewhat amazed.

His head lowered in embarrassment, the man whispers: 'Right before I died, my wife ordered me to line up in this queue.'

Suit Supply 'Toy Boys' advertising poster at a tram stop in Amsterdam, 2016.

11. WHO DOES PUBLIC SPACE BELONG TO?

> Men act and women appear. Men look at women. Women watch themselves being looked at. This determines not only most relations between men and women but also the relation of women to themselves. The surveyor of woman in herself is male: the surveyed female. Thus she turns herself into an object—and most particularly an object of vision: a sight.
>
> John Berger, *Ways of Seeing* (1972)

A poster at a tram stop—a dark woman with closed eyes wearing only a tight-fitting light green corset below the breasts. Two miniature, clothed men slide down her uncovered hills. In other posters from the same advertising series, a woman has one well-shaped breast hanging from a light blue dress to please a man in a tailored suit beside her; or the well-dressed man is in the foreground, in front of a woman with bare torso. In the entire series, the men are carefully dressed and the women, more or less undressed. Sometimes the man is dressed in outdoor gear and reading a book on the couch while a woman in a girdle, one stocking left on, nestles against him. Imagine that: you are happily reading dressed in an attractive suit and you get to look at a near-naked woman as a bonus. Suit Supply company founder

Fokke De Jong defended the campaign against accusations of sexism, telling Buzzfeed: 'Sexism implies inequality, if you want to read any form of sexism in here than it has to be towards the men. They obviously do not have the upper hand here.'[312] The vast majority on social media disagreed—which in truth was probably part of the plan. Variants of such images have become commonplace in the public arena; if their effects on sales were less profitable, we wouldn't see so many of them.

Hello Boys

Like mushrooms in autumn, websites about breasts appear out of nowhere. They teach women sexy tricks or give well-meaning advice. They tell less-endowed women to eat lots of

Eve Seduces Adam by Bernard Salomon, 1561.
Museum of Printing and Graphic Communication, Lyon.

312. https://www.thedrum.com/news/2016/02/25/suit-supply-toy-boys-campaign-accused-being-sexist-towards-women-founder-argues

fruit: strawberries, pomegranates and bananas are all supposed to contain booby benefits. Breasts themselves are depicted as fruits, from peaches and apples to watermelons. In the creation stories of Judaism, Christianity and Islam, the forbidden fruit with which Eve seduced Adam, has always been linked to her seductive breasts. A sixteenth-century Bible illustration depicts Eve offering Adam the apple with her right hand and a breast with her left.

Associating breasts with puddings or cakes is no less popular. In the French film *La Grande Bouffe* (1973), actor Philippe Noiret plays the role of a magistrate dying in the arms of a voluptuous actress while eating a breast-shaped pudding. In contemporary Japan, the breast is touted as a delicious dessert: two pale mound-shaped puddings at chest height of a young girl on the package attract attention; they are packed separately in hard plastic, each with a pink dot in the middle. Above left is the message: 'Eat lovingly' and on the right, a warning: 'The cup is fragile, so be careful.'[313]

Japanese supermarket breast-shaped dessert, 2017.

313. https://weirdasianews.com/2006/12/07/japanese-breast-pudding-yummy/.

In the twentieth century, sexy adverts grew into a global business. Advertisers unceasingly present women as attractive objects. Until Covid-19 caused a slight slump, global advertising grew to an astounding $649 billion a year by 2020, and is predicted to resume its growth anytime soon.[314] It would be fascinating to discover just how much of that output might be seen as objectifying women. Sexy images and slogans are so suggestive and repeated so often that it is hard not to believe in this universal fake reality. The makers of the Wonderbra made a worldwide splash in 1994 with their eye-popping 'Hello Boys' poster campaign that launched model Eva Herzigova's cleavage onto an unsuspecting public. They returned to it twenty-four years later with an 'empowering' twist using the slogan, 'Hello Me'. 'The campaign is aimed to celebrate an era of empowered women; women who decide by themselves and for themselves, women who derive their sexuality from inner confidence. Women who want to feel sexy for themselves, when they want to,' said senior product manager Olivia Capalléra. To illustrate this new-found freedom, they photographed a model in their top-selling skimpy, strapless underwear and supersized her on poster sites tagging the nearest convenient retail outlets.[315]

The advertising industry is trapping women between old rules about chastity and new (but no less demanding) beauty requirements. Among our foremothers, breasts hung bare and carefree as simple food sources for babies, but now glossy magazines, websites and social media apps focus on sexy breasts as erotic objects to draw public attention.

Just like noses, mouths, legs, feet or penises, breasts, bellies and vulvas exist in all shapes and sizes, but the standards of

---

314. https://www.statista.com/topics/990/global-advertising-market/.

315. https://www.lbbonline.com/news/wonderbras-iconic-hello-boys-AD-returns-with-a-twist.

society favour a particular variety. Surf the websites of cosmetic surgeons, and positive comments fly in from all sides: 'I LOVE LOVE LOVE my new natural-looking breasts...Go for it!' Another woman explains that all her life she had wanted breast enlargement, because without it, she was incomplete: 'I am so happy that I have finally found my real self!'

A student who had her vulva trimmed is also happy. After much pleading and begging, her mother, a nurse herself, agreed to pay for the operation—having spent several years doing her best to convince her daughter she looked perfectly normal and would overcome her uncertainty. For weeks before the operation, the girl was in suspense: even though she has to study for exams and write various papers, all that seems so unimportant compared to her labiaplasty. The fear of not meeting the fictive standards of society had grown so large it dwarfed the importance of her school diploma.

Many young women ruin their self-esteem by taking images produced for pornography as prescriptive, unaware that these adolescent-looking, near-uniform vulvas have been digitally manipulated to meet the industry's requirements.

Evolutionary psychologists confirm that men are attracted to young and physically attractive women with symmetrical features—'flawless and youthful skin, full lips, shiny hair, white teeth, graceful step and firm breasts'—these features being interpreted as signs of fertility. Women began responding to those signals with corresponding beautification—and still do.[316]

What expectations does a social order create that mainly emphasises the differences between girls and boys and insists that girls should be beautiful and accommodating and not tough, hard and ambitious like men? For men, the same message means that

316. Vandermassen: 166.

they must suppress alleged female characteristics or behaviours so as not to be dismissed as 'wimps' or 'sissies'.

Freud interpreted female desires for glittering jewellery, an attractive cleavage and seductive make-up as signs of overdeveloped narcissism. In most cultures men used to decorate their bodies as well, but ever since the French Revolution they aspired, first in the Western world and gradually in other places, to a high level of uniformity. The interest in frills and finery they used to share with women has given way to more uniform clothing promoting professional achievements, social benefits and being a valued member of society instead of vain idleness.[317]

Advertising images add further fuel to the fear of not fitting in. Men too are converted to the belief that appearance is everything, but up to now, it has mainly brainwashed women into believing that appearance determines happiness in all areas of life.

Terror of the outside

The perception that their body does not meet the 'ideal' form and norm makes women work harder on their appearance than ever. They spend more money on clothes and make-up, and force their bodies into the corset of fashion.

Mothers are indoctrinated by nightmares about ageing and train their daughters in how to look sexy and apply seductive make-up at a younger and younger age. In children's beauty contests, girls are pitched against each other as miniature femmes fatales in teeny bikinis. Make-up and anti-wrinkle creams are already available for ages eight to twelve and a number of girls believe that growing up means growing old and ugly.[318]

---

317. More in *Naked or Covered*, Chapter 8.

318. Mona Chollet, *Beauté fatale. Les nouveaux visages d'une aliénation féminine*, 2015:43.

How 'natural' female appearance really is in Western societies depends on the context and situation:

> ['Natural' features] are best tolerated in periods when the distribution of gender roles is most self-evident: the women at home, the men outside. The very conservative [European] 1950s still loved plump creatures. Conversely, when women venture into traditionally masculine territories and occupy a larger place in social life, it seems as if they have to make up for the resulting imbalance by reducing the place that their bodies occupy in that very space.[319]

Since the motherly, nourishing female body has through the ages mainly been associated with or imprisoned in the home environment, it looks as if women felt they needed a different type of body to escape from the bonds of history—by adjusting into a body that could no longer be associated with their envy-evoking ability to reproduce. It seems the message going around was that you had to renounce the maternal plump body by looking 'like a boy with small breasts,' in the words of a psychiatrist specialising in eating disorders. Some agencies warn a young model starting to develop hips and breasts to beware: 'you are becoming a woman'—a development to be avoided at all costs. Instead, better to torture yourself with dangerous and sometimes deadly diets and medicines.

Contemporary stories about bone-thin girls show a new variant of unconditional female submission to a condition of being looked at and acted upon instead of looking and acting in the world by themselves.[320]

Looking back through history, one wonders whether there is

---

319. Ibid. 148, referring to Susan Bordo's *Unbearable Weight*.

320. Ibid. 149.

nothing new under the sun. The ideal contours of contemporary female models, stimulating anorexia, are reminiscent of the ascetic practices to which exemplary girls and women in the first centuries of Christianity surrendered to gain respect. At the time, fasting was highly recommended to promote chastity, but women took refusing food as a new way to boost their low-value status.

Some went so far that their breasts shrivelled and menstruation stopped. By wiping out their feminine forms, they became physically more like men, vainly deluding themselves that they would finally be treated as equals in society, as fourth-century bishop and theologian Basil of Ancyra had promised:

> Although clothed in a female body, they have by means of asceticism beaten off the shape engendered from it for the sake of the soul, and have made themselves appear like men through excellence, just as their souls have been created equal. And just as men, through asceticism, pass from men to the rank of angels, so also these women, through asceticism, pass from women to the same rank as theirs.[321]

However, to prevent misunderstandings, the bishop immediately added that equality in earthly life held only for the soul, but in the afterlife both sexes would become 'equal in all ways'. The desperate perspective of anorexia sufferers reminds us of the impossible efforts of their ascetic predecessors. The message is irrevocable: you may try your best to lose your female shape and appearance and functions out of self-loathing, but you will remain a second-class citizen as long as you are trapped in a female body. Medieval ascetic women—some have even been sanctified—served as an example to ordinary women who continued to eat and to

321. Quoted in Theresa Shaw: 237.

bleed when they were not pregnant. Just like in contemporary advertisements, the promoted image of extremely thin ascetic girls without female qualities went hand in hand with negative images of women in society.[322] Does it mean that inside medieval women there was already a little male surveyor watching them?

What advertising today considers desirable or valuable for women primarily deals with their appearance: 'Everyone just wants to be beautiful, don't you think?' says Sofie (who does not want her surname in the newspaper). 'On your mobile phone, on your computer, on Instagram, on Facebook: all models and fit girls with perfect bodies and faces. In the end, you do want to be one of them.'[323]

And you can trust that men will always react 'naturally' to such a sight of perfection: 'I just start kissing them. It's like a magnet. Just kiss. I don't even wait. And when you're a star, they let you do it. You can do anything. Grab 'em by the pussy. You can do anything,' claimed a candid Donald Trump in the years before he was elected President of the United States.[324]

The English poet Frieda Hughes breaks the vicious circle with a poem about the perfect silicone breasts, the possessor of which does not have to utter a word, because everyone instantly understands their wordless language. Until, in the last stanza of the poem, she takes decisive action:

When at last she made the photo shoot,
She gently placed her breasts
Of shiny plastic flesh

---

322. Ibid. More extensive information about negativity towards women's appearance in the Western tradition in Umberto Eco's *History of Ugliness*, Chapter 4.

323. NRC *Handelsblad*, 10-11 September 2016.

324. *The Washington Post*, 7 October 2016.

Upon the table for
The cameraman,
And left.[325]

Bare breasts in a globalised world

From an international conference on the consequences of globalisation in 2000 in Dar es Salaam, two striking statements by Africans have stayed with me. One was: 'Globalisation is like a medicine: taking too much, you get sick, take too little, you'll die.' The other portrayed the immense power of advertising in a grim simile: 'Globalisation is like rape—you can do nothing about it, so it's best to lean back and enjoy.'

Since the twentieth century, information, products and images have been moving around the world at lightning speed. Western commercial messages have an impact worldwide, and the same applies to images of breasts. Less than a century ago, men and women in tropical areas usually walked around naked. Bare breasts were for nursing babies, and that is what the women did without embarrassing anyone—in the market, while working the land or anywhere on the road. Even in regions where breasts were mostly covered because of the cold, children were raised for centuries with the image of mothers with babies on the breast.

Today, ever more working women switch to bottle-feeding when their maternity leave expires, while women breastfeeding their babies in the public space increasingly experience disapproving glances or are made to feel embarrassed in societies where breastfeeding used to be perfectly normal. Erotic advertising images have affected the naturalness of the nourishing breast, not only in the Western world. They spread confusion and reinforce

325. Frieda Hughes, 'Breasts', from the collection *Stonepicker*, 2001. https://www.poetryinternationalweb.net/pi/site/poem/item/555.

the one-sided way in which men now look at women and women at themselves.

On the internet, breastfeeding mothers report their own mixed feelings and other people's, from complaining customers in a restaurant to staring fellow travellers on public transport, reactions varying from annoyance to disapproval or even an outright suckling ban. Comments on breastfeeding and the resulting embarrassment among mothers can be found everywhere.

In 2014, Louise Burns discreetly fed her twelve-week-old baby in the dining room of five-star London hotel Claridge's. The floor manager immediately came up to her to ask her to cover her bosom with a napkin. When Louise posted equally modest before-and-after pictures on Facebook, activist mothers descended on the hotel to stage a public breastfeed protest next to the entrance.[326]

Until recently, breastfeeding was an everyday phenomenon in China. An American researcher wrote in 2000:

> From my research in China, it's very clear that the breast is much less sexualised there than it is in American culture [...]. It's neither hidden nor revealed in any particular way in women's dress or undergarments. In many villages, women sit in the sun with their breasts exposed, and older women will be out washing clothes with their breasts exposed, and it's all completely irrelevant to erotic arousal.[327]

This sounds idyllic, but in contemporary Asia, times are undeniably changing. A Chinese woman who was recently feeding her baby on a crowded train was photographed by a fellow passenger and scandalised on Weibo, the Chinese version of Twitter, with the text: 'Let me remind you that this is the Beijing metro and not

326. https://www.bbc.co.uk/news/uk-england-london-30359606.

327. Emily Martin, in Angier: 139.

the bus that runs through your village.' The photo went viral and sparked a furious debate about breastfeeding. Many rejected the mother's behaviour, because she had openly shown her 'sexual organs'. Others defended her and considered it a shame that this intimate photo had been shared on the internet without her permission, among them a doctor who was also a mother: 'Breasts are not sexual organs and babies need to be fed when they are hungry. She is a great mother.' Apparently Chinese citizens find the sight of a baby on the mother's breast in public just as embarrassing as many contemporary Westerners.

Africa is changing as rapidly as China. In Nigeria, a young mother, afraid of breastfeeding her baby while using public transport, ended up in an embarrassing situation when she kept pretending nothing was the matter, however much her baby cried.'Put the baby on the breast or the breast on the baby'—meaning you can solve a problem in more than one way—is a popular Yoruba proverb. Male passengers loudly addressed the young woman, accusing her of being cruel and insensitive. One of them scornfully yelled: 'Why are you trying to deny this child what is naturally his?' And an old man openly wondered: 'What is in your breast that no eyes have seen? I beg you, breastfeed that child!' Only after much pressure did the woman reluctantly give in.[328] Why was she so unwilling to suckle her baby in public? According to the article in the *Vanguard*, this new development is due to advertisers of imported baby milk and the spreading of erotic breast images making educated women refuse their babies their 'natural right'. In all human memory breastfeeding was nothing to be embarrassed about. But the nourishing and seductive functions of breasts have got in each other's way to

328. https://www.vanguardngr.com/2011/08/exclusive-breast-feeding-whither-nigeria-in-the-campaign/.

the point where it's unclear whether one is acceptable in public, or neither.

India is a huge country, and many Indian mothers confirm that breastfeeding is prevalent and not an issue for discussion. Others complain about lurking men who make breastfeeding women feel embarrassed. Here, as in China, there is a great difference between modern city women and village women who routinely take out a breast to feed a child wherever as soon as it cries. In urbanised areas, upper-class mothers and women with higher education no longer breastfeed in public.[329]

An Afghan doctor writes that in his country breastfeeding is difficult because Islam demands that women completely cover their bodies, even though in Islamic countries discreet public breastfeeding is permitted. In Iran, headscarves are required, but mothers, with part of the chador over their torso and baby, do breastfeed in the streets and on public transport: 'Over here it is not considered a sexual act,' I was told in Tehran, 'but in public, young women are doing it less and less.'

In countries where breastfeeding in public is prohibited, such as Saudi Arabia and the Gulf States, male control over their own desires visibly escalates. An Indian man shares his experience in the region:

> I was travelling to Dubai on a flight. My baby was being breastfed at the time. My wife was hesitant, but upon seeing the baby crying she started breastfeeding. I covered her and the baby with a newspaper. The guy in the other row

---

329. With the exceptions of the observations in Nigeria and Iran, the citations and commentaries in this paragraph on breastfeeding come from https://www.007b.com/public-breastfeeding-world.php. This rich and comforting website shows breasts of every kind to make clear that breasts are completely normal body parts and meant to feed babies.

> was staring like an animal. I wondered how this person could stare so recklessly at a woman who is feeding a baby. I was very angry and at the peak of losing control, I wanted to punch him. But keeping control of myself, I just wondered if someone stared at his own wife's breasts when feeding their baby, what would be his reaction? These guys have to grow up![330]

By contrast, a Saudi from Jeddah is full of empathy for the staring man:

> If a woman feeds her baby and the people are seeing her, of course they like to see her breast more and more and maybe they become hot and like to do sex with that lady who is feeding. And I think it is not good that any lady feed her babies in public places. If she wants, yes, she can move to the place where no one can see her.[331]

What would this chap make of the Icelandic member of parliament breastfeeding her six-week-old daughter in parliament, when she was unexpectedly called forward to elaborate on a proposal she had submitted earlier? The child kept on drinking while the mother gave the requested explanation. Nobody blinked. In Brazil, minister Manuela d'Ávila breastfed her baby in the National Assembly, and in Australia, the House of Representatives recently changed the house rules so that breastfeeding and bottle-feeding, previously not permitted, are now allowed.

Activists continue to claim the right to breastfeed in public. In Hong Kong, a hundred young mothers protested against the increasing intolerance by feeding their babies in public in a

330. https://www.007b.com/public-breastfeeding-world.php#asia; https://www.facebook.com/groups/breastfeeding.muslim.mothers.

331. Ibid.

flash mob. That same weekend in the United States, a group of female soldiers gathered in front of the Jefferson Monument in Washington, D.C. dressed in army uniform, breastfeeding their babies to call attention to the position of young mothers in the army.[332]

The narrow-minded fixation on the erotic function of the breast continues to confuse young mothers. The best advice is to just shrug, and remind yourself of the words of one breastfeeding mother: 'Women who go out to a nightclub show more of their breasts than a mother breastfeeding.'

Are women more respected in societies where the breast is seen as a powerful symbol of nurturing and loving care than in societies where the breast is only seen as an erotic object, asks Margaret Miles, author of *A Complex Delight*.[333] A relevant question in an age where breasts in advertising automatically land in the brain folder of eroticism and sex. No one thinks of a nurturing mother when a woman pops a breast out of her elegant dress in an advert or a tabloid snap. However, going back in time, one does find early examples of that same seduction device. For example, in the Church of the Holy Sepulchre of Barletta in southern Italy, where an early medieval mural shows three beautiful women doing their utmost to seduce Saint Anthony by each offering him an attractive right breast. Having courageously resisted temptation, he was rewarded with sanctification. Back then Satan exploited the female appearance with all his might to seduce believers, and nowadays it's the media. Nothing new, except for the global scale.

---

332. https://www.vogue.com/13435454/breastfeeding-public-womens-rights-hong-kong-flash-mob-jefferson-memorial-active-duty/?mbid=social-facebook.

333. Miles: Afterword.

The way to the top

As long as women merge with their appearance, science will remain more associated with men than with women. The importance of knowledge and learning has always been highly appreciated everywhere. Knowledge is power, knowledge is wealth, knowledge means prestige and privilege, according to worldwide traditional wisdom:

> Knowledge is the enemy of ignorance. (English)
> Knowledge is a treasure following its owner. (Chinese)
> Knowledge is better than goods. (Arabic)
> Knowledge is a treasure that cannot be stolen. (Filipino)
> Not knowing is bad, not wanting to know is worse. (Wolof).

Men took that glowing recommendation to heart, while keeping this fervently desired knowledge from women, claiming this was to protect their virtue:

> The glory of man is knowledge, the glory of woman is to renounce it. (Portuguese, Brazil)
> Men should set knowledge before virtue, women virtue before knowledge. (German)
> Virtuous is a woman without knowledge. (Chinese, Taiwan)

To reinforce the differences between the sexes, two by-now familiar tactics were called into action. On the one hand, women's brainpower was denied or scorned:

> A wise woman is twice a fool. (English)
> The women's side of the house: the side without knowledge. (Burmese)

On the other hand, society was warned about the inherent dangers of female intelligence. Even in the oldest known sources men are advised that clever and capable women were to be condemned:

> A woman's intelligence can cause a catastrophe. (Sanskrit)
> A man doesn't want a woman smarter than he is. (English)
> A dog is smarter than a woman, it does not bark at its master. (Russian)
> To educate a woman is like putting a knife in the hands of a monkey. (Hindi/Portuguese)
> A crowing hen and a woman who knows Latin never come to a good end. (German/Spanish)

Women ought to be silent in the presence of men. Showing knowledge as a woman was unusual and inappropriate, and public success was presented as an unwanted feminine feature.

Objections against university-educated women remained insurmountably high, and more often than not, they still are. If no restrictive laws existed, male researchers concluded that women were unable to perform intellectually—the fact their skull contained fewer brain cells than a man's made them unsuitable for an academic education.

The discussion intensified as more girls went to university. No argument was shunned. Some scholars openly argued that for women, study was 'unnatural'; it caused sterility and perversity. In the nineteenth century, it was suggested that a woman's ovaries would shrivel up as soon as she received higher education. (In the twentieth century, women in Saudi Arabia were told that their ovaries shrink if they drive a car, but more recently this danger seems to have been overcome). Of course, girls were also warned that by studying they would lose their chances of finding a husband. In short, a learned woman was a lost woman.

Although arguments about the inferior female brain have been outdated for over a century, some ultra-orthodox Muslim clerics cling in vain to the notion that women's bodies prevent wisdom:

> No sensible person can deny the fact that man, due to his innate capabilities, is superior to them in so many things. The poor woman passes through such periods or intervals in her life in which she is almost incapable of doing anything and has to look to others for help and cooperation. These periods are romances, pregnancy, bleeding after childbirth and suckling the baby.[334]

Arguments that do their utmost to prove that women are at an intellectual disadvantage have everything to do with the fear of losing an established order. To effectively exclude women, the common message 'keep off, keep off' was directly connected with the female body, as expressed in the Ethiopian Oromo proverb: 'Breasts that contain milk, do not contain intelligence.'

Ironic, then, that in spite of all efforts to prevent women from entering classrooms, so many universities, particularly in Europe, opt for the image of the nourishing mother as their academic emblem. In 1088, the year of its foundation, the University of Bologna was the first to choose *Alma Mater Studiorum* as its motto. Others followed. At the entrance of the Cuban University of Havana, the words 'Alma Mater' are chiselled in heavy letters beneath a colossal black marble statue of a woman with open arms and impressive breasts. Leiden University's Alma Mater has a chastely covered and inconspicuous bosom, but *Alma Mater Cantabrigia*, from 1600, presents a dynamic female figure with rounded breasts, flowing hair and wide-open arms. In her left hand she holds a sacred cup and in her right hand the sun of science spreads its shining light. She effortlessly carries Cambridge's city walls as a crown on her head.

334. Mufti Zaferruddin Miftahi, *Modesty and Chastity in Islam*, 1993:160.

Left: *Alma Mater, Havana* by Mario Karbel, 1919.
Right: *Alma Mater Cantabrigia* by John Legate, 1600.

From those breasts bursting with knowledge, for centuries only students with no breasts of their own benefitted—apart from a few notorious exceptions. In thirteenth-century Italy, Bettisia Gozzadini put on men's clothes, attended the University of Bologna and graduated more dazzlingly than all her classmates. Against all prejudices, she proved that a woman could become a lawyer. In 1296 she even taught law at her Alma Mater—but that had to be from behind a curtain, lest her beauty distract the attention of her male students.

Only since the twentieth century have European Alma Maters been widely sharing their knowledge with daughters as well as with sons. Graduates the world over still call their university their Alma Mater and themselves her *alumni*, literally meaning 'sucklings'. Much has changed for the better, but what about at the top level in science? There are still considerably more male professors than female. In 2013 The American Physical Society published an article about the harrowing discrepancy between

A girl, finally, a girl! Cartoon, late twentieth century. Origin unknown.

the number of male and female Nobel laureates in physics: 196 versus just two. The most famous female laureate is Marie Curie, to whom that honour was awarded together with her husband in 1903 for the discovery and investigation of radioactivity. After the death of her husband, she won a second Nobel Prize in 1911, for her research in chemistry. In 1910 she was nominated as a member of the French Academy of Sciences. After a heated debate, her male counter-candidate was elected; the difference was two votes and the vote had to be done over. Now it was about the admission of women, and the Academy voted against it with an overwhelming majority. Even after Marie Curie's second Nobel Prize, the Academy stayed with their decision, and only in 1979 was a woman allowed to join this illustrious club for the first time. In the UK, before 1945, the only woman in the Royal Society was a skeleton in the anatomical collection. It wasn't until 1972 that a second female physicist was awarded the Nobel

Prize in her field: Maria Goeppert Mayer who, for almost all of her active life, remained unpaid for her work.[335]

By now unfounded claims about women's feeble intellect have finally ended up on the scrapheap almost everywhere, and academic institutions are increasingly aware of how much exceptional female talent has been and is still being lost. Everyone's path to the top begins with reading and writing, and governments that encourage girls and women to get a better education make their countries more prosperous. As long as nonsensical sex-related messages about knowledge, brains and attractiveness echo, stereotyped ideas remain an obstacle for women, but more and more exceptions show that the way up is no longer impassable.

335. The only Nobel Prize category with fewer women is Economics, with one female winner—Elinor Ostrom in 2009: cf. https://www.scientificamerican.com/article/the-last-woman-to-win-a-physics-nobel/; https://en.wikipedia.org/wiki/List-of-female-Nobel-Laureates.

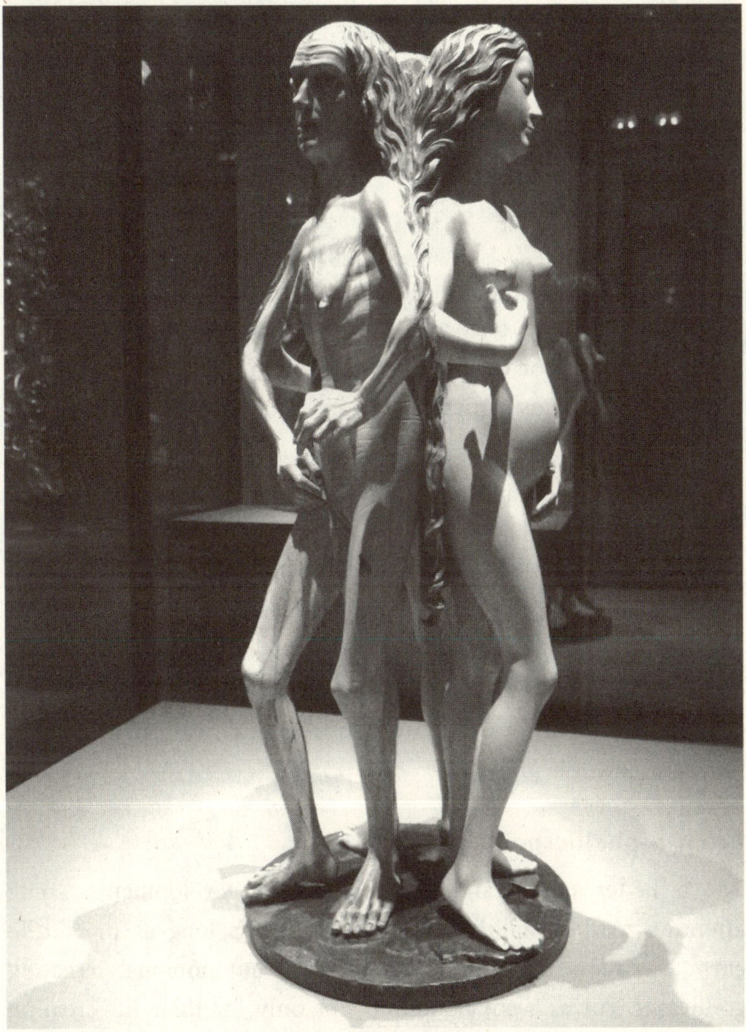

Allegory of Vanity by Michel Erhart or Jörg Syrlin the Elder.
Lime wood, Ulm, *c.* 1470-1480. Kunsthistorisches Museum, Vienna.

12. WORLD IN MOTION

> If the male organ rises up, it is an overwhelming catastrophe, for once provoked it cannot be resisted by either reason or religion. For this organ is more powerful than all the instruments used by Satan against man.[336]

Under the thin layer of contemporary society's asphalt lie the well-preserved and well-entrenched ideas of our ancestors. A search for handed-down views about body parts unique to women not only yields knowledge about past conceptions, but also valuable insights into the present, where the changing position of so many women has caused confusion on multiple fronts. We cannot change history, but we can alter our way of looking at the past and the present.

From a phallic point of view

For a better understanding of historical developments, some attention to the phallus is relevant here. As long as the fertile earth was represented by female gods or autonomously creating goddesses, vulvas were honoured not only for their life-creating powers, but also for their magical protective effect in times of calamity, as we saw in Chapter 4. It is estimated that the worship

336. Ibn Abbas, quoted in Nawal El Sadaawi, *The Hidden Face of Eve*, 1980:206ff.

of the erect penis began in the prehistoric New Stone Age (around 11,000 BC). In cultures where tributes to the penis prevailed, not only did stories circulate about penis gods, but penis images were erected—at home, in the courtyard, in temples and on the street. In myths the phallus often took on the size of an elephant's trunk, as with the Aboriginal Djanggawul (see page 160). Nor was the Egyptian God Atum, who we met in Chapter 2, poorly endowed. A bas-relief on an excavated temple wall depicts him in the acrobatic act of autofellatio, lying on his back with his feet above his head, about to take his extremely long phallus in his mouth. The Chinese emperor Zhou Xin (1105-1046 BC) had such a potent penis that he could walk around a room with a naked woman perched on his erection.[337] There is no shortage of such stories.

Nor is there a lack of images. Hindus worship phallus-shaped stones, columns or pillars representing the creative power of the god Shiva; and in Dorset, England, the Cerne Abbas Giant is a sight to behold: a 180-feet-tall limestone outline of a giant wielding a bludgeon in his right hand and an erection up to his ribs. He is so impressive that many people climb up the hill specifically to have sex on top of the phallus. Often believed to date to prehistoric or Roman times, after extensive research in May 2021, the National Trust concluded that its creation dates from the late Saxon period (700-1100 AD).[338]

Penis festivals are still celebrated in various countries. For example, a giant phallus is carried on participants' shoulders in a predominantly male parade during the annual Festival of the Steel Phallus in Japan. At the Holi Festival in Rajasthan in India

337. Maggie Paley, *The Book of the Penis*, 1999:41-44.

338. https://www.nationaltrust.org.uk/cerne-giant/news/national-trust-archaeologists-surprised-by-likely-age-of-cerne-abbas-giant

a giant phallus is carried around in honour of the local god Eloji. The crowd attending the festival mainly consists of men singing songs in praise of Eloji to stimulate their own virility. But women who want to become pregnant with a male child also venerate Eloji. This God dedicated to sex is depicted as a man with an extravagant moustache and an unnaturally long penis.[339]

Left: Cerne Abbas Giant, Dorset, England, *c.* 700-1100 AD.
Right: Archaic herm with exceptionally intact phallus, Siphnos, Greece, *c.* 520 BC.

Ancient Greek stories and images confirm the public attention the penis enjoyed. In everyday life the phallus was well represented in the streets of Athens thanks to the *herms*, named after the god Hermes: a stone base with a sculpted head, two testicles

339. More festival examples on https://www.scoopwhoop.com/Places-Where-Penis-Is-Worshipped/#.5anbkposd; https://www.newsflare.com/video/189888/entertainment-arts/devotees-take-giant-phallus-in-procession-in-india.

and an erect penis. They were found in front of private houses and marked the boundaries of public and private areas.[340] Here too men carried a giant phallus in procession, as can be seen on painted vases.

Eva Keuls defines phallocracy as a prevailing principle in which 'the human race is essentially male, the female being a mere adjunct, unfortunately required for the purpose of reproduction. The natural consequence of this notion is the elimination of the female from all social processes.'[341] She describes the power of the phallus among the ancient Greeks as a cultural system in which the penis is not represented as an organ of unification or a means of mutual pleasure, but as a weapon:

> [...] a spear or war club, and a scepter of sovereignty. In sexual terms, phallocracy takes such forms as rape, disregard of the sexual satisfaction of women, and access to the bodies of prostitutes who are literally enslaved or allowed no other means of support. In the political sphere, it spells imperialism and patriarchal behaviour in civic affairs.[342]

Greek tradition has stories about the struggle of Greek heroes against the Amazons. These warrior women—according to some their society consisted exclusively of women—were independent and bellicose. Classical images depict Greek heroes slashing and clubbing Amazons to death or chasing them away.

Occasionally, an Amazon threateningly aims her lance at the genitals of a naked Greek man such as Theseus, Athens' hero, but that is quite exceptional. Yet such scenes suggest the threat

---

340. Eva C. Keuls, *The Reign of the Phallus*, 1985:385ff.

341. Ibid. 86-87.

342. Ibid. 2.

Greek warrior in battle with an Amazon queen,
painted on an amphora, c. 500-490 BC.
Walters Art Museum, Baltimore.

of a possible defeat, says Keuls, and unmistakably reflect male fear of female rebellion, as well as the possibility of a weakening of power. Even though the phallus held sway, obsessive fear of women always persisted, and men never sat easily on the throne.[343] Is this not the thief's fear that someone will one day ransack his own house?

Again and again, we have come across this tension between power over and fear of women. Political, cultural and religious traditions still cling on to that power. Thousands of proverbs help allay male fear with stereotypical perceptions of the perfect wife. In short, she should be smaller and younger than him, as well

343. Ibid. 3ff. In her research she compared more than eight hundred images of Amazons in Greek antiquity, especially in Athens. Amazon stories belong to the large category of myths in which a country or the entire world was populated by women only.

as less talented and less educated; she should humbly look up to him, keep quiet and listen, and never contradict her husband.[344]

Insecure men still adhere to this ideal, and when they feel disappointed fear easily turns into anger, often escalating into verbal or physical violence (Chapter 9). But just put yourself in their place, history and position. As a man you have internalised belittling messages about women all your life. And you keep getting the warning that 'they' are unreliable and must be strictly controlled, because otherwise chaos breaks out. This makes it difficult to approach someone of the other sex without prejudice. If, moreover, you have been convinced for centuries that there is a ready-made person in your own sperm and that you are the one introducing it into a womb, then you are almost automatically going to believe that women contribute little or nothing to society and nothing substantial to their own pregnancy either.

The quote at the beginning of this chapter, a statement by a respected companion of the Prophet Muhammad, has often being quoted approvingly. Here Ibn Abbas reveals a formidable fear of the unpredictable behaviour of the most sensitive male body part, while the continuation of his statement, in which he directly addresses women, is no less revealing: 'That is why the Prophet, Allah's peace be upon him, said, "I have not seen creatures lacking in reason and religious commitment more able of overcoming men of reason and wisdom than you."'

As we have seen, this line of reasoning is much older than Islam, and still eagerly practised in all contexts where the belittling and marginalising of women is still the order of things.

344. Cf. *Never Marry a Woman with Big Feet*, Chapter 4.

Misconceptions about sex

Myths, religion and popular culture influence the way in which we look at ourselves and at the other sex. The fact that a man is not responsible for controlling his own drives is a perverse misunderstanding that enjoys unprecedented authority. Women have often ended up going along with that view or even claimed that they are by definition responsible for all male urges, convinced that their role in life is to be subservient to the whims of the unruly phallus.[345] An Islamic student in Egypt answered my question as to why she wore a headscarf: 'We all know that men are beasts, and that's why we need to fully cover ourselves.'

This rather grievous misconception about the male sex has become so ingrained that lack of self-control is confused with 'masculinity'. Women have to give in it, according to the reasoning: 'You caused my arousal, so you have to help get me rid of it.' A man's best remedy for arousal by a female stranger was to rush home and 'discharge the material of that excitement where it rightfully belongs, so that Satan [...] does not entangle him in sin'—advice originating from the writings of Imam Muslim (Muslim ibn al-Hajjaj, 821-875). On YouTube, ultra-orthodox preachers repeat the warning to women that their prayers will not be answered if they do not immediately oblige their husbands when they come home agitated and in need of their wives. Whether a woman has something else on her mind at such a moment is of no relevance: she must let her bread burn in the oven rather than let her husband burn with desire.[346]

This tenacious traditional reasoning is also singed into the minds of countless non-Muslim men and women who earnestly

---

345. More in *Naked or Covered*, Chapter 9: 'Religion and the History of Covering Up'.

346. https://www.youtube.com/watch?v=d55thwza8PU (in Arabic and Dutch); popular preachers such as Al-Qaradawi spread the same message.

state that men cannot help being carried away by their testosterone, as Dutch literary critic and columnist Jessica Durlacher argued in 2018 in a debate at the National Theatre in Amsterdam.[347]

A professor specialising in the philosophy of law was also inclined to sympathise with the ideas of Ibn Abbas in a column about the Weinstein affair, even though he himself is a dogmatic atheist:

> Such a situation—alone with a woman in a room—remains a temptation for many men. Their hormones may strike up, so that their will follows their desire instead of their reason. Irrevocably this will lead to unsavory things. That is why it is better to prevent something like this from happening. Hence, women were supposed to keep their distance from foreign men—that is, any man who is not a husband or brother—and if a tête-à-tête was unavoidable, to take along a trustworthy male. It seems to me that this line of thought was certainly not entirely wrong.[348]

In this way he automatically puts the solution back on to the woman's plate. Just like in the time of Ibn Abbas, it is better for women to be guided! Wouldn't it by now be more reasonable for an adult man who is afraid his hormones might play up—for example, during a thesis meeting with an attractive student—to get himself a testosterone supervisor?

The 'effects' of testosterone continue to be based more on popular opinion than on scientific evidence. In Cordelia Fine's razor-sharp *Testosterone Rex* (2017) she argues that the whole testosterone fable was invalidated a long time ago. Or, in the words of Amsterdam professor of sexology Ellen Laan: 'There is not one

347. Jessica Durlacher in the programme *Sign of the Times*, March 2018.

348. Andreas Kinneging about Weinstein and the well-considered will, in *Novum*, April 2018.

piece of evidence proving that men who conduct unconsensual sexual behaviour have more testosterone than those who do not.'[349]

The cynical reality is that wherever people hold on to the fabled *force majeure* of testosterone, there are men interpreting this view as a licence to do whatever they want. As a result, potential victims are constantly in danger—not only in society, but also at home. According to World Health Organization estimates, one in three women experience some form of physical or sexual violence on the part of her own partner, and 38 per cent of the murders of women are committed by male partners. Reports of such cases are constantly in the news and yet barely scratch the surface in terms of the number of actual occurrences. Recent statistics of women's lack of physical security confront the world with the shocking consequences of fake testosterone logic in societies where men are not brought up to practise self-control from an early age (see Plate 25).

In an extensive interview, Professor Laan corrects a few misconceptions about sexual behaviour, based on her recent research findings:

> Both men and women respond to sexual stimuli. With the man they are visible on the outside, with the woman they can be measured from the inside.
>
> The libido concept from Freud's 'drives' must be thrown overboard: this 'steam boiler' theory saw the man as a barrel full of lust that must be discharged into sex ('he cannot but carry on'), but testosterone is no 'macho hormone'. This substance plays a role in the sexual lust of both men and women.
>
> Power differences between men and women are the

349. Interview in *NRC-Handelsblad*, 17 November 2017. See also: Van Lunsen and Laan, *Seks! Een leven lang leren (Sex! A Lifelong Education)*, 2017.

> main cause of male misconduct. Two surviving ideas play a role in this. First, that it is not the perpetrator who is guilty and responsible for his own arousal, but the woman who sexually arouses him—for example, by wearing a short skirt. Secondly, the myth that a man with an erection must absolutely come, because otherwise he will get 'blue balls'. Eradicate it as nothing but empty talk that has manipulated generations of women. There is no physiological urgency whatsoever for such an ejaculation: a man who has no sex for a while will simply have a nocturnal ejaculation.
>
> Undesirable behaviour can only be prevented by (sexual) education in which equality between men and women is paramount.[350]

That much-needed sexual education is still in its infancy. Only in 2000—in the final document of the Women's Convention of the United Nations in Beijing—was it recorded for the first time that emancipation policy should also be targetted at men. Writing off all responsibility for oné s own desire remains a sign of weakness—from both sides.

The 'overwhelming catastrophe' *à la* Ibn Abbas customarily ignored the question of how women experience forced or obligatory sex. Throughout history, from the starting point of male arrogance or carelessness, a female 'no' is too frequently interpreted unilaterally as a 'yes'.

---

350. Laan, ibid., paraphrased.

The obvious

After a guest lecture in Nairobi, I was invited into a girls' student dormitory. We sat in a circle and had tea. One of the girls was breastfeeding twins and told me how the father, a fellow student, felt zero responsibility for the two babies. How could that be? The story was shared in bits and pieces. At the end of the month all the students received their monthly allowance, everyone was happy and longing to go out at night. The boys knocked on the girls' doors and they went into town together. There the boys treated the girls to a coke, but at the end of the night it was expected that they would be paid back 'in kind'. This had happened to the student with the twins. 'But you girls get your own allowance, right?' I asked. Their indignation shot through the sky like a lightning bolt. Yes, exactly, that was the problem. The boys were deeply offended when the girls wanted to pay for themselves. 'They immediately find you a bitch,' the young mother sighed, now herself unable to finish college. At the end of an increasingly emotional discussion about how bad it was to be called a bitch, she added: 'I once had a teacher at school who warned the girls: "The male world is like a pond full of crocodiles. Never trust them." We did not believe her, and only now I realise how right she was.'

Fortunately, partners can also talk to each other about mutual expectations and reflect critically on their own behaviour. A public confession of the Egyptian doctor and author Sherif Hetata illustrated this. I met him in Utrecht in the 1990s as the husband of writer and activist Nawal El Sadaawi (who was hailed as 'the Simone de Beauvoir of the Arab World' and 'Egypt's most radical woman'). I was asked to interview her after a performance of her play *Woman at Point Zero*.

My first question was: 'Nawal, what's your secret?'

'Oh, Sherif can better answer that one,' she replied.

So I invited him to sit with us on the stage. As a child, he explained, this adored son was so spoiled by his mother that even his slippers were always kept by his bed pointing in the right direction. Once he and Nawal got married and lived in the same house, Sherif began to ask her to do this or that for him, as seemed logical from his perspective. But then her answer was often: 'Sorry, I'm too busy, right now' or 'You know I have a deadline' or 'Not right now, darling!' It annoyed him so much that he began to wonder whether she really loved him: 'Yes,' he confessed to the audience, 'to tell you the truth, it took me a long time to realise that socialism starts at home.' At the end of our conversation, he addressed a serious warning to the young women in the audience: 'Beware if you girls fall in love! You are inclined to do everything to pamper that undoubtedly spoiled by his mother, adorable young man, but if you start living together, please remember that it will be extremely difficult to get back to normal!'

Challenging your privileges and sharing your power on your own initiative never goes without saying. As long as myths and popular culture persist that women have been created for the wellbeing of men, the female body remains an object for a man to handle the way he wishes within the rules of society. Women often go along with it, *nolens volens*, or somewhere in between.

What is the position of a modern-day woman in this long history of power and powerlessness? The Dutch journalist Joyce Roodnat once ended up in a humiliating situation about which she remained silent for years until the #MeToo debate made her think about how bad the experience had been. In 2017 she mainly remembered her confusion during an interview in Paris with Claude Lanzmann, creator of the impressive documentary *Shoa* (1985) about the Nazi death camps—who she regarded as 'A hero, a great artist':

> The conversation took place at his house, he answered every question in great detail. And while he spoke about Auschwitz and the way he exposed camp torturers with a hidden camera, he was fondling me. Refusing him politely, I let him do his thing. I knew my place. He was the great filmmaker, I was a nobody. In any case, I had to finish that interview, going back with unfinished business was impossible. The interesting thing was, neither he nor I said anything about his behaviour. When he started becoming really scary, I stood up and said I had to leave. He insisted on giving me a ride and in the end I even got into his car. Why? I couldn't say. Eventually I came to my senses. I got out at a traffic light. I wrote the article and told nobody. I was silent out of respect for the arts. Later I heard that I was not the only one this had happened to. That helped.[351]

Ultimately such abuse of power, she concluded, is not about sex, but about humiliating women as objects 'you do something with'. Old misconceptions keep sowing confusion and are wrongly interpreted on both sides.

#MeToo and beyond

#MeToo has spread around the world as a swelling tsunami of female outrage over such confusing confrontations and degrading victimisations. It started in 2017 as a small outburst of indignation about the serial impudence and impropriety of American film icon Harvey Weinstein. Revelations by employees about the many years of silently-tolerated behaviour led not only to his arrest,

351. https://www.nrc.nl/nieuws/2017/10/18/metoo-oftwel-hij-ook-13559309-a1577724.

but to a movement calling for sexual harassment and abuse to be stopped. The first women to speak out were well-known and well-to-do Western women, and the first men accused, powerful film magnates and actors. Soon the movement expanded in all directions as a recognisable phenomenon with global resonance. Not only in the film world, but also in sports, education and the medical world, women began to call out their harassers, assailants and rapists by name, with an amazing snowball effect. Here and there accused men were now falling from their pedestal, while more repulsive sexual violence than ever came to light in all layers of the population, with increasingly number of young girls, defenceless toddlers and even babies as victims. Whoever does a search for '#MeToo' alongwith the name of any country on the internet is confronted with a worrisome wildfire of disturbing data.

An open debate is ongoing, with reactions ranging from benevolent to glossing over, from abusively ignoring to hostile denial, as more women speak out and set out their limits more clearly than ever. As usual, a counter-movement started surprisingly quickly. In particular, famous women who dared to scrutinise the behaviour of powerful men were called whores, liars, traitors and opportunists. One of the first women to experience this reaction was the Italian actress and filmmaker Asia Argento. In 1997, at the age of twenty-one, she was raped by Weinstein. When she was one of the first to bring her case out in the open in October 2017, she was disgraced in her native Italy and threatened daily. The same happened to women who revealed what had been going on at the notorious *bunga bunga* parties of Silvio Berlusconi. According to critical journalists, those violent counter-reactions in Italy were due to the silence code that the Mafia imposes on Italian society. According to Argento, #MeToo women who break that taboo are attacked by frustrated men who excitedly detail what they would like do to women who refuse to shut up any longer, if they should find these women somewhere alone.

New information about Asia Argento in *The New York Times* in August 2018 not only led to a fresh wave of scorn and blame for her personally, but also triggered a shock in the #MeToo movement: women, it became clear, could be more than just victims. It was claimed that a few years earlier Argento herself, then aged thirty-seven, had sexually abused seventeen-year-old actor Jimmy Bennett, who she later silenced with a large sum of money.[352] It turned out that power not only corrupts men, but also women. The only difference is that throughout history, women have had considerably less opportunity to practise their abusive power.

Counter-reactions to #MeToo appear everywhere. Some governments even try to deny the existence of sexual abuse within their boundaries. In China the first official commentaries were that such things do not happen 'here', but in the meantime #MeToo echoes continued to resonate. Five girls who wanted to start a campaign against sexual aggression on public transport were sentenced to a few weeks in prison. Women in China and elsewhere in Asia try to explain that their protests are not targetted against the government, but stem from concern for their own safety.

But there are positive signs too. The exposure of sexual violence not only works therapeutically for victims, it also gives new perspectives on sexual abuse in different societies. In November 2017 Cairo was declared the world's most unsafe city for women. Soon after this news came out, a self-confident Egyptian lawyer on a television panel called on men to rape women in jeans with rips that expose their bare flesh 'out of a patriotic sense of duty'. This reaction was criticised in the media and shot down by

---

352. https://www.nytimes.com/2018/08/19/us/asia-argento-assault-jimmy-bennett.html.

both men and women at large. In South Africa men took to the streets alongside women to protest against violence and sexual harassment. Worldwide dimensions of #MeToo can contribute to societies in which manliness is no longer synonymous with sexual possession at last.

In the past women have often been made to believe that their bodies were not theirs, while men were told that a woman's body was meant to have a male owner. Economic dependence led women to present their bodies as seductively as possible, because without the opportunity to develop themselves professionally, the body was their only capital in life. The role of passive, beautiful object has been fed to women for centuries and still holds its power thanks to merciless advertisers. Those images are imposed, no less than binding religious laws, and repeated so often that an ongoing struggle is needed not to submit to it.

Mandatory invisibility of the body in patriarchal traditions and the provocative portrayal of women as consumable lust objects are both forms of external enslavement. They detract attention from female achievements in art, science, sport and other fields from which women were mostly banned until the twentieth century—a legacy left over from their natural headstart as sole birth-givers.

In many places the male-female relationship has already shifted in the direction of more equality. But on the flipside, there are more and more frustrated men—in the US the term 'angry white men' has even been reclaimed as a badge of honour among the far right. They cling to the illusion that there is a way back to the good old past: a deceptive message with the limited view of a dead end. Psychiatrists get more and more such men in their waiting rooms. One of them observes:

> Men have been trapped. From an evolutionary point of view, they are left empty-handed by a decreasing influence on the regulation of their own sexuality, until they really

> no longer matter. They are also mocked and blamed for everything. [...]—indeed, we are in the settlement phase.[353]

Alongside politically correct and silent men rolling along with feminisation, there are angry and bitter men behaving like wronged children, and men who turn away from society, infected by a feeling of being spurned. In extreme situations, such individuals sometimes opt for a violent settlement with women based on an irreparable feeling of inferiority. Just one example:

> 'I actually look good. I dress good, am clean-shaven, bathe, touch of cologne—yet 30 million women rejected me,' wrote George Sodini in a blog that he kept while preparing for this week's shooting in a Pennsylvania gym in which he killed three women, wounded nine others and then killed himself.[354]

The stories and dreams of men who fear women told in contemporary psychiatric sessions are surprisingly similar to events referred to in ancient myths and stories. The heavy stone of the mythical past still weighs down on the back of the present. The projection of destructive urges onto the opposite sex turns women into monsters or witches celebrating their gruesome lust at the cost of men's wellbeing, while in reality, the reverse occurs far more often.

Having worked for years with murderers and rapists, an American prison psychiatrist stated after another shooting tragedy that violence against women almost always originates in a paralysing feeling of inadequacy, when all belief in the

---

353. Margreet Fogteloo, interview with psychiatrist Frank Koerselman in *De Groene Amsterdammer*, 23 March 2017. My translation.

354. Bob Herbert, op-ed column, 'Women at Risk', *The New York Times*, 7 August 2009.

perpetrator's masculinity seems lost. They have no success with women and then come up with a spectacular act of violence that finally generates attention:

> The mainstream culture is filled with the most gruesome forms of misogyny, and pornography is now a multibillion-dollar industry—much of it controlled by mainstream US corporations. One of the striking things about mass killings in the US is how consistently we find that the killers were riddled with shame and sexual humiliation, which they inevitably blamed on women and girls. The answer to their feelings of inadequacy was to get their hands on a gun (or guns) and begin blowing people away.[355]

We all yearn for security and for a role in society. We want to be needed and to be taken seriously. #MeToo was and remains a much-needed movement, but victimisation is not a position for anyone to linger in, and it is too easy to place all the blame on the opposite sex.

It is not always clear who is in charge, as power relations can subtly shift. In the past, women have served as humble doormats to men in powerful positions, and even now many still do. #MeToo rightly points to that power inequality, but overlooks the power that women themselves have in some situations. That this power exists is proven by the many forms of fear we encounterered in the previous chapters: the fear of the mystery and strangeness of a different and appealing being; and fear of the birth-giving power that has for so long disrupted gender relationships, as global oral and written traditions convincingly illustrate. The ineradicable need to belittle women or represent them as a destructive enemy also reflect those ancient fears.

355. Ibid.

Male fear and awe still exist everywhere, and women are too little aware of their power. Power has to be handled with care. The one who has more power—physically, sexually, financially, intellectually—has more responsibility for adopting humane conduct, a golden rule that holds for all human beings.

It has never been easy to overcome resistance and practise autonomy, especially for those who have internalised their submissive position. Women must get rid of their traditional role as a silently pleasing object and claim freedom that is rooted in qualities and talents, qualities that have nothing to do with their appearance.

It is not a matter of degrading the sexuality of men, but of upgrading that of women. The most humane premise is that no one is entitled to sex at the expense of another, or in the words of Stephan Sanders: 'Perhaps there is such a thing as the right to sex, but of course not to sex with someone else.'[356] For Julie C. Suk, 'An Equal Rights Amendment for the twenty-first century is best conceptualised as a right to egalitarian institutions rather than a right against discrimination.'[357] People have always been able to adjust ingrained patterns of life, challenge themselves and each other, and take new directions. Instead of a fixation on phallus monologues or vagina monologues, we can explore dialogues about how people can do better together, with an eye on each other's vulnerabilities. This does not only apply just to sex, but to our daily interactions with each other, in the broadest sense. We can but dream.

---

356. *De Volkskrant*, 23 May 2018.

357. 'An Equal Rights Amendment for the Twenty-First Century: Bringing Global Constitutionalism Home', *Yale Journal of Law & Feminism*, January 2017.

INDEX